LAND OF THE RISING DEAD

A Tokyo School Girl's Guide to Surviving the Zombie Apocalypse

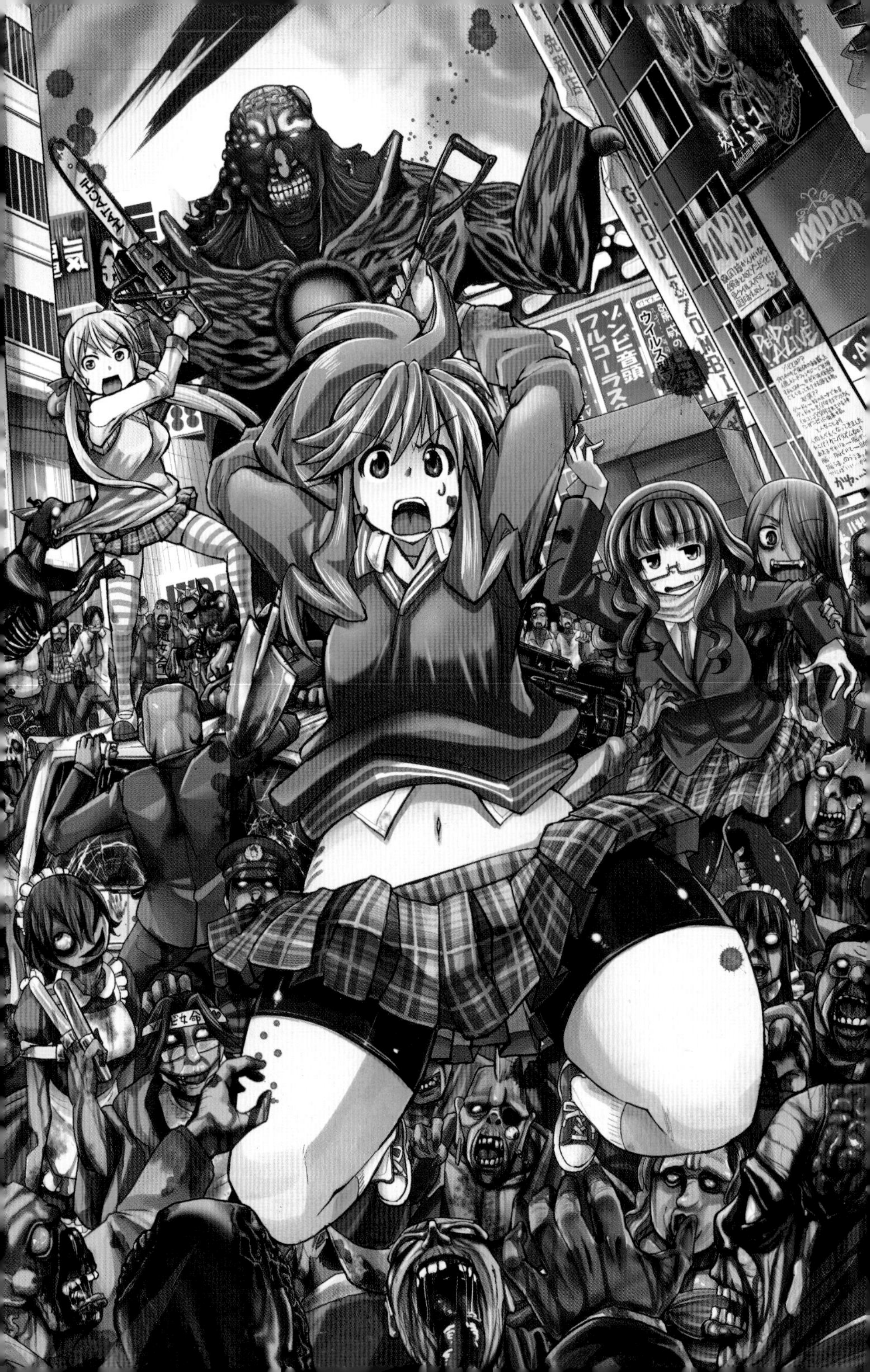
免税店
HATACHI
GHOUL&ZOMBIE
ZOMBIE
VOODOO
DEAD or ALIVE
ゾンビ音頭
フルコーラス
ウイルス

Prologue

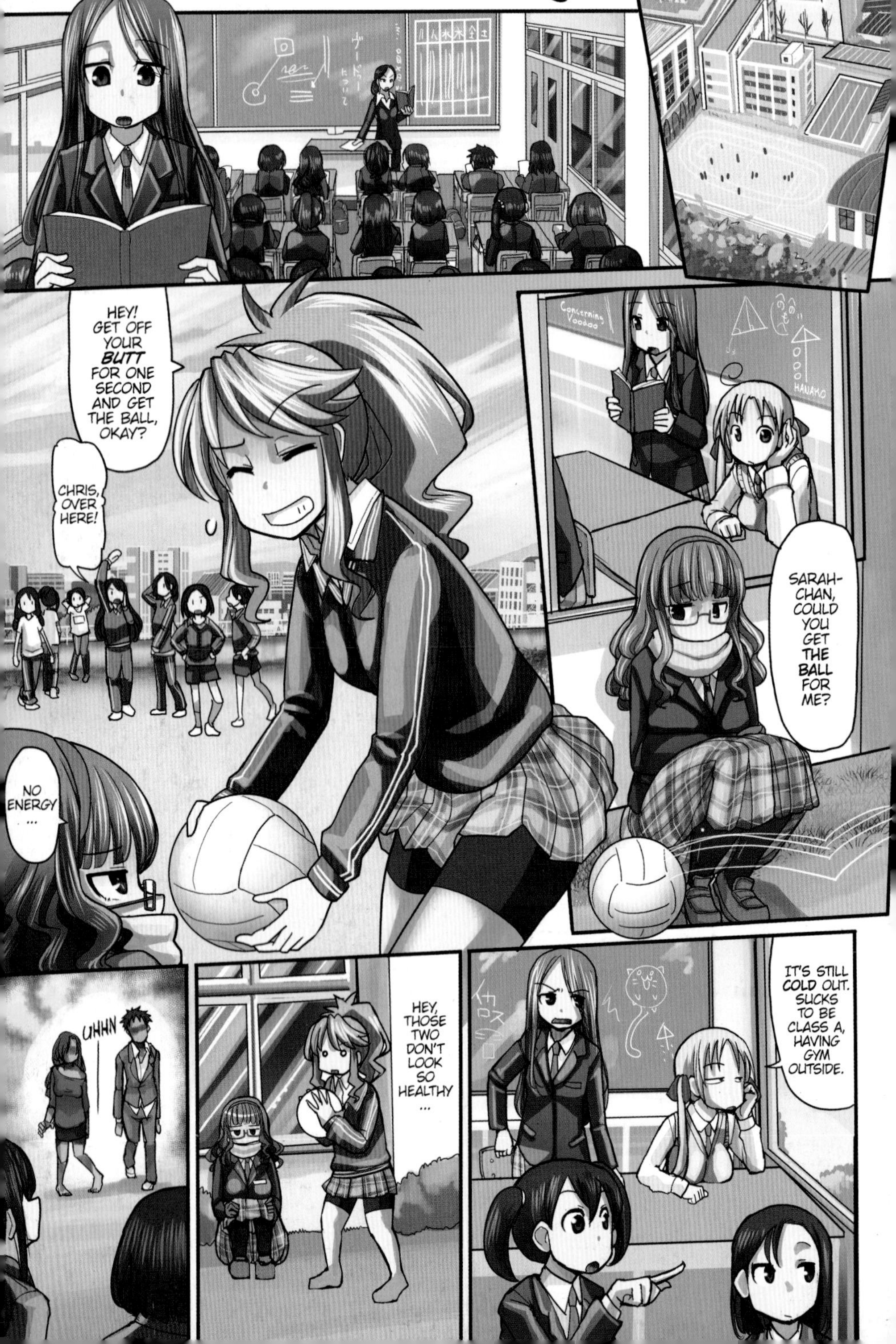

Concerning Voodoo
HANAKO
HEY! GET OFF YOUR BUTT FOR ONE SECOND AND GET THE BALL, OKAY?
CHRIS, OVER HERE!
SARAH-CHAN, COULD YOU GET THE BALL FOR ME?
NO ENERGY ...
IT'S STILL COLD OUT. SUCKS TO BE CLASS A, HAVING GYM OUTSIDE.
HEY, THOSE TWO DON'T LOOK SO HEALTHY ...
UHHN

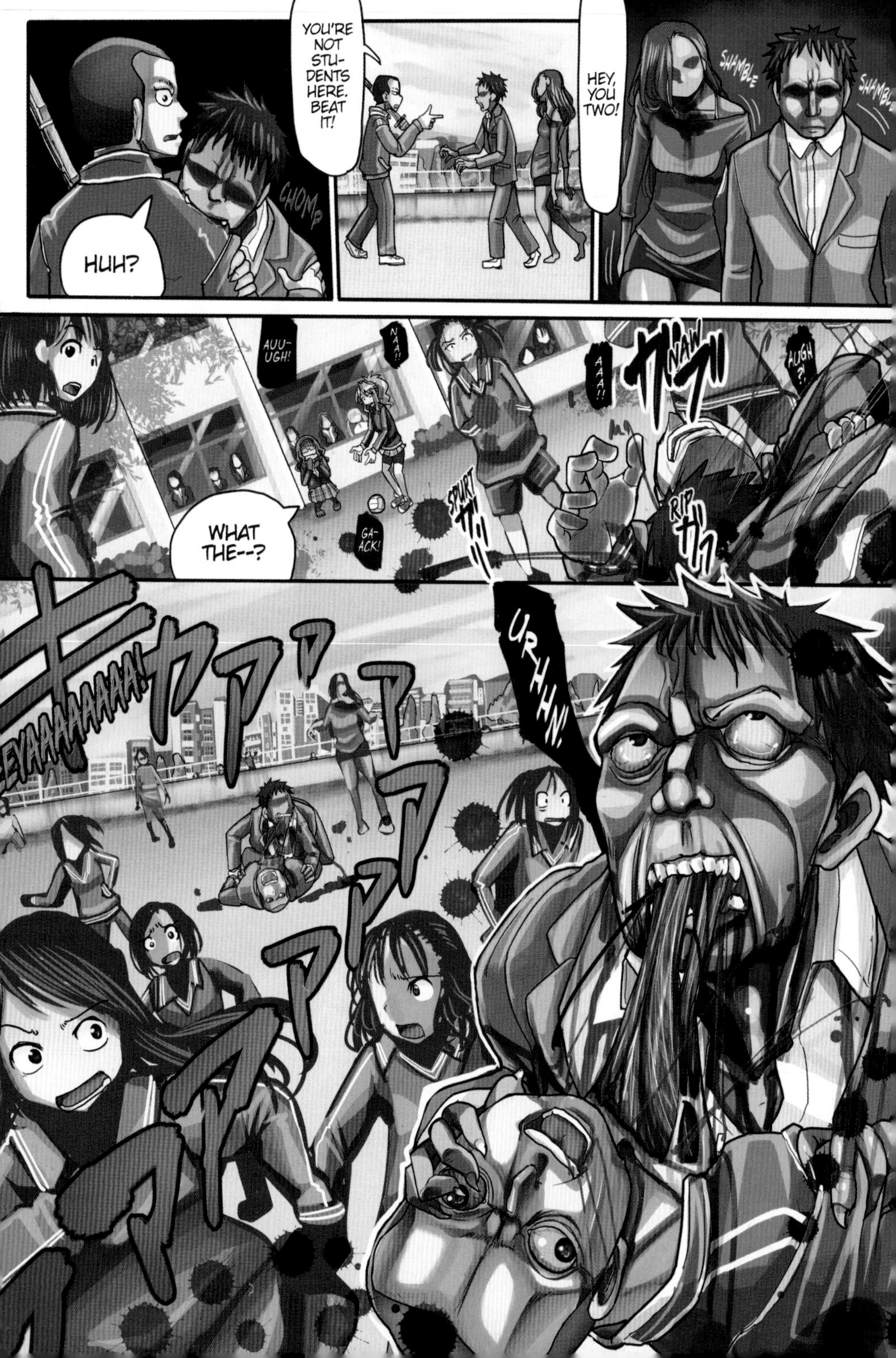

HEY, YOU TWO!
SHAMBLE
SHAMBLE
YOU'RE NOT STU-DENTS HERE. BEAT IT!
CHOMP
HUH?
AUGH?!
NAW
AAA!!
RIP
SPURT
GA-ACK!
NAAA!!
AUUGH!
WHAT THE--?
URHHN!
EYAAAAAAAAA!

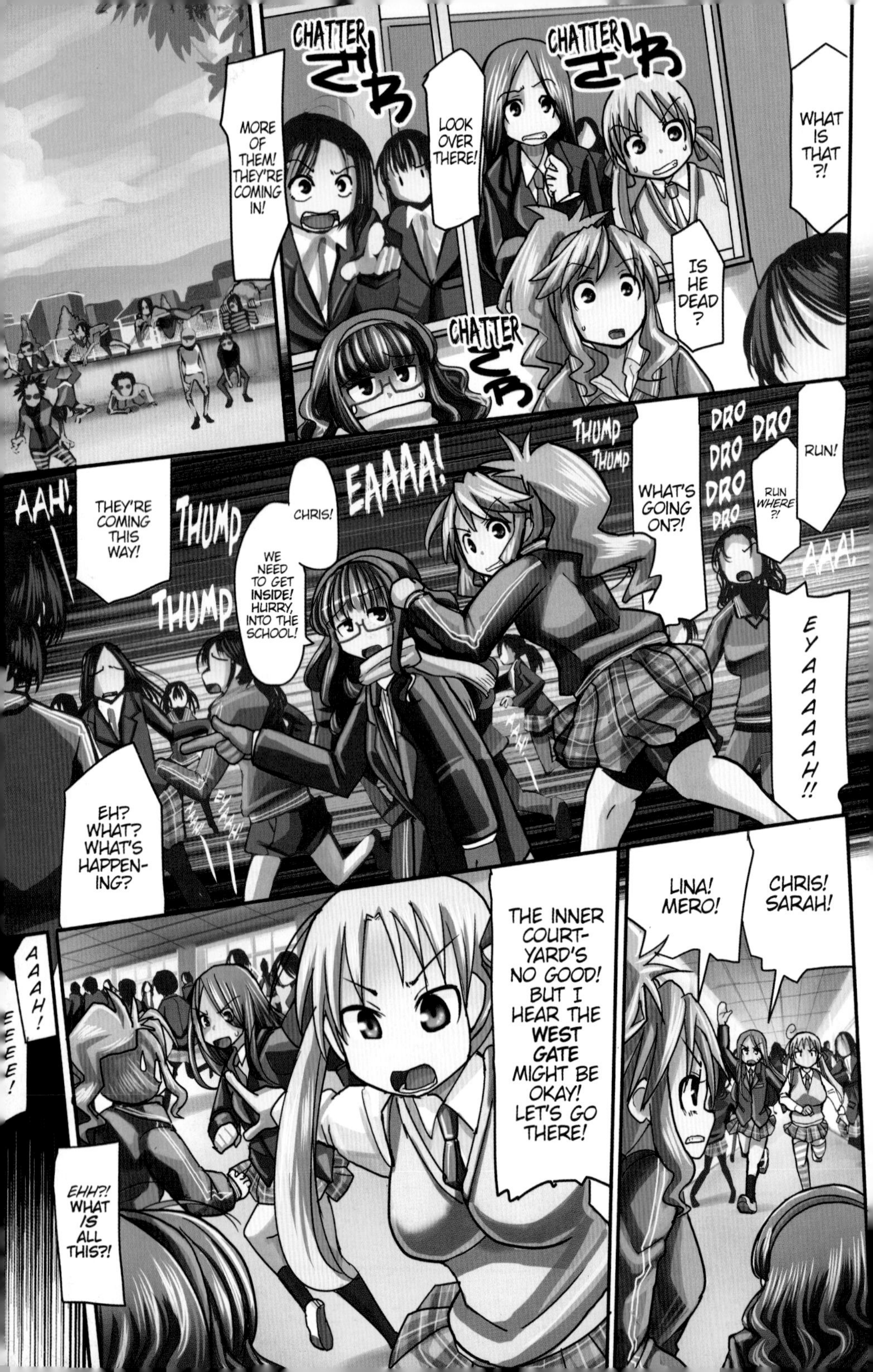

WHAT IS THAT?!
CHATTER さわ
IS HE DEAD?
LOOK OVER THERE!
CHATTER ざわ
MORE OF THEM! THEY'RE COMING IN!
CHATTER ざわ
RUN!
RUN WHERE?!
DRO DRO DRO DRO DRO DRO
WHAT'S GOING ON?!
THUMP THUMP
EAAAA!
CHRIS!
WE NEED TO GET INSIDE! HURRY, INTO THE SCHOOL!
THUMP
THUMP
THEY'RE COMING THIS WAY!
AAH!
AAA!
EYAAAAAAH!!
EH? WHAT? WHAT'S HAPPEN-ING?
CHRIS! SARAH!
LINA! MERO!
THE INNER COURT-YARD'S NO GOOD! BUT I HEAR THE WEST GATE MIGHT BE OKAY! LET'S GO THERE!
AAAH!
EEEEE!
EHH?! WHAT IS ALL THIS?!

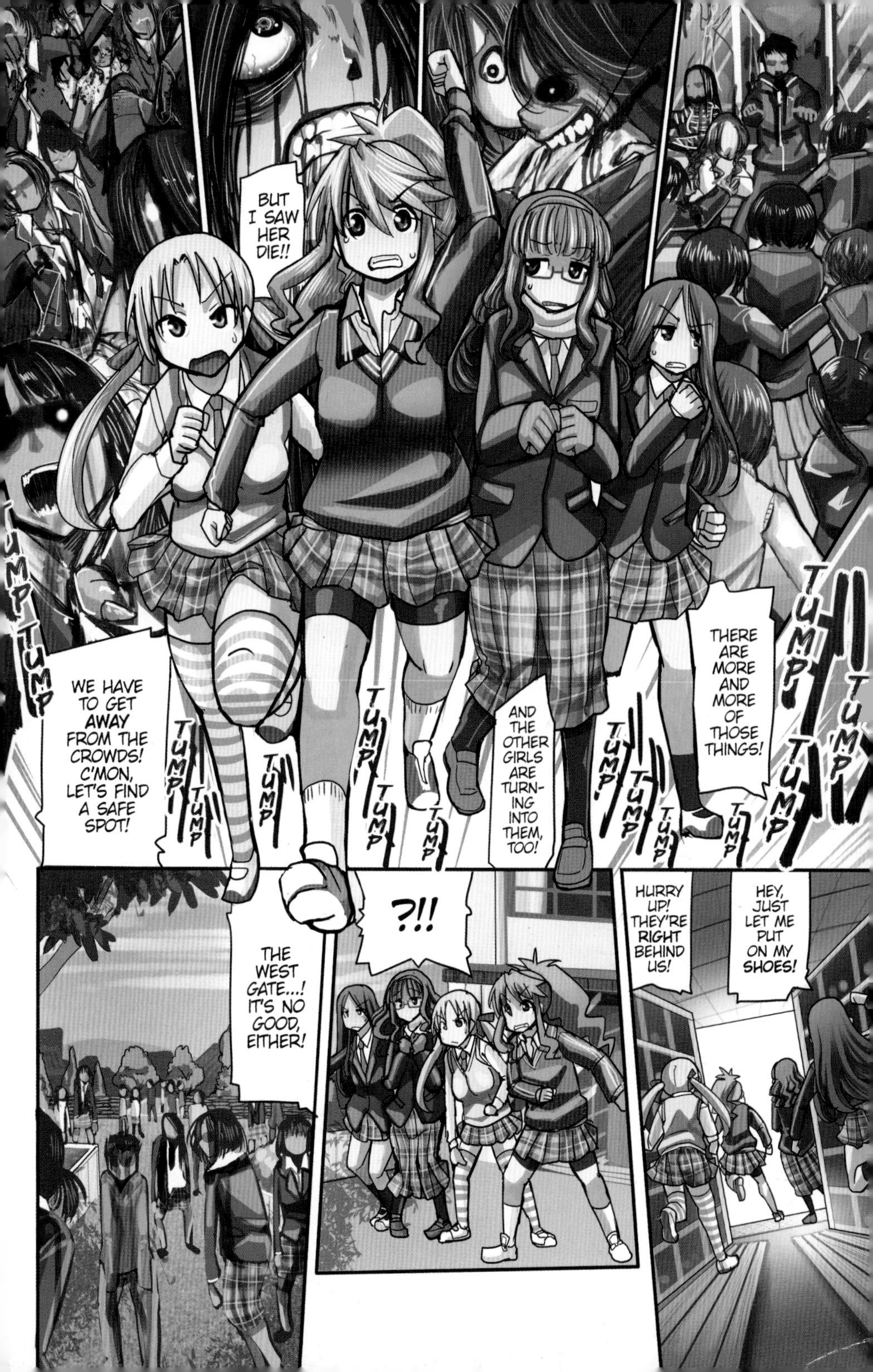

BUT I SAW HER DIE!!
THERE ARE MORE AND MORE OF THOSE THINGS!
TUMP TUMP TUMP
AND THE OTHER GIRLS ARE TURNING INTO THEM, TOO!
TUMP TUMP TUMP
TUMP TUMP TUMP
WE HAVE TO GET AWAY FROM THE CROWDS! C'MON, LET'S FIND A SAFE SPOT!
TUMP TUMP TUMP
HEY, JUST LET ME PUT ON MY SHOES!
HURRY UP! THEY'RE RIGHT BEHIND US!
?!!
THE WEST GATE...! IT'S NO GOOD, EITHER!

THEY'RE SURROUND-ING US!

WE CAN'T GO BACK TO THE SCHOOL! LET'S JUST BREAK THROUGH THEM!

GRAB SOME-THING TO FIGHT THEM OFF!

GRUNCH

?!

MERO!

YAH!

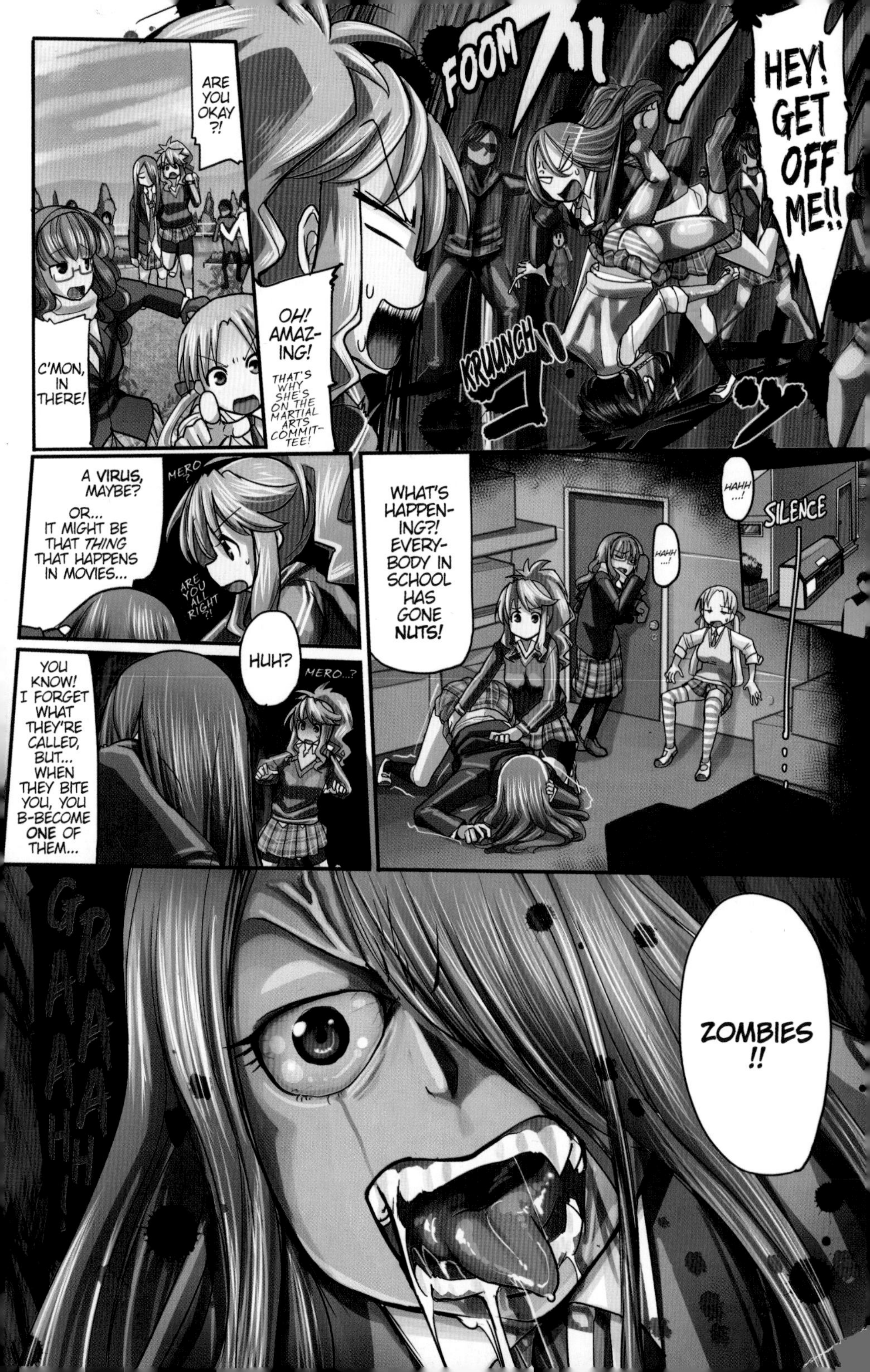
FOOM
HEY! GET OFF ME!!
KRUUNCH
OH! AMAZING!
THAT'S WHY SHE'S ON THE MARTIAL ARTS COMMITTEE!
ARE YOU OKAY?!
C'MON, IN THERE!
SILENCE
HAHH...!
HAHH...!
WHAT'S HAPPENING?! EVERYBODY IN SCHOOL HAS GONE NUTS!
A VIRUS, MAYBE?
MERO?
OR... IT MIGHT BE THAT THING THAT HAPPENS IN MOVIES...
ARE YOU ALL RIGHT?!
HUH?
MERO...?
YOU KNOW! I FORGET WHAT THEY'RE CALLED, BUT... WHEN THEY BITE YOU, YOU B-BECOME ONE OF THEM...
ZOMBIES!!
GRAAAAHH!

LAND OF THE RISING DEAD

A Tokyo School Girl's Guide to Surviving the Zombie Apocalypse

by
**DAI
AKAGANE**

**WATARU
ARAIZAWA**

**NORIMITSU
KAIHO**

**MORIHIRO
MATSUSHIRO**

illustrated by
**FREDDY
SAKAZAKI**

Seven Seas

SEVEN SEAS ENTERTAINMENT PRESENTS

LAND OF THE RISING DEAD

A Tokyo School Girl's Guide to Surviving the Zombie Apocalypse

by DAI AKAGANE, WATARU ARAIZAWA, NORIMITSU KAIHO, & MORIHIRO MATSUSHIRO

TRANSLATION
William Flanagan

ADAPTATION
Dave Howlett

MANGA LETTERING
Bambi & Roland Amago

INTERIOR LAYOUT AND DESIGN
Clay Gardner

COVER DESIGN
Nicky Lim

PROOFREADER
Katherine Bell
Troy McDaniel
Danielle King
Jade Gardner

PRODUCTION MANAGER
Lissa Pattillo

EDITOR-IN-CHIEF
Adam Arnold

PUBLISHER
Jason DeAngelis

ISBN: 978-1-626923-47-8
Printed in Canada
First Printing: October 2016
10 9 8 7 6 5 4 3 2 1

FOLLOW US ONLINE: *www.gomanga.com*

READING DIRECTIONS

This book reads from *right to left*, Japanese style. If this is your first time reading manga, you start reading from the top right panel on each page and take it from there. If you get lost, just follow the numbered diagram here. It may seem backwards at first, but you'll get the hang of it! Have fun!!

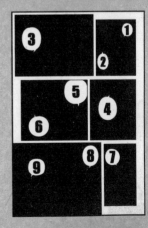

Table of Contents

CAST OF CHARACTERS

Mero Ando

The leader of the group. She was raised in high society and is usually at the top of her class. Her serious attitude has led her to chairmanship of several school committees, and she plans to run for class president next year. She's also a fervent fan of zombie movies. She loves zombies so much, she's turned into one for this book.

Lina Torajima

A naïve, innocent, twin-ponytailed girl with a knack for saying dumb things. Of the four, she is the shortest but has the largest bust size. She seems like a klutz who is terrible at both sports and classes, but she is unusually observant and incomparably lucky.

Sarah Honma

She's a bookish girl who is always calm and not given to extreme emotions. She's a bit of an otaku, and has some interests that would be considered more gross than zombies to most people. When it comes to normal subjects, she tends to keep quiet, but if you happen to get her started on a topic she's really interested in, you can't shut her up.

Chris Kureno

Stands out from the crowd with her athletic build and her eagle-like eyes. Boasting herculean strength, she excels at all sports. She's passionate, which can come across as foolhardy or belligerent. She's the type who learns better by doing than by thinking, so her school grades aren't great, even if she often does jump to the correct conclusion.

1 Origin of Zombies
and Later Development

By Wataru Araizawa

The Ever-Propagating Zombies

Since the beginning of this century, the number of zombies has been steadily increasing. In movies, television series, novels, comics, manga, games… In fact, across all media, the walking dead have been spreading like a plague.

As late as the mid-1990s, zombies were not a common sight on the average person's TV screen, with the exception of RPGs, where the grotesque appearances of the walking corpses were watered down and deformed by pixelated graphics, or in the zombie-infused tape collections of rabid horror aficionados or ardent Japanese fans of western movies. Horror and splatter movies gained instant popularity in the 1980s, and in venues like the *Thursday Night Movie of the Week* TV show, zombies became a subject of conversation for fans both old and young, and grade-school students started playing zombie games in the parks. This writer particularly remembers the posters for *Return of the Living Dead*—which had the Japanese name *Battalion*—pasted over every available phone pole, and within the story, the half-corpse woman the Japanese called "Obamba" gained particular popularity. This character gave rise to a new word, Obattalion, which means a pushy middle-aged woman.

But even so, zombies were overshadowed in popularity by other major monsters like vampires and werewolves, relegating zombie offerings to B-movie, cult-classic status. Bucking

that trend was the *Resident Evil* movie, based on a game of the same name, which made over a hundred million dollars worldwide. The popularity of each successive sequel made the property a tent-pole franchise for the studio.

In 2010, the manga-cum-anime *High School of the Dead* aired on television, and despite long hiatuses between manga volumes, both the TV series and the manga are still popular.

In June of 2013 (August of that year for Japan), the PR department of the movie *World War Z* courted controversy by trying to hide the fact that the film had zombies in it. Nevertheless, in its opening weekend, it was viewed by over 200,000 people in Japan alone, and went on to become a blockbuster hit, grossing $540 million worldwide. But why? Well, before we talk about that, let's start with a discussion on what zombies are.

The Debut of Zombies

In western culture, a journalist named William Seabrook introduced the idea of zombies into the mainstream. He had spent several years in Haiti and wrote a sensationalized account of his experiences with Voodoo and zombies in his book *The Magic Island* (1929). Eyes began turning to Haiti when American forces occupied the island in 1915. At that time, there was a secret religion that grew among the black slaves of the island, who had been forcibly brought there in French colonial days from Africa. The religion is a hybrid of many African beliefs mixed with Chinese Taoist ideas.

William Seabrook was a journalist who loved the still-hidden worlds (of that era), cultures, religions, and occultism of other cultures. He was highly influenced by books such as 1927's *Adventures in Arabia*, in which they introduce the Yazidi religion, which worships the Peacock Angel Melek Taus, as well as tales of devil worship and other occult practices introduced by such names as Robert W. Chambers, Seabury Quinn, and Howard Phillips Lovecraft. He developed deep connections to celebrated, often infamous, occultists such as Alistair Crowley

and George Gurdjieff, and Seabrook himself is sometimes counted among their number.

Following an interest in cannibalism, he listened to the stories of the Guere tribe of Ethiopia. Unsatisfied with their answers, his intellectual curiosity led him to the Sorbonne University in Paris, where an intern procured some human flesh for him. Seabrook then cooked it and recorded his thoughts on the taste. (He wrote frankly about the experience in his 1931 book, *Jungle Ways*.)

According to Seabrook, zombies are the "living dead" who are resurrected by Voodoo priests, and then, having no will of their own, are put to work as slaves. He postulated that the name derives from the western region of central Africa and that area's belief in the supernatural beings, *nzambi*. *Nzambi* was originally the name of the gods who created and controlled the world, but no longer reveal themselves because of humanity's sins. Eventually, the name began to be used to refer to certain supernatural powers, and it's believed that black slaves brought the word to the islands of the Caribbean.

With the introduction of the word zombie in the late 1920s, onscreen appearances in films soon followed. One of the earliest was in director Victor Halperin's 1932 film *White Zombie*. The following dialogue is from an opening scene of that movie, in which a Caucasian couple is confronted by zombies.

Worker: *They are not men, Monsieur, they are dead bodies!*
Main Character: *Dead?*
Worker: *Yes, Monsieur. Zombies. The living dead.*
Worker: *Corpses taken from their graves, who are made to work in sugar mills and fields at night.*
Worker: *Look! Here they come!*

These zombies were essentially living corpses that could not even be stopped after being shot with a handgun. Even so,

they only moved at all on orders from Legendre, a practitioner of black magic (Bela Lugosi, made famous a year earlier for his starring role in *Dracula*). They did not eat human flesh, nor did they increase their numbers by biting people. They were little more than pitiful puppets.

Soon after, zombies would appear on the printed page as well. The earliest appearance of zombies in mystery fiction was in the January 1937 issue of *Weird Tales*, a pulp magazine (so called for the cheap, low-quality paper on which the mass-market magazines were printed). The story, titled *The Disinterment,* was co-written by Duane W. Rimel with none other than H.P. Lovecraft, author of the stories that popularized the Cthulhu mythos.

The short story was written in September 1935, and although it never included the word "zombie," the narrator claims

THE FIRST ZOMBIE MOVIE

 BY THE WAY, THE ZOMBIES IN WHITE ZOMBIE WEREN'T REALLY "THE LIVING DEAD," BUT LIVING HUMANS REDUCED TO A HALF-DEAD STATE BY ZOMBIE POWDER.

to have been revived from near death by a doctor who used medicine acquired in Haiti. However, it is revealed his brain was in fact brought back in someone else's dead body. While not directly a zombie story, "The Disinterment" was clearly inspired by tales of zombies and Voodoo medicine.

Incidentally, H.P. Lovecraft wrote a serialized short story titled *Herbert West: Reanimator*, in which a mad doctor uses scientific methods to revive the dead as grotesque monsters. Eventually, he meets his own gruesome end at the hands of his vengeful creations.

Lovecraft's story was adapted into the 1985 film *Re-Animator* (released in Japan as *Zombio*), and is known worldwide as a zombie movie. But the story was actually written in 1921, eight years prior to the release of Seabrook's *The Magic Island*, which popularized the concept of the zombie for most readers.

And truthfully, the idea of the "walking dead" was well known in the horror genre in the west long before zombies ever came along.

The Pedigree of the Walking Dead

Since this book deals with the modern idea of zombies (specifically, the Romero zombie), I'd like to delve into the roots of this idea a bit more first.

Before the rise of Christianity, many burial rites in ancient Europe were connected to folklore that centered on the idea of the walking dead. This included many of the oral-tradition sagas of the Germanic tribes in ancient times.

Most of these stories involve dead people who still harbor strong emotions or attachments to the living or societal outcasts who, after their death, cause destruction and damage to the living people around them. If the living feared that a dead person might come back, for example, they might cut off the dead person's head and place it between its legs. Even so, in the Icelandic *Eyrbyggja* saga, cutting off a person's head and

even burning his body did not necessarily prevent the dead person from coming back and causing widespread destruction.

In ancient Rome, offerings were made to the souls of the dead on the third day after the mourning period when the souls are said to finally depart the earthly plane. It was believed that, if the proper rituals weren't observed or that if the person died a violent and unnatural death, the soul of the deceased would be unable to reach the realm of Pluto and would be cursed to wander the earth forever.

Europe was faced with an unusual number of dead bodies upon the arrival of the plague and the Little Ice Age in the 14th century. People at the time took comfort in the idea that angels guided the souls of the dead up to Heaven. Death loomed large in the consciousness of the time as the concept of *Memento Mori* ("remember that you must die") came into fashion, and artists of the period mixed images of the living and dead in their paintings. This preoccupation with death popularized the art style known as *Danse Macabre* ("dance with death"), a depiction of hell that featured a line of the dead marching like something out of the film version of *World War Z*. Other monstrous versions of the "walking dead" could be found in European culture of this period, different from the ones we have already discussed yet still representing the same fear of death. So now, let's introduce some of these other monsters, many of whom share traits with the creatures we know as zombies.

VAMPIRES

If you think of walking dead things in Eastern Europe, vampires will quickly come to mind. Modern images of the vampire are reflections of John Polidori's *The Vampyre* or Bram Stoker's *Dracula*, but the original vampires were mud-streaked monsters who crawled out of their graves to inflict harm on the living.

Amongst the Greek myths surrounding such blood-sucking monsters as Lamia and Empusa, there is the legend of the

vampiric Vrykolakas—humans who have come back from the grave. At first, the Vrykolakas were carcasses that came out of their graves searching for a new soul, and they were not considered to be very dangerous. But about the time that belief in Christianity began to spread, these monsters became the corpses of people who had died in isolation, were improperly buried, or corpses of those who had never been baptized, who had risen from the dead to seek revenge on the living. In their unlives, they thirsted for human blood. The bodies of the Vrykolakas did not decompose but instead hardened, and every part of their bodies had swelled until their joints could not bend. The devil himself was believed to have entered their bodies.

When night fell, the Vrykolakas would climb out of their grave and knock on the door of their former home, hoping to draw their family out. The only way to stop this vampire was to burn its corpse to ash.

The Christian church in Eastern Europe (the Eastern Orthodox Church) taught these legends of the walking dead and presented Christian teachings as a practical way to combat the monsters which were known by different names in various regions. In Romania, they were called *Moroii*, and in the Balkans, the Vrykolakas were called *Vukodlak*. And thus, the vampire legend spread across Europe, until in the 11th Century when, during a council of clergy in Limoges, France, the Bishop of Cahors spoke of witnesses who had observed the corpse of an excommunicated knight in a place very far from his grave.

MUMMIES

Mummies, corpses who come back to life seeking revenge on those who break into their tombs and disturb their sleep, are another example of the "walking dead."

Mummies are corpses who have, through artificial or natural processes, had their decomposition halted through drying and are preserved in something close to their original state

over long periods of time. The most commonly-known type of mummy is usually someone who has been wrapped in bandages and mummified in accordance with ancient Egyptian tradition.

Europeans and Americans first came to witness the preservation and mummification techniques used by the ancient Egyptians in the 18th century. Interest in ancient Egypt was popularized in French high society in 1781, following the publication of Antoine Court de Gebelin's book series *Le Monde Primitif* (The Primeval World).

Over the course of the 18th and 19th centuries, disreputable salesmen sold what was claimed to be Egyptian mummies, which went on to become tourist attractions. In 1821, Jane C. Webb-Loudon attended one such attraction in a Piccadilly theatre where the bandages of one such mummy were removed for the audience. Using that experience as a basis, she wrote about a mummy out for revenge in the novel *The Mummy*.

A new type of monster was born, one that would later be written about by such prestigious authors as Louisa May Alcott and Arthur Conan Doyle.

FRANKENSTEIN'S MONSTER

There is a crescent-shaped lake straddling France and Switzerland called Lake Geneva where the English Romantic poet Lord George Gordon (Noel) Byron had a vacation house, Villa Diodati. An infidelity scandal had forced him to flee his native England to live abroad. In the summer of 1816, he was living at the villa, and he surrounded himself with four others who were either living with him or summering nearby. One was a doctor, Dr. John William Polidori, who was interested in disorders of the blood and sleepwalking—subjects that brought him to Byron's attention. Also nearby were Byron's lover, Clair Clairmont, her half-sister Mary Wollstonecraft Godwin, and the man she had run away with, the poet Percy Bysshe Shelley.

On the night of June 15th, this entire group gathered at

CHAPTER 1

the Villa to wait out a rainstorm while Lord Byron read a French translation of some German ghost stories. Someone made the odd suggestion that they should all write scary stories themselves. The aforementioned Dr. Polidori used the suggestion to pen what would become *The Vampyre*, but the real surprise came from Mary Godwin, who wrote the story that would eventually become *Frankenstein: or, The Modern Prometheus*. In Godwin's story, the young scientist Victor Frankenstein pieced together a patchwork of corpses to create a man-made monster.

Once published, this work inspired other authors to write about the "risen dead" in a different way than vampires or mummies. In this case, it was about life given to corpses dug up out of the ground. One of these later authors using this same motif was the aforementioned H.P. Lovecraft, in his story *Herbert West: Reanimator*.

FORERUNNERS OF ZOMBIES

IN JAPAN, BODILESS SPIRITS LIKE GHOSTS SEEM TO BE MORE POPULAR. MAYBE IT'S SOME KIND OF CULTURAL DIFFERENCE?

VAMPIRES ARE LIKE ZOMBIES IN THAT THEY BOTH LIKE TO BITE PEOPLE.

EVEN BEFORE ZOMBIES, SEVERAL TYPES OF "RISEN DEAD" WERE ALREADY PRETTY POPULAR IN THE WEST.

 GOOD GUESS, BUT IN THE EDO PERIOD (1603-1868), IT WAS CUSTOMARY TO BURY THE DEAD. CREMATION DIDN'T BECOME THE NORM UNTIL MORE MODERN TIMES.

 I KNOW WHY! IN EUROPE, THEY BURY THEIR BODIES AS THEY ARE, BUT IN JAPAN, BODIES ARE CREMATED, SO THERE'S NO BODY TO BE REVIVED.

The Arrival of Romero Zombies

With the ingredients gathered in the kitchen, it was only a matter of time before the right cook appeared—a filmmaker named George Andrew Romero. The dish he cooked up was a film that would come to be titled *Night of the Living Dead*.

Romero had been a fan of movies from a very young age, especially monster movies such as Bela Lugosi's *Dracula* and Boris Karloff's *Frankenstein*. But one film that really caught his attention was 1964's *The Last Man on Earth*, a black-and-white movie starring Vincent Price. A unique, impressive actor with an exaggerated style that could be played as either eerie or campy, Price had appeared in countless horror films. In this movie, all of humanity had been turned into vampires, with the exception of Price's Robert Neville, the last living human. Based on the novel *I Am Legend* by Richard Matheson, the movie would be remade with Charlton Heston in 1971 as *The Omega Man* and once more as *I Am Legend* in 2007 starring Will Smith.

Romero founded the movie production company Latent Image in 1963, and inspired by the concept of *The Last Man on Earth*, he made his low-budget, black-and-white feature film debut, *Night of the Living Dead*. In the film, as the revived corpses of the recently dead start to attack humans, a group of survivors tries to wait out the crisis in a deserted farmhouse. Strangely enough, the word "zombie" is never mentioned in the film.

Romero's plot borrowed certain elements from *The Last Man on Earth*. In Romero's film, the living dead lay siege to the farmhouse, in much the same way that the vampires surround and besiege the house where Price's Neville is holed up. Other similarities, borrowed for the first movie or added later, include the creatures' shambling pace, their taste for human flesh, the way their bites transmit their affliction, and the fact that their heads are their weak spot.

At first, Romero had planned for his movie's monsters to be called vampires, but Romero and John Russo's script

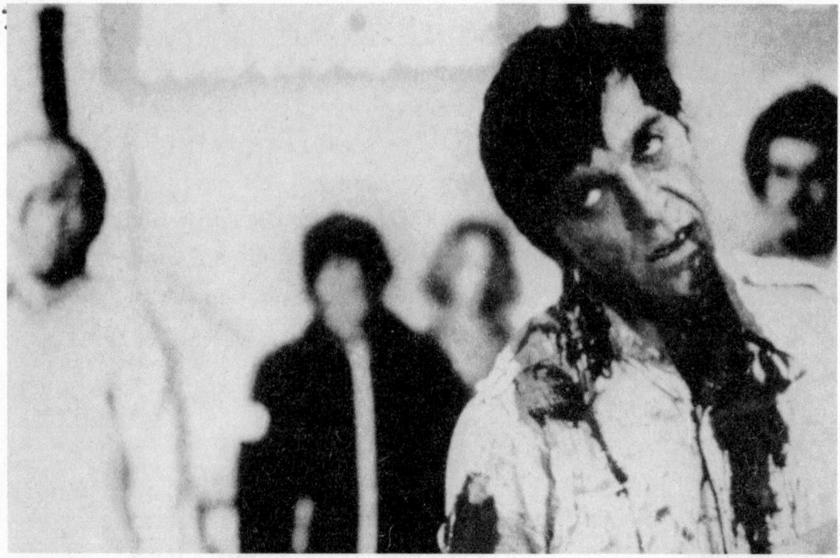

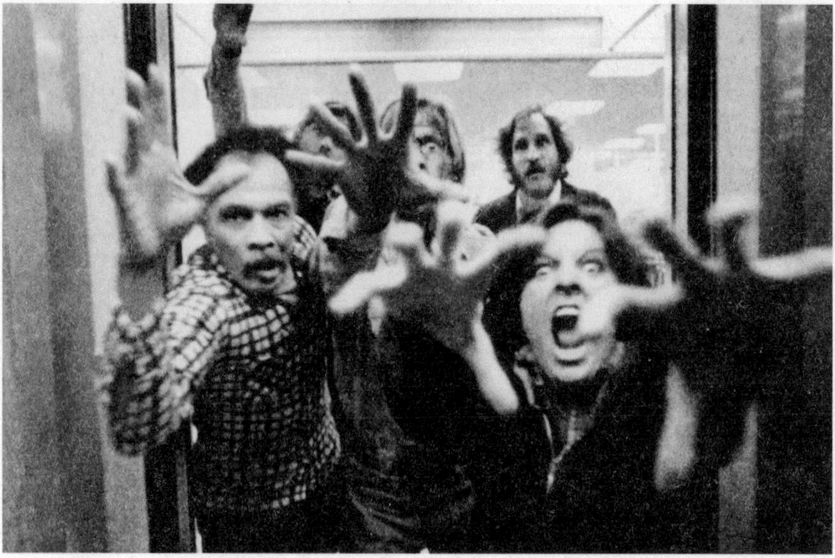

PHOTO CREDIT: KAWAKITA MEMORIAL FILM INSTITUTE

Zombies as seen in the movie *Dawn of the Dead*, in which the portrayal of the zombie-like creatures of *Night of the Living Dead*, continued to evolve. The sequel's zombies moved in a slow, shambling manner, often walking with their arms reaching out before them. After *Night of the Living Dead* and *Dawn of the Dead*, a third movie in the series debuted in 1985, *Day of the Dead*. These films are often referred to as Romero's *Trilogy of the Dead*.

refers to the corpses as "ghouls" (a man-eating monster that appears in the legends of the Arabian peninsula). Romero's walking corpses would not be called zombies onscreen until the 1978 sequel, *Dawn of the Dead* (known internationally as *Zombi*).

Neither *Night of the Living Dead* nor *Dawn of the Dead* offers any solid explanation for why the dead were returning to life. The most satisfying attempt at an answer comes when a character in *Dawn of the Dead* states, "There's no more room in Hell. When there's no more room in Hell... the dead will walk the Earth."

In any case, *Dawn of the Dead* had a huge influence on how zombies were depicted worldwide: a shambling gait, a taste for human flesh, the spreading of the plague through bites, destruction of the brain their only weakness... The Voodoo

THE ARRIVAL OF ROMERO ZOMBIES

THEY'RE ZOMBIES! WHY ARE THEY SO **FAST**?!

HUMANS BECOME ZOMBIES AFTER THEY'RE BITTEN BY A ZOMBIE-- AN OUTBREAK THAT THREATENS ALL OF HUMAN SOCIETY. LIKE A DISASTER MOVIE!

THE MOVIE THAT SOLIDIFIED OUR IMAGE OF ZOMBIES IS ROMERO'S *NIGHT OF THE LIVING DEAD!*

 WELL, THE STANDARD IMAGE OF ZOMBIES HADN'T REALLY BEEN SOLIDIFIED YET. YOU'LL HAVE TO WAIT UNTIL *DAWN OF THE DEAD* BEFORE YOU GET TO WHAT WE ALL IMAGINE AS STANDARD ZOMBIES...

 THE ZOMBIES IN *NIGHT OF THE LIVING DEAD* CAN USE TOOLS AND WALK NORMALLY, AND THEY'RE A LOT MORE DEXTEROUS THAN WE'RE USED TO!

origins of the zombie have now been replaced in the public consciousness by the attributes of Romero's creations. In *Night of the Living Dead*, the living dead were able to move somewhat quickly when a potential victim was nearby, but the standard shambling zombie didn't make its debut until *Dawn of the Dead*.

The pose where the zombies have both hands thrust out ahead of them also never appears in *Night of the Living Dead*; instead, it can be first found in *Dawn of the Dead*. Most people seem to think that this pose was derived from the way Boris Karloff played Frankenstein's monster in *Frankenstein*, but Karloff himself accredited the way Conrad Veidt played the sleepwalker Cesare in the 1920 German film, *The Cabinet of Dr. Caligari*.

As a side note, there is another work that is cited as a possible influence on *Dawn of the Dead*. Richard Matheson, author of *I Am Legend*, also penned a story that featured moving corpses following World War III, *Dance of the Dead* (the author's son, Richard Christian Matheson, would go on to adapt the story for a 2005 installment of the television series *Masters of Horror*). The "lifeless undead phenomenon" (LUP) from the story resembles Romero's zombies very closely. Not only that, but the title is *Dance of the Dead*. This has been widely reported in review sites worldwide as being a possible influence on Romero's films, but this has never been officially confirmed as fact.

Derivations and Scientific Interest

The arrival of Romero zombies is the beginning of a new epoch in horror movie history.

Before *Night of the Living Dead*, zombie-like walking corpses occasionally appeared in films, but Romero's film treated the outbreak of the walking dead as a swiftly moving plague. This idea was terrifying to audiences and a source of inspiration for generations of filmmakers. Individually, a zombie is

slow-moving and easily overpowered if you can destroy or re-move its head. The real threat comes from being overwhelmed by the sheer number of walking corpses as the zombie plague spreads. (If you really want a taste of that kind of fear, Capcom's zombie survival game *Dead Rising* is a good place to start.)

Once they get close, they're easily dispatched, but several more zombies are quick to take their place. Soon, you find yourself surrounded on all sides and backed into a corner; a horde of zombies is like a flood of infectious disease, a disaster that escalates with frightening speed.

Before long, relatives of the Romero zombies, with slight alterations, began to appear in droves on the movie screens. In 1979, an unauthorized sequel, *Zombie (Sanguelia)* led to a dispute between its director Lucio Fulci and Romero collaborator Dario Argento. In 1985, Dan O'Bannon wrote and directed a movie that promoted itself as a *Night of the Living Dead* sequel, entitled *Return of the Living Dead*. And a shorter film with a considerably higher profile would take its cues from Romero zombies: Michael Jackson's 1982 music video "Thriller."

"Thriller" director John Landis was no stranger to the horror movie genre (the opening sequence features an elaborate werewolf transformation, an homage to the director's 1981 film *An American Werewolf in London*). The video features corpses rising from the grave to chase after a heroine who is forced to take refuge in a deserted house, much like the protagonists of *Night of the Living Dead*. The massive popularity of "Thriller" ensured that even viewers who weren't horror fans had a good idea of what a zombie was.

And as the popularity of the Romero zombie grew, there was renewed interest in the original Voodoo zombies. A Canadian anthropologist and ethnobotanist, Wade Davis, made his way to Haiti in 1982. He had lived among the aboriginal populations of Latin America, collecting many of the plants used for medicinal herbs. In Haiti, he discovered something called "zombie powder," a drug that was supposed to induce

asphyxiation. In reality, zombie powder suppresses the metabolism to an extent to where the subject could be mistaken for a walking corpse. If modern medicine could bring a patient back to his or her normal metabolic state, the substance could be used as a general anesthetic.

Acting on a request from the eminent pharmacologist Nathan S. Kline, Davis went to Haiti. His experiences led him to pen two books, *The Serpent and the Rainbow* and *Passage of Darkness: The Ethnobiology of the Haitian Zombie*. Effectively, he became the second Seabrook, approaching zombies and the Voodoo religion from a scientific point of view.

Davis collected examples of zombie powder from every part of Haiti that had actually been used in Voodoo rituals, and the ingredients of the powder varied from region to region. However, some ingredients were common to virtually every example of the powder, such as:

- Ingredients from the pea family and other nut families such as cashew or sumac
- A bit of human flesh burned until it was black
- Skin and entrails from a fish related to the pufferfish

The flesh may not have actually been from a human, but its chemically inert state means that it was likely only for ceremonial, not scientific, purposes anyway.

The element that Davis concentrated on was pufferfish poison—or more precisely, tetrodotoxin, an alkaloid neurotoxin. This nerve poison creates a death-like state in which the brain undergoes oxygen deprivation, giving the appearance that the affected person has become a zombie. Davis's conclusion was widely accepted as a scientific explanation for real world zombies, and soon other studies of this phenomenon would follow. However, Davis's conclusions don't explain the long length of time the shamans have control of their zombies, nor do the numbing effects of tetrodotoxin account for the delirium and crawling movement of zombies. Even today, psychologists

◂ Lucio Fulci's *Zombie (Sanguelia)* is known for scenes of extreme gore, featuring swarms of decomposing zombies and a heroine getting her eyeball skewered. As a side note, the scene in which a zombie does battle with a shark is considered a classic moment by fans of the horror genre.

❮ Dan O'Bannon's *Return of the Living Dead* is a cult-classic zombie parody that effectively mixes scares and laughs. This photo depicts the scene where the remaining upper half of an old woman (nicknamed "Obamba" in Japan) explains why she is compelled to eat people. The movie also features a number of other unique and memorable zombie characters, like the grotesque "Tar Man."

such as Terence Hines are disputing that element of Davis's explanation.

In more recently published books related to the practice of the Voodoo religion in Haiti, it is noted that the culture tends to isolate people suffering from mental disorders as they are said to be unable to take on traditional employment. These books cite several cases where family members returned to their homes after years of labor as zombies, but when DNA tests were performed on these people, they were found to be unrelated to their "families."

In any case, these are part of the real-life culture of Voodoo and zombies, and they have little to do with fictional zombies. The zombies that George A. Romero created have already taken on a unique identity among the pantheon of movie monsters.

So, Why Zombies Now?

Future *World War Z* author Max Brooks released his first book, *The Zombie Survival Guide,* in 2003. The 2009 movie *Zombieland* offered even more tips on how to make it through a zombie outbreak via a list of 32 rules the film's protagonist, Columbus, has compiled. It seems that new guides on how one would survive a zombie apocalypse are popping up all the time these days. But it was a 2004 parody of Romero's zombie movies, *Shaun of the Dead*, which kicked zombie mania into high gear. (It didn't hurt that a *Dawn of the Dead* remake was released the same year.)

In recent zombie offerings, the "running zombie" has gained popularity. Starting with first-person shooter games such as *Left 4 Dead* and *Dead Island*, depictions of zombies running at full speed have become more and more the norm. The turning point for zombie depictions, where the infected come barreling at you full tilt, seems to have been 2002's *28 Days Later* (even though more lively and aggressive living dead were featured in *Night of the Living Dead,* and the zombies in

Return of the Living Dead could run quite fast when food was nearby). The increased speed at which zombies pursue their prey seems to be just another step in the living dead's natural evolution. In Romero's own 2005 film *Land of the Dead*, some zombies display a crude form of intelligence, even appearing to mimic activities from when they were still alive.

Hirohiko Araki (creator of the hit manga *JoJo's Bizarre Adventure*) wrote in his book *Hirohiko Araki's Bizarre Horror Movie Critique*, "It's the lack of individuality—the fact that anyone who is bitten can become one...anyone can become a zombie. It's that they are hordes of nameless creatures that makes it so creepy." To Araki, this was the essence of why we fear zombies, and why we are fascinated by them. In essence, a zombie is a human who has become a monster, yet is still recognizable as having once been human—a frightening yet compelling concept. Zombies represent the end of society as we understand it.

They wear the faces of friends, acquaintances, and loved ones of the characters within these stories, but now they are twisted parodies of themselves. Their actions bring about the destruction of everything mankind has accomplished. Even if they weren't attacking humans or trying to spread a contagion, the very idea of dead humans rising and walking around would eventually lay waste to the human soul and lead to society's downfall. That was the premise of a book by Mamoru Oshii (director of *Ghost in the Shell*) entitled *Zombie Nikki* (*Zombie Diary*), which portrayed the twilight years of the human race.

Still, the key to the massive mainstream popularity of zombie entertainment remains elusive. Writer and game designer Yuriko Shibamura offers an interesting opinion on the subject. She said, "In America, they have this thing called a story cycle. When they're at war, they start doing fantasy and war-style entertainment. When fantasy gets big, they go through a recession, and horror starts gaining popularity. When horror gets popular, mystery starts gaining popularity. Then when mystery

reaches its peak, science fiction starts gaining popularity. Then things get rough again, and we go back to fantasy." This quote was taken from an interview from *The Myth of Cthulhu: Dark Navigation*.

A recession directly after a war? Certainly the economy suffered following the first Gulf War. And after the 9/11 terror attacks and the war in Iraq, the preoccupation with fantasy Shibamura describes came to pass, heralded by a wave of interest in fantasy cinema like the filmed adaptations of *The Lord of the Rings* and the *Harry Potter* series. We could also be said to be currently experiencing the horror craze that inevitably follows. And in most cases, just a few years after a trend takes off in America, it soon spreads to Japan as well.

On March 11, 2011, northeastern Japan was wracked by a massive earthquake and tsunami. The impact of this disaster can still be seen and felt today. One can't see the images of people waiting for rescue on tops of buildings without thinking of the beginning of the game *Dead Rising,* even if the connection is inappropriate and unbidden.

Apocalypse Now? In stories of a zombie apocalypse, we are seeing a new vision of the end of the world—only this time, it isn't caused by war. Is there some meaning in facing the living dead, knowing their nature and taking measures to stay alive? The answer to that cannot be found in this or any other history of the zombie genre. You must ask that of yourselves, dear readers.

SPECIAL THANKS

The author would like to thank Ryou Morise, the editor-in-chief of the Japanese edition of Max Brooks' The Zombie Survival Guide *for all his help and use of his research materials.*

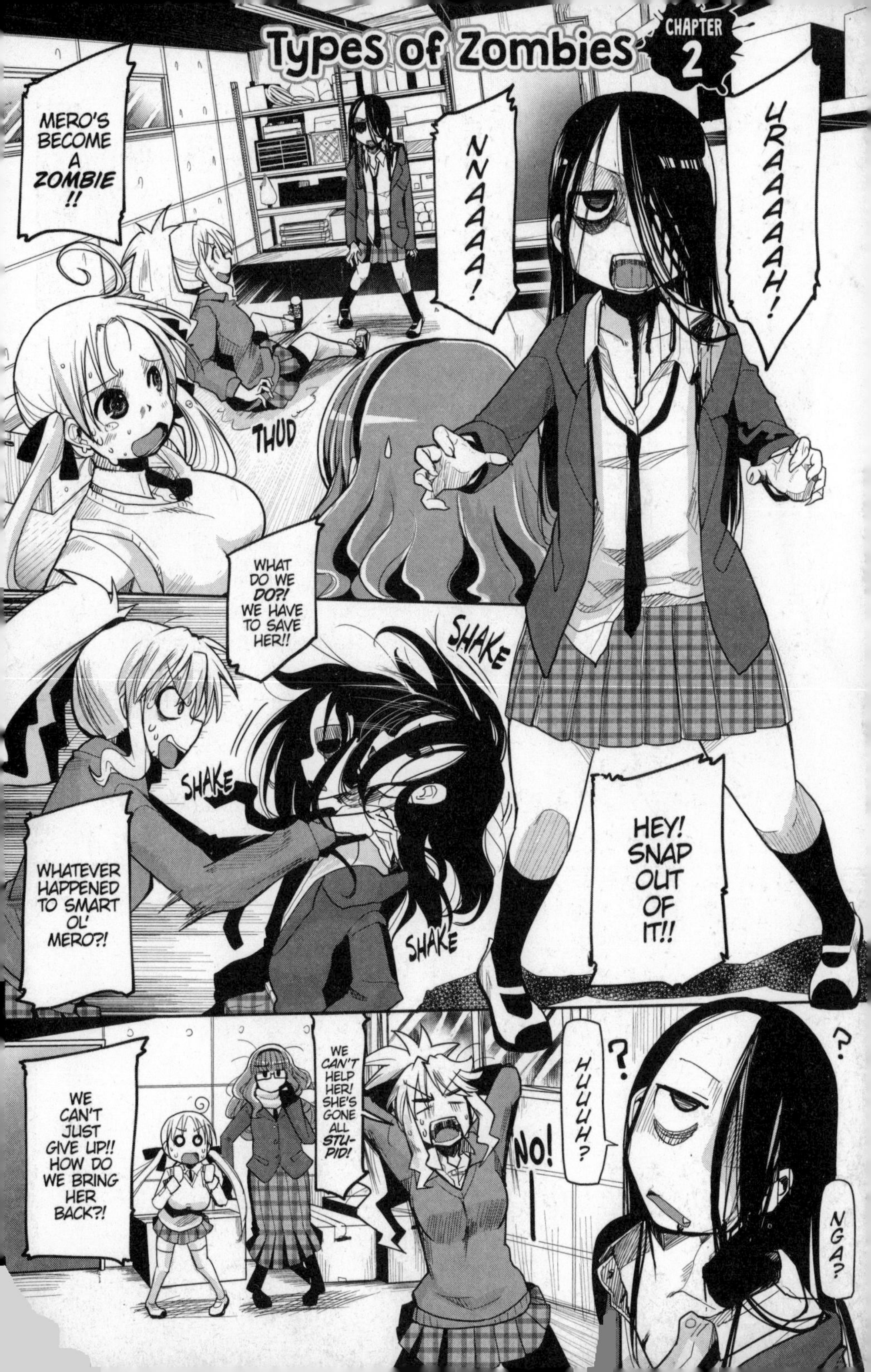
Types of Zombies
CHAPTER 2
MERO'S BECOME A ZOMBIE!!
NNAAAAA!
URAAAAAAH!
THUD
WHAT DO WE DO?! WE HAVE TO SAVE HER!!
SHAKE
SHAKE
SHAKE
HEY! SNAP OUT OF IT!!
WHATEVER HAPPENED TO SMART OL' MERO?!
HUUUH?
?
?
NGA?
NO!
WE CAN'T HELP HER! SHE'S GONE ALL STUPID!
WE CAN'T JUST GIVE UP!! HOW DO WE BRING HER BACK?!

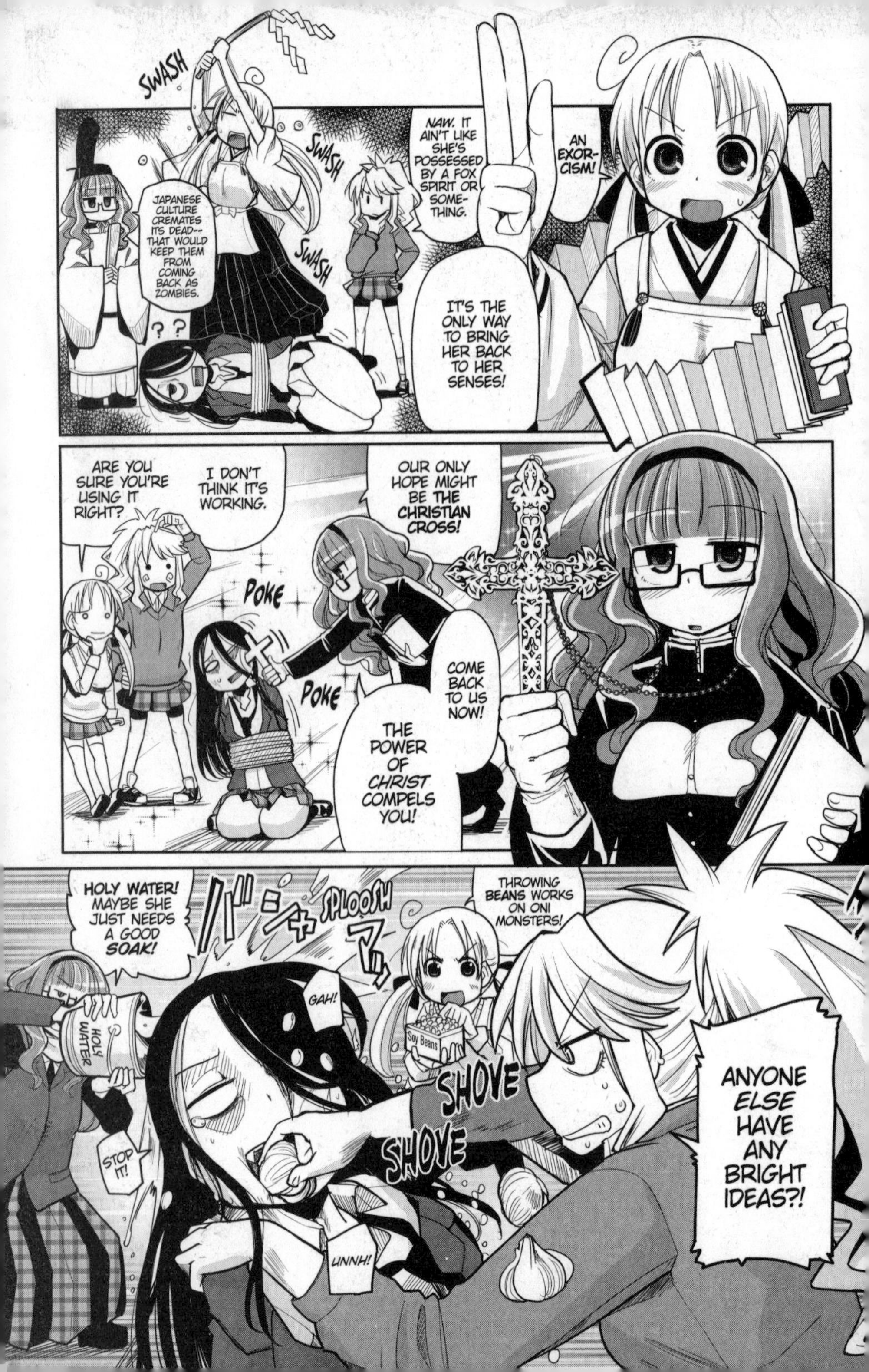
AN EXORCISM!
NAW. IT AIN'T LIKE SHE'S POSSESSED BY A FOX SPIRIT OR SOMETHING.
IT'S THE ONLY WAY TO BRING HER BACK TO HER SENSES!
SWASH
SWASH
SWASH
JAPANESE CULTURE CREMATES ITS DEAD-- THAT WOULD KEEP THEM FROM COMING BACK AS ZOMBIES.
? ?
OUR ONLY HOPE MIGHT BE THE CHRISTIAN CROSS!
COME BACK TO US NOW!
THE POWER OF CHRIST COMPELS YOU!
POKE
POKE
I DON'T THINK IT'S WORKING.
ARE YOU SURE YOU'RE USING IT RIGHT?
THROWING BEANS WORKS ON ONI MONSTERS!
SPLOOSH
HOLY WATER! MAYBE SHE JUST NEEDS A GOOD SOAK!
GAH!
Soy Beans
HOLY WATER
SHOVE
SHOVE
ANYONE ELSE HAVE ANY BRIGHT IDEAS?!
STOP IT!
UNNH!

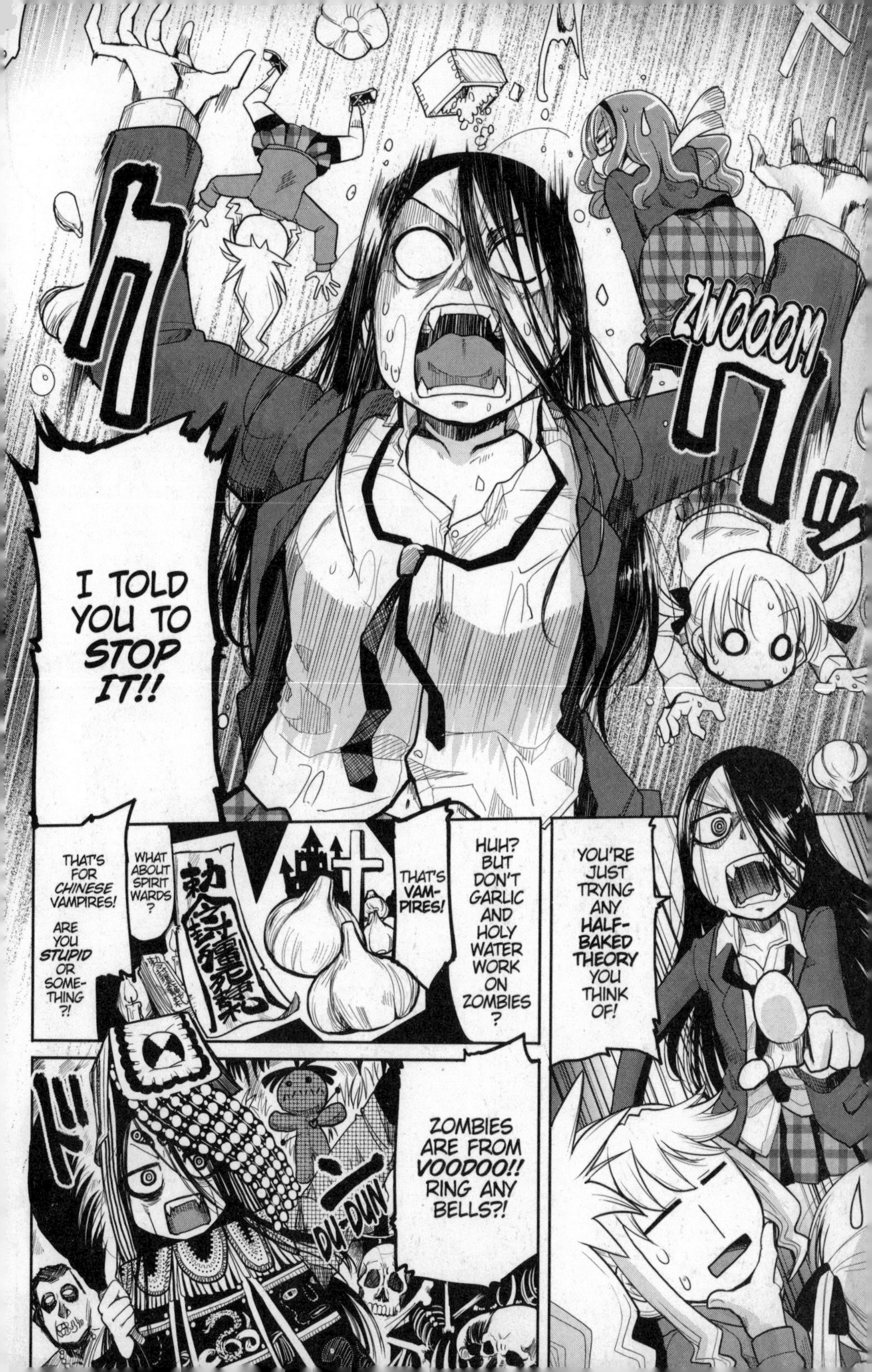
ZWOOOM
I TOLD YOU TO STOP IT!!
YOU'RE JUST TRYING ANY HALF-BAKED THEORY YOU THINK OF!
HUH? BUT DON'T GARLIC AND HOLY WATER WORK ON ZOMBIES?
THAT'S VAMPIRES!
WHAT ABOUT SPIRIT WARDS?
THAT'S FOR CHINESE VAMPIRES!
ARE YOU STUPID OR SOMETHING?!
ZOMBIES ARE FROM VOODOO!! RING ANY BELLS?!
DU-DUN

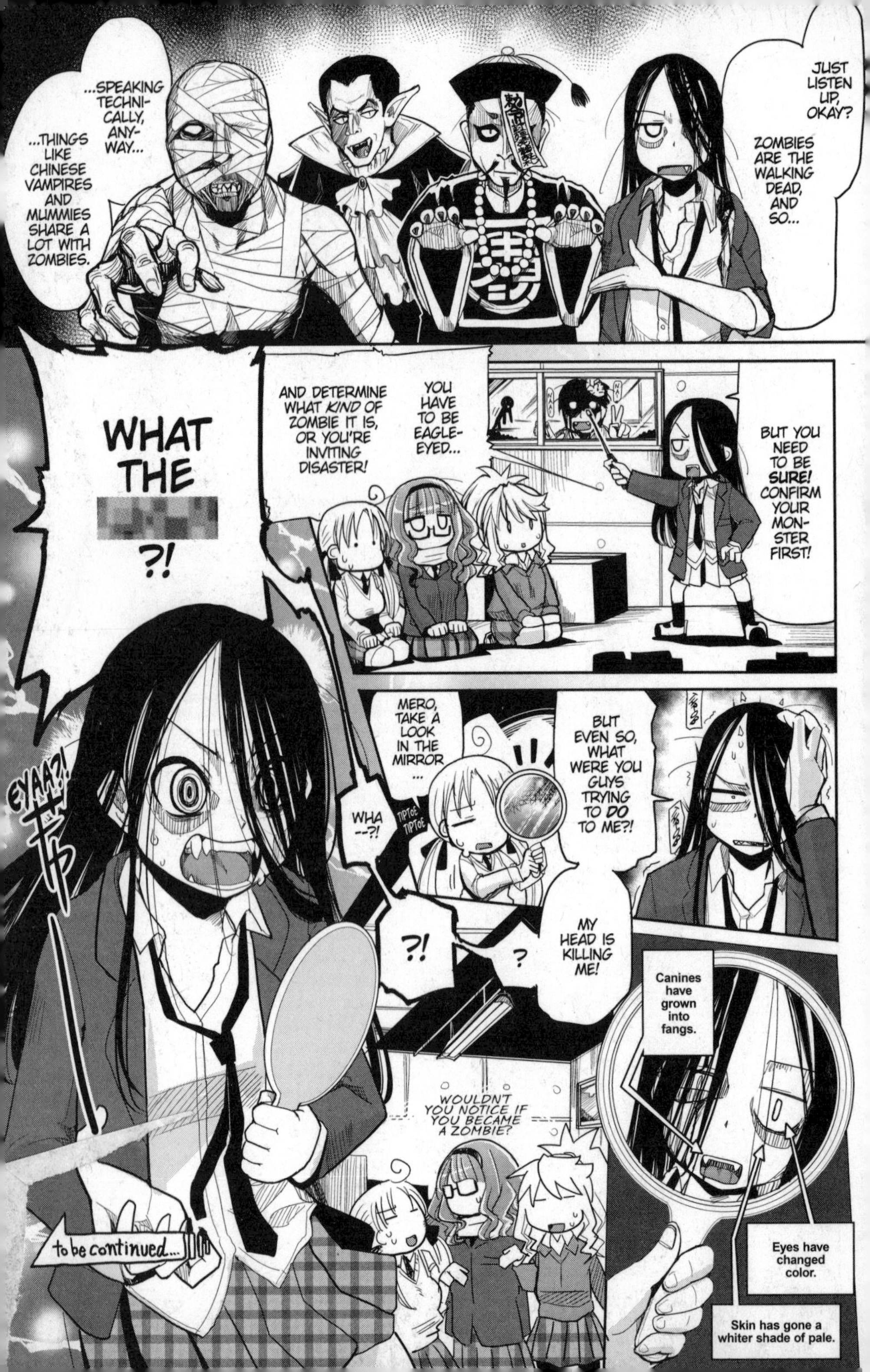

JUST LISTEN UP, OKAY?
ZOMBIES ARE THE WALKING DEAD, AND SO...
...SPEAKING TECHNICALLY, ANYWAY...
...THINGS LIKE CHINESE VAMPIRES AND MUMMIES SHARE A LOT WITH ZOMBIES.
BUT YOU NEED TO BE **SURE!** CONFIRM YOUR MONSTER FIRST!
YOU HAVE TO BE EAGLE-EYED...
AND DETERMINE WHAT *KIND* OF ZOMBIE IT IS, OR YOU'RE INVITING DISASTER!
BUT EVEN SO, WHAT WERE YOU GUYS TRYING TO *DO* TO ME?!
MERO, TAKE A LOOK IN THE MIRROR ...
WHA--?!
TIPTOE TIPTOE
MY HEAD IS KILLING ME!
?
?!
Canines have grown into fangs.
Eyes have changed color.
Skin has gone a whiter shade of pale.
WOULDN'T YOU NOTICE IF YOU BECAME A ZOMBIE?
WHAT THE ?!
EYAA?!
to be continued...

WAIT! DOES THIS MEAN THAT *I'VE* BECOME A ZOMBIE?!

 (REALLY? SHE DIDN'T NOTICE?)

 BUT THANK GOODNESS, YOU'VE COME TO YOUR SENSES!

 Y-YEAH... LET'S IGNORE THE WHOLE BODY THING FOR A MINUTE. AT LEAST YOUR BRAIN IS WORKING AGAIN.

 TRUE. I DO FEEL A TINY BIT SLUGGISH, BUT I ALSO FEEL KINDA GOOD, TOO. I GUESS I'VE BECOME ONE OF THOSE SELF-AWARE ZOMBIES.

 SO SHE *IS* STILL INSANE! SHE'S DEAD! SHE'S ALL MESSED UP! *WAAAH!*

 HEY, I'M AS SANE AS ANYBODY!! IF YOU ASK ME, I'M SANER THAN ANYONE WHO WOULD READ SUTRAS OR TRY TO PERFORM AN EXORCISM ON A ZOMBIE!!

 WAIT A MINUTE--IF YOU'RE SAYING YOU'RE SANE, ARE YOU SAYING YOU *WANTED* TO BECOME A ZOMBIE?!

 WELL, I'VE BEEN PLAYING THE STRAIGHT-A STUDENT ACT AT SCHOOL ALL THIS TIME, BUT ACTUALLY, I'VE REALLY BEEN INTO ZOMBIE MOVIES EVER SINCE I WAS A LITTLE KID. I EVEN USED TO DREAM ABOUT BECOMING A ZOMBIE-- I JUST NEVER EXPECTED MY DREAM TO COME TRUE!

 I NEVER WOULD HAVE GUESSED. BUT IF IT WORKS FOR HER, ALL'S WELL THAT ENDS WELL, HUH?

 BY THE WAY, MERO, DIDN'T I HEAR YOU IMPLY THAT THERE ARE SEVERAL TYPES OF ZOMBIES OUT THERE?

 YES, EXACTLY! JUDGING BY HOW YOU GUYS ACTED BACK THERE, YOU CLEARLY KNOW NOTHING ABOUT ZOMBIES. ON THE OTHER HAND, I'VE DONE THE RESEARCH AND HAVE BEEN MENTALLY PREPARING FOR HOW TO SURVIVE A ZOMBIE ATTACK FOR YEARS NOW. WOULD YOU LIKE TO KNOW THE SURVIVAL METHODS I'VE COME UP WITH?

 AN OFFER THAT'S BOTH NICE AND TERRIBLY ARROGANT AT THE SAME TIME!

 I-I HAVEN'T BEEN DOING IT FOR *YOUR* SAKES! DON'T GET ME WRONG HERE!!

 I THINK THAT'S "TSUNDERE."

TEXTBOOK EXAMPLE.

 WHO'RE YOU CALLING "TSUNDERE"?! WELL, ANYWAY... FIRST, YOU HAVE TO SEPARATE ZOMBIES INTO THEIR DIFFERENT GENERAL TYPES AND COME UP WITH METHODS OF CONFRONTING EACH TYPE. ONCE YOU UNDERSTAND THE ZOMBIE TYPES, YOU CAN FIGURE OUT THE BEST WAY TO FIRST FIND SAFETY--*THEN* YOU CAN FIND THE MOST PRACTICAL METHODS OF BATTLING THEM.

2 Types of Zombies

By Norimitsu Kaihou

Magically Cursed Slave-Type Zombies
~THE OLDEST TYPE~

DEFINITION AND HISTORY

Magically Cursed Slave-type zombies are corpses that have been put to work as slaves after having been revived through supernatural means. They are simply being manipulated.

Originally in Haiti's Voodoo religion, "zombie" means "snake soul." A shaman (Bokor) uses the power of that soul to force the body into slave labor. One theory is that zombies are people who only *seem* dead but have instead been brainwashed through drugs or hypnotism and put to work. (This follows the theories espoused by Wade Davis in *The Serpent and the Rainbow* and others elsewhere.)

These days the meaning of the word "zombie" has broadened to mean many different things, but it could be said that the Magically Cursed Slave-type zombie is the closest to the original meaning. Although some opinions differ, this is basically the type found in the first zombie movie, *White Zombie* (1932).

Of course, the Voodoo religion isn't the only force that has enslaved dead bodies as servants in written stories and oral traditions. You could probably say that one of the earliest horror-movie monsters, the mummy, is also a zombie brought back to life through curses and magic. In the 1999 remake of

The Mummy, The Book of the Dead is accidentally read in the middle of an excavation of historic ruins. This leads to the resurrection of the mummy of the high priest, Imhotep. In the 1940 film, *The Mummy's Hand*, as in later films, the descendants of high priests use manipulated mummies against parties who are trying to explore ruins.

There is also the tradition of what in the West is referred to as the Chinese Vampire, *Jiangshi*. The word is said to have originally referred to a laborer who has died far, far away from his home, and his family does not have the means to transport the body back for burial. A Taoist priest would perform rites that would reanimate the body, manipulating it to return home. The word itself refers to the hardening of the body due to rigor mortis.

In the 1980s, there was a boom of *Jiangshi* movies, and within those could be found a wide range of types of *Jiangshi*.

STRENGTHS AND WEAKNESSES

The strengths of the Magically Cursed Slave-type zombie depend on the kind of curses that have been used. The image of zombies in Haiti is pretty close to what everyone thinks of as zombies: strong, but slow on the job, and difficult to wound or damage.

With *Jiangshi*, the Chinese Vampire, rigor mortis has set in, so their arms have hardened into a thrust-out pose in front of them. The only way they can move is by jumping. But they are much stronger than humans, and they change humans into *Jiangshi* when they bite them.

The Magically Cursed Slave-type zombie's weak point is the curse itself in most cases. For example, in the Voodoo religion, it's believed that, if you stuff the zombie's mouth with salt and sew it shut, you can break the curse. In the case of *Jiangshi* Chinese vampires, a spirit ward by a Taoist priest can stop them (but if it's removed, they will go on a rampage). In the legends, the *Jiangshi* vampires are blind, but they can hear

MAGICALLY CURSED SLAVE-TYPE ZOMBIES

 IN THE VOODOO RELIGION, THEY CALL THE PRIEST/PRIESTESS CONTROLLING ZOMBIES "BOKOR." BUT IN RECENT FICTION, A FIGURE WHO CONTROLS DEAD BODIES OR THE SPIRITS OF THE DEAD IS REFERRED TO AS A NECROMANCER.

 THE BEST WAY TO DEFEAT THESE ZOMBIES IS TO JUST TAKE DOWN THE GUY CONTROLLING THEM, RIGHT?

your breathing. So if you can hold your breath, you might be able to avoid them.

For other zombies, belief in God (or related gods) or sanctified ground (of temples, shrines, churches, etc.), and crosses can be a weakness. Mainly, though, when you're dealing with Magically Cursed Slave-type zombies, your main enemy is not the zombies themselves. You should use methods for defeating highly functioning attack zombies, but since your main opponent is a human, you might be able to negotiate yourself out of the situation. Even when you cannot avoid battle, knowing the magician's goals might give you an edge.

DISTINGUISHING THEM, AND WHEN YOU MEET ONE

When you see a zombie and there's a shaman or magician nearby, you may be dealing with a Magically Cursed Slave-type

zombie. Study up on their native lands for telltale signs and confirmations. The savvy survivalist will already have investigated the zombie traditions native to wherever he or she intends to travel. You should be extra careful when entering unknown historic ruins or excavation sites. Find the shaman or magician as quickly as possible, and start taking measures against him or her. After all, if the magician can control one zombie, he/she can probably control many. As time goes on, the number of zombies under his/her control will increase.

However, one problem is that Magically Cursed Slave-type zombies can be very difficult to distinguish from Vengeful Spirit-type zombies, which we will discuss below. If you are confronted with Vengeful Spirit-type zombies, it's best to consider retreat. Although by that time, it might be too late…

Explosive Pandemic–Type Zombies
~THE ROMERO PEDIGREE~

DEFINITION AND HISTORY

Explosive Pandemic-type zombies mostly spread a contagion through wounding or biting humans, and in that way, they increase their numbers. Because they multiply so quickly and explosively, they can destroy all human civilization in a very short time. For this reason, we'll refer to them as Explosive Pandemic-type zombies.

The person responsible for Explosive Pandemic-type zombies is none other than George A. Romero, who created them in 1968's *Night of the Living Dead*. Zombies represent the possibility of global catastrophe, heralding the end of human civilization. This is a prospect that is both fascinating and horrifying to moviegoers, but it's a compelling concept that has elevated zombie fandom from cult interest to worldwide phenomenon.

The image the word "zombie" conjures up in our consciousness (for example, the walking dead wandering aimlessly,

EXPLOSIVE PANDEMIC—TYPE ZOMBIES

SO YOU'D BETTER PAY CLOSE ATTENTION TO THIS TYPE!

THIS BOOK IS BASICALLY ABOUT HOW TO SURVIVE THE EXPLOSIVE PANDEMIC-TYPE ZOMBIE.

RRRRRROOOOOOHHH

WHEN MOST PEOPLE THINK OF ZOMBIES, *THIS* IS USUALLY THE TYPE THEY'RE THINKING OF. THEY OFTEN APPEAR IN GAMES AND MANGA, TOO!

GRR! ARG!

BUT THE HUMANS WHO ARE BITTEN BECOME ZOMBIES THEMSELVES, AND THEIR NUMBERS INCREASE EXPONENTIALLY. THAT IS THE BIGGEST THREAT.

BUT THEY'RE SLOW, RIGHT? AND THEIR SKULLS ARE PRETTY FRAGILE, HUH? WE CAN HANDLE THIS...

 I'LL TURN YOU ALL INTO ZOMBIES...!

 I HATE HOW ONE ZOMBIE BITES A HUMAN AND THAT HUMAN TURNS INTO A ZOMBIE, WHO ATTACKS *ANOTHER* HUMAN WHO BECOMES A ZOMBIE, AND SO ON. AS THE NUMBER OF ZOMBIES GROWS, THE NUMBER OF HUMANS SHRINKS.

expanding their numbers by spreading the contagion), is indisputably attributed to Romero's original film. However, there are films that pre-date *Night of the Living Dead* that feature some of the aspects of this type of zombie. In the movie *Things to Come*, adapted from a novel by H.G. Wells, a spreading infection causes humans to lose their reason and become like beasts. In 1954's *I Am Legend* by Richard Matheson, human civilization has been destroyed by vampires (anticipating the end-of-the-world scenario depicted by Romero). In 2007, a new film adaptation of the novel was released in which the enemies weren't vampires but just plain zombies (created by a virus).

In Romero's zombie movies, such as *Night of the Living Dead* and *Dawn of the Dead*, the cause of the zombie plague is never clearly identified. All that's known is that it's happening all over the world. One of the characters speculates that Hell is

full and overflowing—a mystical, rather than scientific, explanation. If you accept that theory, then Romero's zombies could be considered Vengeance Spirit-type zombies.

Many of the zombie stories that followed attributed the spread of zombies to a virus, parasite, or some other scientific cause. The *Resident Evil* series of games and movies followed in that pattern.

STRENGTHS AND WEAKNESSES

Explosive Pandemic-type zombies tend to be slower than the average human, but what they lack in speed, they make up for in physical strength. The theory is that, while normal humans observe limits on their strength to keep their bodies functioning, the zombies have no sense of self-preservation beyond their need to feed. Therefore, this gives the illusion of zombies having super-human strength.

Although it isn't known how zombies sense the living, in many instances they seem to rely on sound. A zombie will, in most cases, keep moving until its cranium has been crushed and its brain destroyed. They move quite slowly, so a living human can often simply run away. They also have extremely limited intelligence, making them susceptible to traps.

COPING METHODS

The easiest way to know if you're dealing with Explosive Pandemic-type zombies is by their numbers. If there are countless zombies wandering about as far as the eye can see, these will likely be Explosive Pandemic-type zombies. If they get their hands on you, you will probably wind up infected (if the situation is that far gone, then there's not much we can do for you at that point). The chances of becoming infected increase if there is a military laboratory or pharmaceutical experiments happening nearby.

By the time you meet a zombie, the contagion has probably spread to a point where there is little an individual can do

about it. Large-scale zombie extermination requires systematic removal methods. Your best chance at survival is to run, stay hidden, and try to find other survivors. At that point, you may be able to wait for the government or military to deal with the problem, but if that doesn't pan out, you may have to recreate human society with your surviving companions.

In the case of zombies appearing in villages and small towns or if the contamination is discovered and isolated at an early stage, then it might be possible to prevent the spread of the infection. In those cases, the first order of business is to build barricades and try to keep the zombies contained.

One possibility is to ask the government or military for assistance. However, asking the police for assistance will probably turn out to be a futile effort. Police aren't likely to believe your story, and they may destroy your barricades, only to find themselves surrounded. This will considerably exacerbate the problem.

One drawback of relying on the government or military is that they may decide the best way to deal with the outbreak is to quarantine the area and destroy everything in it. You may find yourself having to decide whether or not to make yourself a martyr to the cause of preserving the rest of mankind.

The first consideration in coping with Explosive Pandemic-style zombies is to keep from being surrounded. As long as an escape route is still available, you should be able to outrun them. Stay calm and stick to your escape route, if you can. If you should find yourself attacked, take special care not to become infected. The careful survivor wears garments that cannot be penetrated by teeth or fingernails. For this purpose, leather jackets and safety boots are standard wear, as they should be easy to procure.

Take care to observe the physical abilities of the zombies. Most zombies are unable to climb stairs or ladders. If that is the case, then an effective strategy is to take refuge on the top floor of a building. In the same way, you should also carefully

observe how the zombies react. Some theories say they are attracted to sounds, heat, smells, or carbon dioxide. Once you have a good idea of their capabilities, you will be able to more effectively hide or otherwise throw the zombies off your trail.

You must also prepare for the possibility that you or one of your comrades could become infected while fleeing or fighting zombies. In most cases, there is no treatment for a zombie infection, so you may need to make some tough choices to avoid the infection spreading even further.

Vengeance Spirit–Type Zombies
~THE BLOOD RELATIVES OF FULCI~

DEFINITION AND HISTORY

The Vengeance-Spirit-type zombies are caused by a supernatural phenomenon, in which grudges or regrets of the dead can cause countless dead bodies to return to life. In many of these cases, sorcery is involved, but unlike the Magically Cursed Slave-type zombie, this type of outbreak may be too big for any one shaman or magician to control. This is more like a zombie cataclysm, similar in scale to any possible natural disaster.

From time immemorial, the province of resurrecting the dead has always belonged to one force that goes far beyond the powers of man—the gods themselves. For example, Christian teachings speak of an "end of days," where the dead will be revived for a "final judgment." It is believed that, at this time, God will decide the fate of humanity. The image of the dead being revived on a massive scale seems to have been a key influence on many zombie stories.

In Japanese myth, when the Goddess Izanami died, her husband, Izanagi, searched for her in the land of the dead, only to find that she was now a rotting corpse. His horrified reaction angered Izanami, causing her to send an army of the vengeful dead past the border and into the land of the living

VENGEANCE SPIRIT-TYPE ZOMBIES

THEY GAVE THEIR LIVES TO SAVE MINE...!

TRY NOT TO MAKE THE SAME MISTAKE AS THESE GIRLS--MAKE SURE YOU DON'T CLOSE THE GATES OF HELL WHILE YOU'RE STILL ON THE HELL SIDE. AFTER ALL, SURVIVAL MEANS LIVING ALL THE WAY UNTIL THE END! ★

in Yomotsu-hirasaka. Izanagi pushed an enormous boulder in the way to close off this border. If the dead start rampaging, it would mean the boulder and wards protecting the border have somehow come undone.

Director Lucio Fulci drew on these mythical, fantastical stories of Vengeance Spirit-type zombies to create a series of movies that included *Zombie* (*Sanguelia*), *The Beyond* (*Biyondo*), and *City of the Living Dead* (*Paura Nella Citta del Morti Viventi*). For example, in 1980's *City of the Living Dead* (aka *Gates of Hell*), the suicide of a priest named Father Thomas opens the gates of Hell, allowing the living dead to invade our world. The only way to stop the invasion of zombies is to close the gates again, but when the spirit of Father Thomas appears out of the mist, whoever meets his eyes becomes a zombie. The film is filled with grotesque, nightmarish imagery, such as a storm of

maggots that fall like snow. Fulci's movie favors surrealism and a hopeless, menacing tone over rational storytelling.

Films like *City of the Living Dead* often don't follow a traditionally logical plot. Even if the gates of Hell can be closed, there's no guarantee that the march of the risen dead will stop, so how are the heroes supposed to come up with a strategy for solving the problem? More than anything, these zombies seem to be simply a manifestation of mankind's deepest fears, and as such aren't subject to rational analysis.

Aside from the work of Lucio Fulci, other works such as *The Evil Dead* (1981) and *Pet Sematary* (1989) feature a mythic power that emanates out of ancient, defiled ground, causing the dead to rise. These films also feature the Vengeance Spirit-type zombie. Of course, in every instance, they are not easily dealt with.

STRENGTHS AND WEAKNESSES

Vengeance Spirit-type zombies are tremendously difficult to destroy. In fact, destroying them may not even be a solution, since even the ones you have already taken care of have a tendency to reappear again, much like ghosts or spirits. It's best to approach these creatures as though they exist in a realm beyond human understanding.

It is possible for bad weather to follow the appearance of Vengeance Spirit-type zombies. This may not be caused by the zombies themselves, but by the balance of weather being thrown off as the border between the world of the living and the world of the dead becomes more vague. This may even affect more than the weather—day and night may become reversed, or other supernatural transformations may also occur.

If there is a weakness to Vengeance Spirit-type zombies, it can be found in legends and myths. Perhaps you can dispel the desire for revenge that spawned the zombies in the first place, or there may be secrets within the myths that, when understood, may hold clues to finding ways to defeat the zombies. However,

in most cases, the actions that need to be taken are often beyond the intellects and abilities of normal human beings.

DISTINGUISHING THEM, AND WHEN YOU MEET ONE

If the zombies you meet conform to local oral traditions, then it's safe to assume that these are either Magically Cursed Slave-type zombies or Vengeance Spirit-type zombies. If the weather suddenly turns foul with the arrival of the zombies, or if dawn never comes, or some other supernatural phenomenon occurs, then you may assume that these are Vengeance Spirit-type zombies.

The moment you come across a Vengeance Spirit-type zombie, the first thing to do is immediately run away. If running away is absolutely impossible or if the entire world is affected, there won't be anywhere to run. At that point, you must start thinking of ways to solve the dilemma.

Your best chance is to appease the enormous grudge that led to this catastrophe or find a way to close the gates of Hell. In the case of a grudge, it's best to discard humane half-measures of appeasement. This may mean finding the descendants of the one who incited the grudge and sacrificing them (unfortunately, it may be that *you* are that particular descendant). In the case of the gate, let's first check to make sure which side of the gate we are on before shutting it, shall we?

Deathless—Type Zombies
~LEGIONS OF THE END OF THE WORLD: RE—ANIMATOR~

DEFINITION AND HISTORY

With most zombies, their brains are their vulnerable spot. Destroy the head, and they stop moving. If you destroy the brain and they're still moving, chopping them into pieces or engulfing them in flames should do the trick. However, Deathless-type zombies have a life force that defies even the

most extreme methods. You can destroy their brains, but they still move. Chop them up, and the pieces keep coming. Burn them to cinders, and even the ashes will contain some residual life force.

The signature film for Deathless-type zombies is Dan O'Bannon's 1985 outing, *Return of the Living Dead*. In the film, a military experiment produced a gas called 2-4-5 Trioxin that, when leaked out, caused the zombification of many corpses. These zombies have a bizarrely strong life force, which allows them to move even without their heads. When they are cremated, the rain that falls afterward is suffused with their ashes, which creates new zombies and increases their numbers. In the end, not even a nuclear missile could stop these zombies—the clouds themselves were seeded with the zombie plague, and the subsequent rain spread the infestation worldwide.

Deathless-type zombies call to mind the Book of Revelations in *The Bible* when depicting the demise of human culture. Interpreted this way, zombies are angels doing the work of God as His representatives. As such, it is only natural that they be impervious to mortal intelligence or strength. This version of zombies calls to mind the effects of a catastrophe that renders humanity powerless, in much the same way we lack control over enormous tidal waves and earthquakes. Either way, one of the attributes of Deathless-type zombies is that they have absurd power, and man is no match for them.

When talking about oddly strong life forces, one cannot overlook Stuart Gordon's 1985 film, *Re-Animator*. The film features the twisted genius doctor Herbert West whose research develops a medicine that can bring the dead back to life. This medicine creates zombies, but they are zombies with an unusually strong life force, so strong that every portion of the body acts of its own will. For example, one zombie uses its own intestines as a whip with which to attack the living.

In the sequel, *The Bride of Re-Animator*, zombified body

CALLING THEM "DEATHLESS" IS KIND OF WEIRD, SINCE ZOMBIES ARE DEAD TO BEGIN WITH. BUT I GUESS COMPLAINING ABOUT IT WILL ONLY MAKE ME SOUND LIKE A POSER, HUH?

IF YOU CAN'T TAKE THEM DOWN, THEN THE ONLY THING LEFT TO DO IS RUN, RIGHT? THAT DOESN'T SEEM FAIR...!

parts are gathered together to form new zombies, and in one case, bat wings are added to a severed head to make it fly. This is a new type of life force, incomprehensible to human knowledge.

Of course, if you are confronted with this kind of zombie, any slicing, dicing, and pulverizing activities will do nothing to stop it. The only way to avoid calamity is to wait for the effects of the active agent to fade. Still, even Dr. West, the creator of the re-animating medicine, has no idea how long it will take for its effects to fade.

STRENGTHS AND WEAKNESSES

Deathless-type zombies' strength is, of course, their inability to be put down, but aside from that, they follow most of the attributes of Explosive Pandemic-type zombies and Athletic-type zombies (described below). The problem is that since they

cannot die, you can't even stop them by cutting them into tiny pieces. All that will do is create a bunch of tiny body-part zombies. If you burn them and their ashes are released with the resulting smoke, you may end up creating many, many more zombies.

For those reasons, Deathless-type zombies don't have any special weaknesses.

COPING METHODS

Coping methods follow the same pattern with Explosive Pandemic-type zombies and Athletic-type zombies, with the exception that their deathless state makes attacking them rather meaningless. You can smash their brains or crush their hearts, but they still won't stay down. If you rip apart their bodies, you'll end up with an increased number of zombified body parts. Burning them to ashes risks the ashes being blown away by the wind, creating countless new zombies. If it weren't for the fact that some of them were successfully sealed inside drums of radioactive waste, it's possible that there might not have been a way to stop their attacks. Don't even try to fight them. Just run. When trying to escape, be wary of zombified body parts and zombie rain.

Body parts of Deathless-type zombies may move of their own will, entering small cracks and crevices, and it is quite possible that they will attack from hard-to-see areas. If you are taking refuge underground, you must still keep careful watch, especially for ventilation shafts and other areas where the pipes connect to the sewers.

Rain mixed with zombie ash can not only cause damage to humans, but if it rains on a graveyard or if ash-infected water gets into someplace like a mortuary, it may have the effect of turning those corpses into zombies.

Try to avoid being surrounded, even in places where that seems unlikely. And if it is raining, or it looks as though it might rain, do your best to stay indoors. However, there's no possible

way to exterminate Deathless-type zombies, so even if you are successful in your escape attempts, the destruction of humanity is really only a matter of time. It is possible that you may simply resign yourself to this fate, and find a quiet spot where you can wait for the end to come.

But if you won't give up, then you'll want to resort to scientific research in order to find a way to permanently kill the zombies. Unfortunately, the kinds of laboratory facilities you'll need for this research are usually among the first places to be overcome by the living dead…

Athletic-Type Zombies
~THE NEW GENERATION OF ZOMBIES~

DEFINITION AND HISTORY

Athletic-type zombies are, as the name implies, a fast and dexterous type of zombie. In most cases, these are a subspecies of the Explosive Pandemic-type of zombie, with a high enough contagion rate to cause the swift collapse of human civilization. We call them "athletic," but some have speeds surpassing those of ordinary humans, while others are slower. But since all have unlimited muscle power, it will take a Herculean effort to outrun them.

Opinions differ on who exactly originated the Athletic-type zombie, but in Danny Boyle's *28 Days Later*, the zombies aren't actually dead. More precisely, they are infected living humans who have lost their reason and gone on a rampage. They aren't corpses. But the film is still considered a zombie movie, and taking into consideration that Haiti's zombies in real life were probably not dead either, these zombies could be thought of as "zombies who aren't dead." Meanwhile, Director Zack Snyder's 2004 remake of the breakthrough Romero zombie movie, *Dawn of the Dead*, really brought the running zombie into the mainstream.

ATHLETIC-TYPE ZOMBIES

 AS THE PERSON DOING THE RUNNING AWAY, I PREFER MY ZOMBIES SLOW AND CLUMSY!

 EITHER WAY, IT SEEMS THAT ZOMBIE MOVIE FANS ARE SHARPLY DIVIDED ON THE SUBJECT OF RUNNING ZOMBIES.

As fast-moving zombies became popularized, these depictions quickly outpaced the dull, slow-moving Romero-created zombie, while still focusing on the end of society as we know it. And in that way, these films marked a pivotal change.

Whenever a major release comes along that changes the game, it often spawns spin-offs, sequels, and imitators, eventually becoming a genre unto itself. However, when an idea becomes tied to a genre, it can become stuck in a rut, losing some of its original vigor. At that point, fans of the genre start to wish for something that effectively breaks the previous rules. Zombie entertainment is no exception. We're not simply talking about the game-changing debut of the Athletic-type zombie, but the hope for even further innovations within the zombie genre.

STRENGTHS AND WEAKNESSES

The strengths and weakness of the Athletic-type zombies follow most of the rules of the Explosive Pandemic-type zombie, but naturally their increased speed is a distinguishing factor. If you think of zombies as an infectious disease, then the difference in the speed of the zombies reflects the difference in the speed of the contagion's spread.

With slow-moving zombies, as soon as the military is alerted, they can set up barriers to contain them. But with the high-speed zombies, the zombies may have already scattered into other neighborhoods by the time the military learns what is happening. This very speed that could be the factor that determines whether human civilization is able to survive.

COPING METHODS

You can use most of the Explosive Pandemic-type zombie techniques to battle the Athletic-type zombies as well. You will probably want to keep leather clothes and safety boots handy too. The methods that will kill a slow-moving zombie will also stop an Athletic-type zombie.

Although a spot on level ground with a good view of the surroundings are excellent for slow-moving zombies, you will prefer a spot where it is not as easy to get surrounded when dealing with Athletic-type zombies. When you're trying to find shelter, be advised that the Athletic-type zombies can sometimes overcome simple barricades and obstacles such as staircases and ladders.

The best chance for survival against Athletic-type zombies is a detailed reading of a local map by which to plan your movements. You'll need a plan to avoid being surrounded by approaching zombies at every possible location on the map, as well as designated places you can hide out and rest. Although such a plan is helpful even against slow-moving zombies, it is indispensable when combating Athletic-type zombies.

Moreover, you will need to make contingency plans that can

quickly be put into action if your situation worsens. If your reaction time is slowed by panic, your slowed pace will only make you more vulnerable to the zombies.

Also, you'll need to prepare for the possibility of one of your group being turned into a zombie. In the case of slow zombies, you and your group will have time to look at its expression, realize that your friend is no longer human, and finish off the newly-formed monster before it can infect anyone else. But in the case of Athletic-type zombies, by the time you've realized what's happening, the zombie may already be gnawing on the windpipe of a doomed comrade.

Self-Aware-Type Zombies
~ANOTHER TYPE OF HUMANITY~

DEFINITION AND HISTORY

Self-Aware-type zombies are, as the name implies, zombies who retain a certain amount of self-awareness and reason. The level of self-awareness varies widely: some zombies are basically just animals, while others have the brain power of a toddler, and others still come close to normal human intelligence. Some zombies are even possessed of an intelligence beyond humanity.

We could look to many sources for the origin of the Self-Aware-type zombie, depending on our definition. For example, since Count Dracula is certainly intelligent and self-aware, while also fitting the definition of the walking dead, one could reasonably classify him as a Self-Aware-type zombie. And because the enemies in the 1954 book *I Am Legend* spread their explosive pandemic through biting, the line that separates zombies and vampires (as the book describes) is extremely vague.

So you could say that vampires are monsters of the incredibly "dangerous enemy" variety, while still being a variation on the Self-Aware-type zombie. This type might represent

SELF-AWARE-TYPE ZOMBIES

WHEN THEY'RE LIKE THIS, THEY MAY BE LESS LIKE ZOMBIES AND MORE LIKE ALIENS...

I TEND TO HESITATE BEFORE KILLING AN ENEMY THAT I CAN COMMUNICATE WITH. WE MAY HAVE DIFFICULTY DEALING WITH THEM, EVEN IF THEY AREN'T ENEMIES.

YOU HUNGRY? CORPSE FLESH IS GREAT!

THAT'S RIGHT. AND SINCE A LACK OF INTELLIGENCE IS A WEAKNESS IN OTHER ZOMBIES, BY COMPARISON WE'RE A WHOLE NEW LEVEL OF TROUBLE.

IF YOU THINK ABOUT IT, MERO, YOU'RE THE SELF AWARE-TYPE ZOMBIE, AREN'T YOU?

NOT MUCH PUSH FOUND OF FLESH WILL DO. CAN YOU SELL US SOME?

DO YOU THINK WE COULD HAVE SOME HUMAN MEAT FOR MY CHILD?

THERE HAVE EVEN BEEN RECENT WORKS WHERE A ZOMBIE AND A NORMAL HUMAN FELL IN LOVE, HUH...?

IF THEY FEEL EMOTIONS LIKE LOVE AND AFFECTION, IT'S POSSIBLE WE COULD ALL BE FRIENDS!

the mastermind, or final boss, of a zombie entertainment, with power and intelligence far exceeding the scope of its minions (those being the slow-moving zombie). This type of Self-Aware-type zombie is perfect for games, and as such, it is often found in zombie games or the works from other media that zombie games are based on. An example might be from the Capcom series *Resident Evil*, and its chief antagonist Albert Wesker. He retains his intelligence, even though his is the brain responsible for the virus that spreads zombies all over the world. That brain resides within a superhuman zombie body as he stands in the way of the player character.

The Self-Aware-type zombie is also sometimes used to confront humanity with a philosophical dilemma. The average type of zombie has no more intelligence than an animal, and since communication with them is impossible, the human characters

don't hesitate to destroy them. But if those zombies had real intelligence, they could be considered sentient beings. At that point, is it still morally acceptable to simply kill the zombies?

This kind of dilemma is presented in the 2005 Romero-directed film, *Land of the Dead*, by the self-aware zombie known as Big Daddy. Because humanity is exterminating the zombies, the zombies in this film are presented as a persecuted minority. Since Romero has always examined aspects of human society through the lens of zombie movies, you could say that making a movie where the self-aware zombies are seen as objects of sympathy was inevitable.

Finally, we would like to mention the Hero-type zombie. For some, it's possible that becoming zombified is a good thing. This sort of zombie is immortal and incredibly strong. If the character is able to keep his or her intelligence and manage to make peace with being dead, zombification has its advantages. This idea opens up lots of possibilities for stories where the zombie is the hero.

In the manga *3x3 Eyes* by Yuzo Takada, the third eye and the strong magic powers of the Sanjiyan Unkara clan can seal a soul within a body, causing it to become immortal. This "Wu" becomes a protector, living a rather zombie-like existence. And in Shin'ichi Kimura's novel *Kore ha Zombie Desu ka* ("Is This What You Call a Zombie?"), a pretty young necromancer and a guy she brought back from the dead as a zombie team up to fight all sorts of enemies.

STRENGTHS AND WEAKNESSES

Because there are all types of Self-Aware-type zombies, this is the one type where their lack of intelligence makes them vulnerable.

Their most important characteristic is that they have their reason, and they are able to learn. As such, a method that defeated them once may not work as well, or at all, the next time you try to use it.

COPING METHODS

The Dangerous Enemy version of the Self-Aware-type zombie is to be especially feared. They're too intelligent to fall for simple traps or stratagems. You'll have to work especially hard to outwit them. On the other hand, you may wish to try to communicate with them. It may be possible to deceive them or guide them in a direction beneficial to you. When you are dealing with an enemy who feels a lot of pride, you may be able to trick them into doing what you want by making them angry or flattering them. Of course, your goal is to have it do as you wish, but if you're not careful, you may end up doing what *it* wants instead...

To deal with the Dilemma version of the Self-Aware-type zombies, you will need to decide on your attitude regarding these zombies before engaging them. Are you going to end up fighting them no matter what? Or can you try to live in harmony with them? If you wish to live with them, what kind of living arrangements is possible? If the rest of your human community doesn't agree with you, in a worst-case scenario, it could lead to discord among normal humans.

Non-Human-Type Zombies
~THE CHILDREN OF GAMES~

DEFINITION AND HISTORY

The vast majority of Non-Human-type zombies will be something other than human beings. These are divided into two different variations, the first of which occurs when things like animals become zombified. The second occurs when a human is zombified, but the human's form is changed to something other than the human shape during the zombification process. Since Non-Human-type zombies are on the boundary between zombies and some other kind of monster, a strict definition and pedigree for this type is difficult to settle on. Simply put, if you're

thinking of works that come after the Romero movies, most of these began life as games rather than movies.

Filmmakers are often attracted to zombie movies because they are cheaper to make than the creatures of other horror movies. If a filmmaker doesn't have a big budget, all they need are an appropriately distressed wardrobe and a dirty face, combined with a believable performance from the actor, to create a zombie. This is why a lot of young talent try their hands at different kinds of zombie movies, which is one of the reasons that the present boom has come about. To put it in purely financial terms, a Non-Human-type zombie would be outside the budget of most zombie movies.

On the other hand, the situation is different in games. In the early days of computer games and tabletop role playing games, zombies appeared in fantasy worlds inspired by myths and legends, and in later generations, fighting games that used zombies in modern settings quickly became plentiful. The huge success of games such as the *Resident Evil* series spawned a host of imitations, where zombies were the featured enemy. And although they all shared the idea of the player characters fighting enemy zombies, they also featured many different types of zombies as enemy characters. It also became commonplace for the boss character to be some kind of transformed zombie, with strength far exceeding that of humans.

Thus it can be said that Non-Human-type zombies debuted in games, where they quickly gained popularity as antagonists. Also, in movies adapted from games, such as *Resident Evil* and *House of the Dead*, Non-Human-type zombies soon began to appear in film as well.

STRENGTHS AND WEAKNESSES

Because Non-Human-type zombies come in all shapes and sizes, we cannot make any unconditional rules. However, on the whole, they have greater physical abilities than humans. As if that weren't enough, some are even highly intelligent.

NON-HUMAN-TYPE ZOMBIES

OF COURSE, IT CHANGES EVERYTHING IF THE ZOMBIE ANIMALS HAVE THEIR SAME ATTRIBUTES AS WHEN THEY WERE ALIVE OR IF THEY'VE BECOME SLOW AND CLUMSY LIKE HUMAN ZOMBIES.

YEAH, THE LITTLE ANIMALS ARE QUICK AND HARD TO FIND, SO THEY'RE A PAIN. STILL, NOT NEARLY AS DANGEROUS AS THE HUGE-WILD-ANIMAL TYPE OF ZOMBIES, HUH?

This type of zombie has its own unique weakness as well—for example, some of them are abnormally large, which can make them unstable.

COPING METHODS

To effectively deal with Non-Human-type zombies, you must first understand their nature. If they have the ability to change their shape, then you'll need to figure out what triggers the change. If you're not careful, you might find yourself changing shape before long.

If these zombies were developed as part of some experiment to create a living weapon, your best bet for survival is to defeat the scientist who was behind it all. Another possible origin comes in the form of space aliens who have sent zombies as an advance invasion force. In that case, you'll need to

investigate the aliens by infiltrating their spacecraft in the hopes of finding a way to disable their zombie-creating technology.

Unfortunately, the odds are overwhelming that whoever was behind the experiments was killed during the zombies' original rampage. In that case, you will want the instigator's computer files and research notes. When analyzed, they might hold the key to the zombies' weaknesses or point the way towards some sort of self-destruct sequence you can possibly activate to take out the base where the zombies were created.

Since most Non-Human-type zombies are basically a physical presence (as opposed to Vengeance Spirit-type zombies listed above), they can usually be fought with such things as high-powered weapons, cave-ins, explosions, or other game-style methods of combat. When fighting Non-Human-type zombies, keep your eyes open for helpful clues in the periphery of your environment.

No matter if it's weaponized animals or zombies that can suddenly transform, they all have (or have been given) high-level fighting abilities. At the same time, in most cases, these zombies have instabilities that match their improvements. But because of these instabilities, further transformations may take place. And because of the unstable nature of these zombies, their transformations come with the risk of sudden self-destruction. Some of these zombies may evolve into something even worse or into a more elusive form. At this point, you'll waste valuable time trying to locate them again. And, as mentioned before, those that have evolved too much have the possibility of explosively self-destructing and taking you with them.

AND THOSE ARE THE SEVEN TYPES OF ZOMBIES YOU WILL FIND IN ZOMBIE MOVIES AND OTHER ENTERTAINMENT.

 THOSE VENGEANCE SPIRIT-TYPE ZOMBIES ARE PRETTY AWFUL! THEY'RE SO POWERFUL, AND HUMANS CAN'T DO ANYTHING TO STOP THEM...!

 BUT ALL YOU HAVE TO DO IS SHUT THE GATES TO HELL, RIGHT? I THINK THAT MEANS WE HAVE A CHANCE!

 YEAH, BUT THAT'S ONLY ASSUMING THAT OPENING THE GATES TO HELL BROUGHT THE ZOMBIES TO LIFE IN THE FIRST PLACE.

 AND THE DEATHLESS-TYPE ZOMBIES WON'T DIE NO MATTER WHAT YOU DO, SO ALL YOU CAN DO IS RUN.

 I STILL THINK THEY'RE BETTER THAN THE VENGEANCE SPIRIT-TYPE ZOMBIES, SINCE YOU CAN PHYSICALLY TAKE ACTION AGAINST THEM.

 BUT HEY, IT LOOKS LIKE THE MAGICAL CURSED SLAVE-TYPE ZOMBIES ARE PRETTY WEAK, HUH? THANK GOODNESS!

 YEAH, BUT IN THE END YOU STILL HAVE TO STOP THE SHAMAN OR MAGICIAN IN A FINAL BOSS-STYLE SITUATION, AND THAT PROBABLY WON'T BE EASY.

 IN THAT CASE, WHY DON'T WE OFF THE SHAMAN OR MAGICIAN FIRST? THAT'LL MAKE THINGS EASIER.

 IT'S THE EXPLOSIVE PANDEMIC-TYPE ZOMBIE THAT SEEMS THE MOST POPULAR. WHEN MOST PEOPLE THINK OF ZOMBIES, THAT'S WHAT THEY IMAGINE.

 BUT WITH EXPLOSIVE PANDEMIC-TYPE, ONE ZOMBIE BY ITSELF ISN'T SO TOUGH, RIGHT?

 THE ATHLETIC-TYPE ZOMBIES ARE LIKE EXPLOSIVE PANDEMIC-TYPE ZOMBIES, ONLY TAKEN TO A MORE DANGEROUS LEVEL, AREN'T THEY?

 OH, THAT'S JUST GREAT! AT LEAST WITH EXPLOSIVE PANDEMIC-TYPE ZOMBIES, YOU CAN RUN AWAY FROM THEM!

 STILL, THEY CAN BE KILLED PRETTY MUCH THE SAME AS THE EXPLOSIVE PANDEMIC-TYPE ZOMBIES, RIGHT? I THINK THEY'RE STILL MANAGEABLE.

 THE NON-HUMAN-TYPE ZOMBIES ARE SPLIT INTO TWO DIFFERENT CATEGORIES: THE HUMAN-TRANSFORMED-INTO-SUPERHUMAN TYPES AND THE ORIGINALLY NON-HUMAN VARIATIONS.

 BUT BOTH TYPES HAVE ABILITIES THAT GO FAR BEYOND WHAT A REGULAR ZOMBIE IS CAPABLE OF, SO YOU HAVE TO BE ESPECIALLY CAREFUL WITH THEM.

 I DON'T WANT TO HAVE TO FIGHT ANYTHING THAT SEEMS LIKE IT COULD BE THE FINAL BOSS IN A GAME...

 AND THE FINAL REMAINING TYPE IS THE TYPE THAT *I* REPRESENT. CAN YOU GUESS WHAT THAT IS?

 WELL, SINCE YOU BECAME A ZOMBIE AFTER BEING BITTEN BY ONE, THEN YOU'D BE AN EXPLOSIVE PANDEMIC-TYPE ZOMBIE, RIGHT?

 NO. JUDGING FROM HOW QUICKLY SHE CORRECTS US AND HOW QUICKLY SHE GETS ANGRY, I WOULD DEDUCE A HIGH POSSIBILITY OF HER BEING AN ATHLETIC-TYPE ZOMBIE...

 SHE ACTS ALL SCARY, BUT SHE'S BEEN UNUSUALLY NICE TO US, SO...I KNOW! SHE'S THE TSUNDERE-TYPE ZOMBIE, AMIRIGHT?!

 I'M *TALKING* TO YOU RIGHT NOW!! WHAT ELSE COULD I BE BUT A SELF-AWARE-TYPE ZOMBIE? HERE I AM BEING NICE ENOUGH TO EXPLAIN IT ALL, THE LEAST YOU COULD DO IS GET THE HINT!

 AH, OF COURSE. FROM THIS DISCOURSE, I CAN CONCLUDE THAT AN EFFECTIVE TACTIC AGAINST SELF-AWARE-TYPE ZOMBIES IS TO UNDERMINE THEIR CONFIDENCE WITH BITING SARCASM AND BARBED CONVERSATION.

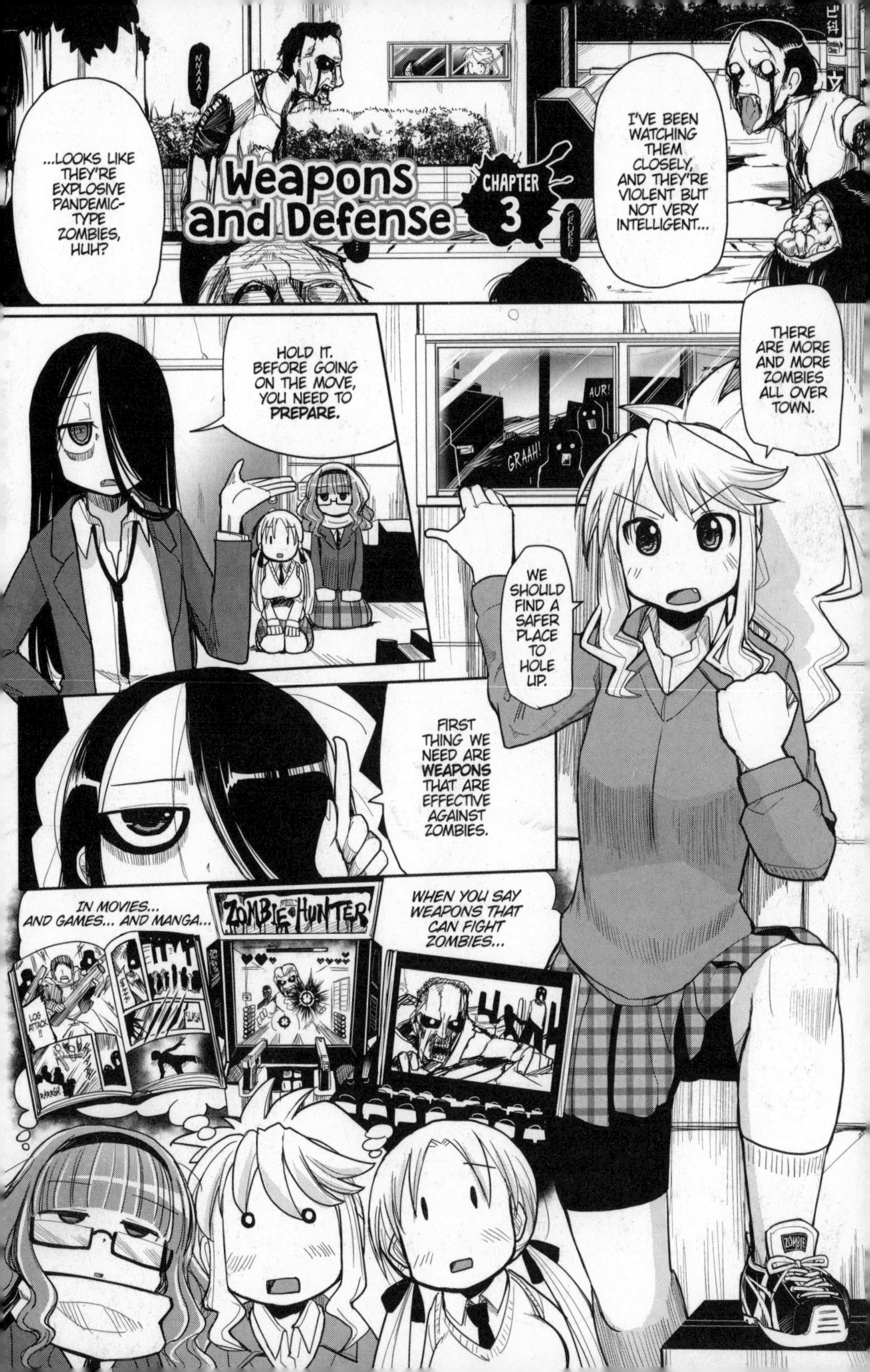

I'VE BEEN WATCHING THEM CLOSELY, AND THEY'RE VIOLENT BUT NOT VERY INTELLIGENT...
Weapons and Defense
CHAPTER 3
...LOOKS LIKE THEY'RE EXPLOSIVE PANDEMIC-TYPE ZOMBIES, HUH?
THERE ARE MORE AND MORE ZOMBIES ALL OVER TOWN.
AUR!
GRAAH!
WE SHOULD FIND A SAFER PLACE TO HOLE UP.
HOLD IT. BEFORE GOING ON THE MOVE, YOU NEED TO PREPARE.
FIRST THING WE NEED ARE WEAPONS THAT ARE EFFECTIVE AGAINST ZOMBIES.
WHEN YOU SAY WEAPONS THAT CAN FIGHT ZOMBIES...
ZOMBIE HUNTER
IN MOVIES... AND GAMES... AND MANGA...
LOG ATTACK!!

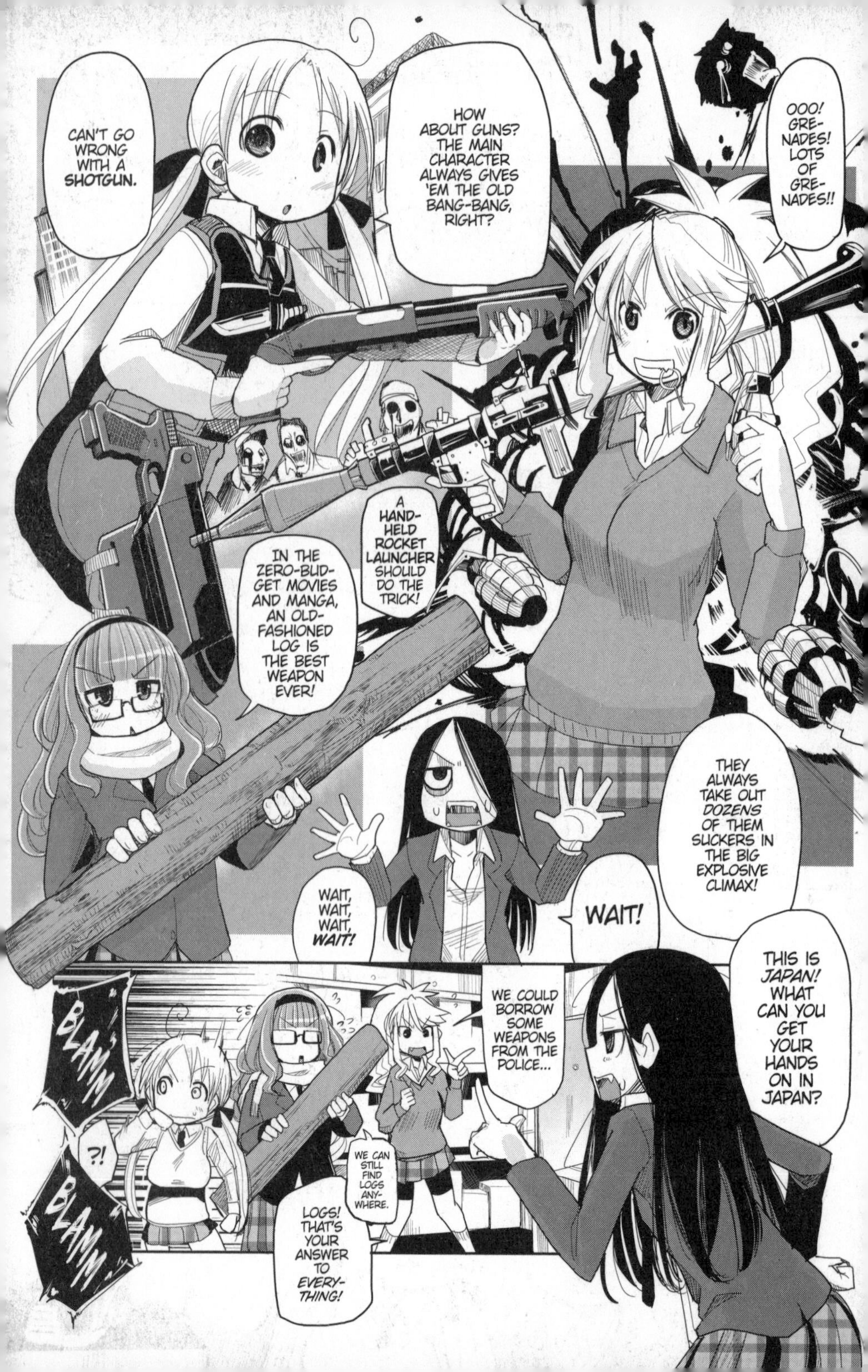
OOO! GRENADES! LOTS OF GRENADES!!
HOW ABOUT GUNS? THE MAIN CHARACTER ALWAYS GIVES 'EM THE OLD BANG-BANG, RIGHT?
CAN'T GO WRONG WITH A SHOTGUN.
A HAND-HELD ROCKET LAUNCHER SHOULD DO THE TRICK!
IN THE ZERO-BUDGET MOVIES AND MANGA, AN OLD-FASHIONED LOG IS THE BEST WEAPON EVER!
THEY ALWAYS TAKE OUT *DOZENS* OF THEM SUCKERS IN THE BIG EXPLOSIVE CLIMAX!
WAIT!
WAIT, WAIT, WAIT, ***WAIT!***
THIS IS *JAPAN!* WHAT CAN YOU GET YOUR HANDS ON IN JAPAN?
WE COULD BORROW SOME WEAPONS FROM THE POLICE...
BLAMM
?!
BLAMM
WE CAN STILL FIND LOGS ANYWHERE.
LOGS! THAT'S YOUR ANSWER TO *EVERYTHING!*

AHHH! GET AWAY! GET AWAAAY!!

HUUGGHH!!

HELP ME! MOMMY!!

DOESN'T LOOK LIKE WE CAN COUNT ON MUCH HELP FROM THE POLICE.

PLACES LIKE POLICE STATIONS WILL FILL UP QUICKLY WITH PEOPLE... AND THOSE ARE THE PLACES THAT ARE USUALLY **COMPROMISED** FIRST.

PEOPLE WHO HAVE BEEN INFECTED WILL BE MIXED IN AMONGST THE LIVING-- AND AS MORE AND MORE OF THEM TRY TO GET IN, MORE ZOMBIES ARE LIKELY TO GET IN WITH THEM.

KA-CHAK...

COME TO THINK OF IT, WE HAVEN'T CHECKED THIS ROOM YET.

UGH. I THINK SHE'S ASLEEP.

MM... MMM...

SNORE ZZZZ

WE NEED A SAFE HAVEN, ONE WITH WEAPONS WE CAN ACTUALLY GET OUR HANDS ON.

YEAH, BUT WHERE?!

SAY, GUYS... ISN'T THIS KINDA WHAT WE'RE LOOKING FOR?

?

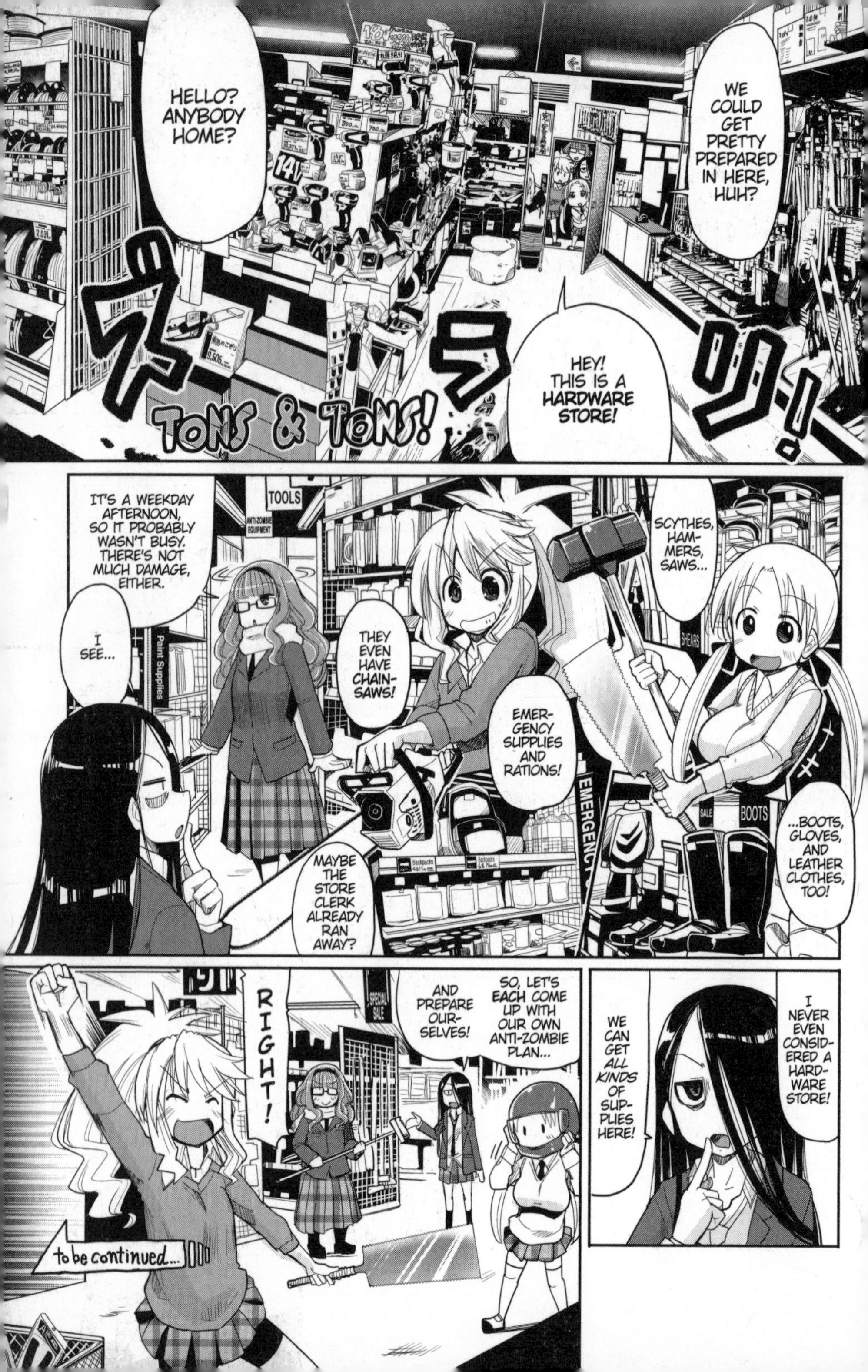
WE COULD GET PRETTY PREPARED IN HERE, HUH?
HELLO? ANYBODY HOME?
HEY! THIS IS A HARDWARE STORE!
TONS & TONS!
TOOLS
ANTI-ZOMBIE EQUIPMENT
SCYTHES, HAM-MERS, SAWS...
THEY EVEN HAVE CHAIN-SAWS!
IT'S A WEEKDAY AFTERNOON, SO IT PROBABLY WASN'T BUSY. THERE'S NOT MUCH DAMAGE, EITHER.
I SEE...
Paint Supplies
SHEARS
EMERGENCY
...BOOTS, GLOVES, AND LEATHER CLOTHES, TOO!
EMER-GENCY SUPPLIES AND RATIONS!
MAYBE THE STORE CLERK ALREADY RAN AWAY?
BOOTS
SALE
Backpacks
I NEVER EVEN CONSID-ERED A HARD-WARE STORE!
WE CAN GET ALL KINDS OF SUP-PLIES HERE!
SO, LET'S EACH COME UP WITH OUR OWN ANTI-ZOMBIE PLAN...
AND PREPARE OUR-SELVES!
RIGHT!
SPECIAL SALE
to be continued...

 I NEVER EVEN THOUGHT ABOUT IT, BUT A HARDWARE STORE SELLS ALL SORTS OF THINGS THAT CAN BE USED AS WEAPONS... SHARP THINGS AND POWER TOOLS... ALSO DEFENSIVE GEAR, LIKE LEATHER CLOTHES AND BOOTS.

 I DON'T SEE ANY LOGS ANYWHERE...

 LISTEN, AND LISTEN GOOD, LOG LADY. THIS WOOD FETISH MIGHT BE CUTE IN *TWIN PEAKS*, BUT IT SURE AIN'T GONNA CUT IT HERE. BESIDES, THERE ARE A LOT OF THINGS IN THE SPORTING GOODS AND CAMPING SUPPLY SECTIONS THAT COULD BE USEFUL.

 YEAH! IT'S ALMOST LIKE THE PERFECT ANTI-ZOMBIE WEAPON SHOP!!

 SO, WE'RE AGREED--THIS IS WHERE WE'LL PREPARE?

 HM, WHAT'LL I TAKE WITH ME? WHAT HAS THE MOST FIREPOWER?

 YOU AND THE FIREPOWER OBSESSION! SURE, FIREPOWER IS GOOD, BUT YOU ALSO WANT SOMETHING WITH A BIT OF REACH! BUT ABOVE ALL, MAKE SURE YOU PRIORITIZE PORTABILITY AND DURABILITY, OR YOU'LL BE OUT OF LUCK!

 PERFORATION AND DAMNATION? WHAT'RE THEY?

 PORTABILITY AND *DURABILITY*. DURABILITY IS HOW LONG YOUR WEAPON WILL LAST. WHETHER YOU'RE CLOSE TO A SAFE SPOT OR STILL HAVE A WAYS TO TRAVEL, ZOMBIES COULD SPRING ON YOU AT ANY MOMENT, DESTROYING YOUR PLANNED ROUTE. YOU'LL HAVE TO FIND A NEW PLACE TO HOLE UP OR ELSE GO A LONGER WAY AROUND.

 IT'S TRUE! WHAT NORMALLY TAKES JUST MINUTES BY TRAIN CAN BE A REALLY LONG WALK!

 RIGHT. SO WHILE YOU'RE ON YOUR WAY, YOU'LL BE IN TROUBLE IF YOU WIND UP UNARMED, RIGHT? MAKE SURE YOU'RE NOT CARRYING ANYTHING THAT'LL BREAK EASILY. AND FOR WEAPONS THAT NEED RECHARGING, RELOADING, OR FUEL, IF YOU DON'T HAVE THOSE PREPARED, YOUR WEAPON WILL BE USELESS. THAT'S WHAT DURABILITY IS ALL ABOUT.

 WHEN WE'RE ON THE MOVE, THINGS THAT ARE TOO BIG, TOO LONG, OR TOO BULKY WILL JUST GET IN THE WAY, HUH? SO THINK ABOUT HOW YOU'RE GOING TO CARRY YOUR WEAPON BEFORE YOU GO!

 EXACTLY! AND WHEN YOU CARRY SOMETHING FOR LONG PERIODS OF TIME, IT TIRES YOU OUT. YOU'RE GOING TO WANT WEAPONS THAT WON'T WEIGH YOU DOWN TOO MUCH. THAT'S THE MEANING OF PORTABILITY.

 THE MOST POWERFUL-LOOKING WEAPONS TEND TO BE BIG AND HEAVY. BUT THE LIGHTEST WEAPONS LOOK LIKE THE MOST FRAGILE. IT'S KIND OF LIKE A GAME, HUH?

 IS THAT ALL WE NEED TO WORRY ABOUT PREPARING?

 MAKE SURE TO BE REALISTIC--CHOOSE WHAT YOU CAN CARRY BASED ON YOUR STRENGTH AND BODY TYPE. YOU ALSO NEED TO BE EXTRA CAREFUL REGARDING THE NATURE OF THE ZOMBIES. IF WHAT YOU BRING IS LOUD OR GIVES OFF LIGHT, IT COULD END UP ATTRACTING ZOMBIES TO YOU IN LARGE NUMBERS.

HMM... I THINK I'VE NARROWED DOWN WHAT I WANT TO CARRY, BUT IT'S GETTING TO LOOK MORE AND MORE LIKE MEDIEVAL WEAPONS NOW...

How to Choose
Weapons and Defenses

By Morihiro Matsushiro

Wooden Swords and Bamboo Swords
THE MAIN WEAPON OF KENDO CLUBS

There are all sorts of non-lethal practice swords such as wooden swords and bamboo swords that are used to train in the use of Japanese-type swords. These are certainly easier to find and wield than metal pipes or wooden beams, and their strength in battle should not be underestimated. The problem is in the durability and stamina of the wooden weapons—simply put, it is very difficult to break a zombie's skull with a wooden sword. For this reason, the most effective attack is to thrust the weapon through an eye into the zombie's brain.

CONCRETE BATTLE TACTIC

It is possible to break through a zombie's skull with a heavy wooden sword, but it is a lot of work trying to hit the skull over

and over. With a bamboo practice sword, it is basically impossible. However, if a thrust is aimed at an eye, you might destroy the zombie's brain, so the most effective tactic is to pick up this easy-to-wield weapon and actively aim for these weak points.

ESSENTIAL PROFICIENCIES

It's easy to wave a sword around, but using it as a weapon requires a certain amount of training. Maintaining your posture after a thrust is quite difficult when you aren't used to it, so be especially careful. Also, anti-zombie tactics require that the weapon be used in a thrusting fashion. This style isn't taught in Japanese kendo-style fencing classes, so special training will be needed.

PRE-CRISIS TRAINING METHODS

The foundation moves are the same as kendo, but aiming at your opponent's eye is forbidden in kendo practice. You must practice that part on your own. No matter what form you practice, make sure you build muscles in your arms and lower back; otherwise any other training will be useless. Therefore, daily training is necessary.

OBTAINING THE WEAPON

Since nearly all Japanese junior high and high schools have kendo clubs or martial arts clubs that include kendo, these weapons should be readily available in any school. Also, any Japanese store that sells sports equipment will likely have them in stock, and there are even shops that specialize in kendo in large cities. You may even find these weapons in souvenir shops in tourist locations. Many have wooden swords as souvenirs, but you'll find that these are decidedly inferior to those wooden swords available in shops that specialize in kendo equipment.

Japanese Swords and Replica Swords
THE SOUL OF THE SAMURAI AND ROOM DECORATIONS

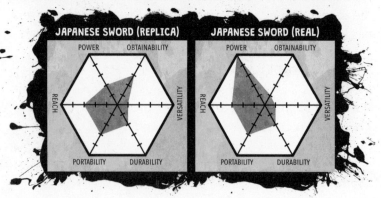

Japanese swords can be divided into two general groups: types with sharp edges that are true swords and those with dulled edges for decorations. The real swords are weapons with a highly lethal potential and can exhibit great power against zombies. But even certain replicas or heavy sword types used in sports have enough power for battle, especially if they are used to destroy zombie brains through thrusts. However, most swords used as decorations are built for showing off rather than battle and therefore may be unreliable.

CONCRETE BATTLE TACTICS

We know what actual swords can do, but even certain replica swords have the power to crack through a zombie skull. However, with a real sword, there is the possibility that breaking through skulls could damage the blade, so a full beheading is the recommended method. Also, like the wooden swords, one should train to stab through the eye into the brain with both real and replica swords, since the method is so effective. And since a real blade with a ruined edge is about as effective as a replica sword, dedicating yourself to aiming for zombie weaknesses is a must.

JAPANESE SWORDS

THIS IS THE SAMURAI SWORD WHICH, TO PEOPLE OVERSEAS, IS SEEN AS SOMETHING *MYSTICAL.*

WAIT! OW?

SPLAK

I-IT'S REALLY NOT A "COOL" WAY OF HANDLING IT, OKAY?!

STOP THAT, WILL YA?!

SPLAK

IF YOU TRY A CUTTING MOTION, YOU'LL DAMAGE THE BLADE.

USING A THRUSTING MOTION IS MOST EFFECTIVE.

WHEN FACING ZOMBIES, GO FOR WEAK SPOTS LIKE EYES.

 WHY ARE YOU LOOKING AT A KATANA AND DROOLING? YOU HUNGRY?

 KATANA... I JUST *LOVE* KATANA...!

ESSENTIAL PROFICIENCIES

The biggest problem with the Japanese sword is how difficult it is to master. If an untrained amateur were to wave it around, not only would it not be wielded effectively, the wielder would be likely to lacerate his or her own arms or legs. So one should learn basic swordsmanship such as drawing the weapon, and try to become an advanced student of the sword. Similarly with replica swords, you need training to make you fit to use it as a weapon. And, we'll mention again that since the thrusting attack that is so effective when fighting zombies is not taught in kendo practice, some special training in that area will be required.

PRE-CRISIS TRAINING METHODS

Aside from training yourself in the methods of drawing your sword, you will need to learn how to do thrusting attacks at

CHAPTER 3

a zombie's eye. At least a certain amount of self-study will be required. To wield a real Japanese sword, you will need even more arm and lower-back strength than using a wooden sword. Unfortunately, few places in Japan will allow you to train with even a replica sword, let alone an actual Japanese blade. So you will probably be forced to substitute a wooden sword in your practices anyway.

OBTAINING THE WEAPON

In Japan, it is extremely difficult to obtain a real Japanese sword with an edge. The same is true for the type of replicas with an edge that are used to practice drawing and swinging. And even if you are lucky enough to find an antique dealer or a sword dealer, they will likely have their swords locked away in cases under high security, and often they will be as *shirasaya*. The *shirasaya* are naked blades without a hilt or guard, and as such, they are difficult to use and should be handled with caution. On the other hand, it is extremely easy to find replica swords used for decoration or as props in plays and other dramas.

Empty Hands
YOUR FIRST WEAPON AND YOUR WEAPON OF LAST RESORT

MARTIAL ARTS WITH BARE HANDS

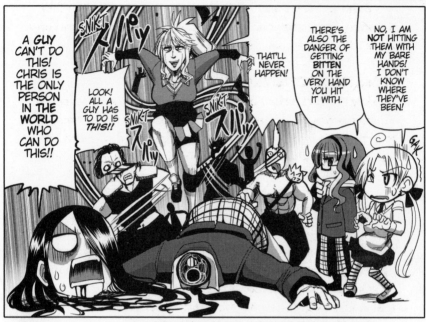

 NO... PLEASE STOP...!

 SHE'S USING THE OPPOSITE ASSASSINATION ART FROM *FIST OF THE NORTH STAR*--FIST OF THE SOUTHERN CROSS!! HER MOVEMENTS ARE LIKE A BIRD FLOATING ON THE WATER'S SURFACE! ITS ELEGANCE IS DIRECTLY PROPORTIONAL TO THE LETHAL POWER IT EXHIBITS!!

Your own bare hands are the most basic of weapons, and at times, they may be the last weapons you have. As far as zombie survival goes, taking on the undead with them is a good way to get yourself zombified, so we cannot recommend it. Even so, at the beginnings of a zombie outbreak or during a surprise attack by zombies, there may be many cases where your fists are all you have left to rely on.

CONCRETE BATTLE TACTICS

Since the Judo techniques for attacking a person's joints are useless against zombies, you'll have to try to do something to either destroy the skull or tear off the head. Still, if you crush an eyeball or strike a strong blow to the head, you may stop its movement for a brief time. Your best target, as always, would be the zombie's head.

Brass knuckles and leather gloves may help, but in their absence, wrapping your hands in cloth and keeping a grip on the ends is better than nothing.

ESSENTIAL PROFICIENCIES

The key to effective barehanded martial arts is directly reflected in one's physical abilities, so a heavy regimen of daily training is a must. You will want to build your physical strength and agility, which will allow you to master the most effective martial arts moves.

PRE-CRISIS TRAINING METHODS

There are plenty of different training methods, but nearly all of them forbid head attacks or attacks that could blind a person. You must choose a martial art that will give you a good chance to kill your opponent. Still, there are very few dojos in Japan that teach martial arts meant for military personnel, so the only thing to do is to practice on your own. Since martial arts techniques such as Karate use some of the same striking techniques as military martial arts, we suggest you enroll in a Karate dojo to start your training.

OBTAINING THE WEAPON

Of course, most people are born with these "weapons," but there does tend to be an unusually large number of arm amputations during a zombie apocalypse, so use caution! Scenes where a zombie bites someone's arm, which then needs to be amputated, are quite common. Sometimes characters find themselves fitted with chainsaws or shotguns as artificial limbs. But as these are not bare hands, we will cover these weapons in their own sections.

Frying Pans (Or One-Handed Chinese Pots)
YOU WON'T BE DISAPPOINTED IN THEIR POWER

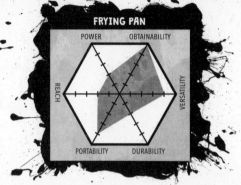

Because of their round shape, frying pans give the impression of only being good as shields. But the types used by professional chefs are heavy, and have an unexpected amount of power. One advantage of searching restaurants for them is that there are usually a variety of frying pans in their kitchen, and you can choose based on your own strength. When choosing, make sure to separate those with heft, power and a good, strong handle from those that do not look like they would make good weapons.

CONCRETE BATTLE TACTICS

For a basic attack, hold the frying pan by the handle and swing so that the flat bottom of your weapon will make contact with your opponent. Swinging it edge-wise may cut well, but it might also easily break. So the best tactic is to swing it so the flat part hits the zombie. An edge-swing is your attack of last resort. And of course, your target is the zombie's head.

ESSENTIAL PROFICIENCIES

Even the comparatively lightweight aluminum pans still weigh in the 500-800 gram range (1 to 1 3/4ths pounds), so you will need practice to be able to swing them effectively with one hand. But frying pans are quite simple to use, so once you have the muscle strength, you will quickly master it.

FRYING PANS

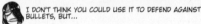
I DON'T THINK YOU COULD USE IT TO DEFEND AGAINST BULLETS, BUT...

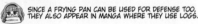
SINCE A FRYING PAN CAN BE USED FOR DEFENSE TOO, THEY ALSO APPEAR IN MANGA WHERE THEY USE LOGS.

PRE-CRISIS TRAINING METHODS

Fry up soybeans without oil and make sure they don't burn. Also practice swinging it in the kitchen on a daily basis. The basic training for this is waving the pan up and down and side-to-side, and when you become used to its weight, bring it down with force.

OBTAINING THE WEAPON

If you go to the kitchen of any restaurant, you will almost be sure to be able to find a frying pan—just make sure you don't pick one with a loose handle. Also, the Teflon home-use frying pans tend to be light and fragile, so they don't make good weapons. And it goes without saying that the type where the handle clicks on or off is out of the question.

Umbrellas and Canes
FOR BEST RESULTS, USE YOUR IMAGINATION

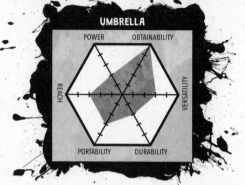

Umbrellas and canes are common everyday tools, but it doesn't take much to use them as weapons. However, since umbrellas have almost zero durability, it's best to think of them as one-use items. Cane-style items like trekking poles can be used not only for stabbing but also bludgeoning. They are formidable weapons that should not be discounted. On the other hand, canes for the aged can't really be used as weapons, so choose carefully.

CONCRETE BATTLE TACTICS

Both umbrellas and canes are basically thrusting weapons, and the most effective place to thrust is at the zombie's head (or, more specifically, the eye). You'll lose some reach if you grip it with both hands, but at the same time, you might not be able to get enough power behind a one-handed thrust to do much damage. Use whatever method is best for you and your particular situation. You can also use an ice pickaxe or trekking pole with one hand, swinging them like a club. Even then, you'd still do best to aim for the head.

ESSENTIAL PROFICIENCIES

An umbrella is a light weapon, and even the more muscularly challenged of us can swing it to drive off the zombies. However,

UMBRELLAS

UM-BRELLAS ARE SO LIGHT, EVEN I CAN USE THEM!

VOOM

THUMP

HYAH!

GRUNCH

TP TP TP

GRUNCH GRUNCH

CHOMP

AAAA!!

...WOULD BE OF NO USE WHATSO-EVER.

SHOULDA KNOWN A FOLDING UMBREL-LA...

UMBRELLA ARSENAL

YOU CAN GET THEM EASILY AT ANY CONVENIENCE STORE, AND SINCE THEY AREN'T HEAVY, YOU SHOULD TAKE *ALL* THAT YOU CAN CARRY.

DEPENDING ON HOW YOU USE THEM, **UMBRELLAS** CAN BE A WEAPON, TOO!

 THANK YOU, MS. OTAKU!

PERHAPS SOMEONE SHOULD TEACH LINA HOW TO FIGHT WITH A FOLDING UMBRELLA. FIRST, YOU PUT AN EYE PATCH OVER YOUR RIGHT EYE AND SAY THESE MAGIC WORDS: "YOU AND YOUR NORMAL LIFE SHOULD JUST DIE--"

it doesn't have much might, so you'll need to be accurate with your blows when fighting a zombie with it. It takes great skill to aim at an eye, so you'll have to get in close and be both tough and courageous (especially if you're wielding it with two hands).

PRE-CRISIS TRAINING METHODS

There are no well-known methods of training with an umbrella, but an effective method might be to get a mannequin and do many thrusting repetitions. When training, try to combine upward thrusts from below and downward stabs from above. We'd also suggest that practice with a trekking pole or ice pickaxe by swinging them one-handed would be effective.

OBTAINING THE WEAPON

Obtaining an umbrella is extremely easy, but they won't become weapons without some work. The umbrella should be closed with tape wrapped around the spokes to secure and strengthen them, and the point needs to be sharpened. Whether you want to strip off the cloth/ plastic covering of the umbrella depends on the quality of the cloth. Home use canes are readily available, but we would suggest a wooden trekking pole instead. Flexible or folding canes should not be used as weapons.

Knives and Carving Knives

REMEMBER, THEY CUT BOTH WAYS

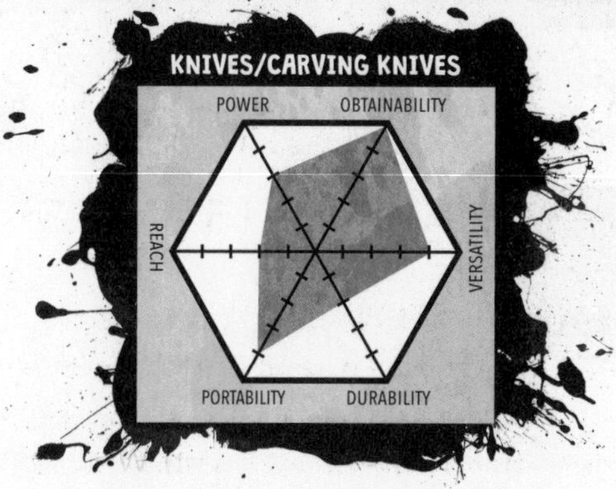
KNIVES/CARVING KNIVES
POWER
OBTAINABILITY
REACH
VERSATILITY
PORTABILITY
DURABILITY

Both utility knives and cooking knives are basically used for slicing, but durability can vary wildly among them. Also, there are a lot of knives that are far superior to carving knives for their thrusting ability. But since knives are strictly controlled in Japan, obtaining knives of the large, double-edged variety is exceedingly difficult. As a result, the remaining knives are not very convenient for fighting zombies.

KNIVES & CARVING KNIVES

 BASICALLY, THE PROBLEM IS THAT A ZOMBIE'S ONLY REAL WEAK POINT IS ITS HEAD. BUT EVEN IF YOU DON'T FINISH IT OFF, YOU CAN SLOW IT DOWN BY CUTTING OFF ITS ARMS AND LEGS. THEN AGAIN, THERE ARE SOME ZOMBIES THAT CAN GROW THEM BACK.

 THIS IS ALSO TRUE OF OTHER WEAPONS, BUT TRYING TO CUT ANY ZOMBIE BODY PART OTHER THAN THE HEAD WON'T GET YOU VERY FAR.

CONCRETE BATTLE TACTICS

As cutting off zombie limbs is relatively ineffective, the best you can do is aim a thrusting blow at the zombie's eye or attempt to crush its brain (its weakest point). Wielding the knife two-handed makes it difficult to reach the zombie's head, so the best moves are single-handed downward slices or slashing thrusts. Since this means close combat against the zombies, you must attack while also avoiding the zombie's counter-attacks.

ESSENTIAL PROFICIENCIES

They seem like light, easy-to-use weapons, but in reality, their use requires practice. In knife-based close combat, thrusting is an advanced technique, so thrusting through those eye sockets will require a lot of daily training. And since you will be within the zombie's reach, you'll need to harden your nerves as well.

PRE-CRISIS TRAINING METHODS

This mainly follows the same kind of thrusting-style, knife-based close combat training, but because of the difficulty of thrusting with a carving knife when held the normal way, you may have to hold it backhand instead. Let's build up our skills by practicing the downward thrusts on a mannequin or similar object. Sideways slicing movements have some effect, so be sure to practice those as well.

OBTAINING THE WEAPON

Carving knives can be found in just about any household kitchen, but since home-use carving knives don't quite match the durability of professional-grade knives, you might do better to check the kitchen of professional chefs. And since you need a sharpened point for stabbing, those flat, square-type cleavers don't make effective weapons against zombies. On the other hand, a type of cleaver that is used to cut meat in Chinese food can be used like a hatchet. It's also possible to find the type of knives used for slicing giant tuna in fish markets, but it's unlikely that an amateur could use it effectively.

Metal Pipes and Baseball Bats
BRING YOUR RAGE DOWN ON THE ZOMBIE'S HEAD!

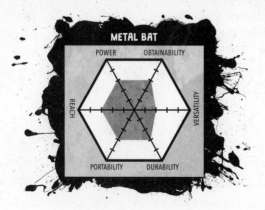

METAL BAT

POWER
OBTAINABILITY
VERSATILITY
DURABILITY
PORTABILITY
REACH

Metal pipes and baseball bats are both easy to obtain, so they're very popular. Metal pipes used in scaffolding have a lot of power and high durability, but they aren't easy to handle. Bats, on the other hand, are easily wielded but have less durability. Also, support poles used in home DIY projects can be used much like pipes and bats.

CONCRETE BATTLE TACTICS

Try to swing as hard as you can for the zombie's head, but in general, you will want to use a full swing as is used in baseball. Still, however you use it, your best bet will be a two-handed swing, since single-handed swings are lacking in both power and accuracy. Metal pipes can be effective when thrust out like a spear, and in such cases, aim for the head. However, you need

THAT THING YOU SEE IN MANGA

 ITS MANY DRAWBACKS QUICKLY BECOME OBVIOUS...   THE NAIL BAT ISN'T ANY HELP AT ALL!

muscle strength to thrust with a pipe, so be sure to work on your muscle strength.

ESSENTIAL PROFICIENCIES

If you're only interested in swinging, you can learn to do so easily without extensive training or injury to yourself. The problem lies with maintaining your posture after the swing while planning your next move, especially with heavy bats or long pipes where the momentum of the swing may throw off your balance. To combat that, you will need to strengthen your overall physique.

PRE-CRISIS TRAINING METHODS

The basic moves for a bat or short pipe are similar to baseball and kendo. But since the only attack that is ultimately effective on zombies is a blow to the head, you will need lots of practice in that area. And with a long metal pipe, you need to study methods when using a *naginata* (Japanese halberd) in which downward thrusts may be emphasized over thrusting attacks. Aside from that, it is imperative that you improve your physical fitness with special emphasis on the muscles in your lower back, waist, and legs.

OBTAINING THE WEAPON

You may be able to obtain a bat easily from a school gym or any store that sells sports equipment, but be sure to choose a metal bat meant for baseball. Wooden bats and bats made for softball do not make good weapons. It's possible to find metal pipes in stores that contain building supplies, but they may be heavy and hard to use. Instead, we would recommend support poles used in home DIY projects. These can be found in hardware stores, as well as in some homes and offices.

Crowbars and Similar Objects
TOP-CLASS WEAPONS FOR ONE-HANDED CLOSE COMBAT

CROWBAR

POWER
OBTAINABILITY
REACH
VERSATILITY
PORTABILITY
DURABILITY

There are several different types of crowbars, but the majority have a flat-spiked end and a split end for removing nails. You can also use a large wrench, or in a pinch, you can take apart a bicycle for its handlebars. However, wrenches and handlebars don't have sharp ends, so they are a bit inferior to an actual crowbar.

CONCRETE BATTLE TACTICS

The basic attacks are to bring the crowbar down on the zombie's head with as much force as you can muster or give it a strong swing from the side. With an actual crowbar, you may use the sharp end in a thrusting attack. However, if you thrust with too much strength, you run the risk of getting your crowbar stuck in the bones of the skull, which will make it difficult to extract. Therefore, if you need to thrust, twist the bar sharply upon completion of the thrust and pull it out as quickly as you can.

ESSENTIAL PROFICIENCIES

If you're only interested in swinging, that is easily learned. Even without extensive training, you should be able to do it with little chance of injuring yourself. Like with metal pipes, the problem

CROWBARS & SIMILAR ITEMS

 THERE ARE LAWS ABOUT WALKING AROUND WITH A CROWBAR, SO WAIT UNTIL THERE'S A CRISIS!

 NOW WE KNOW WHY A CERTAIN CLOSE-QUARTERS-FIGHTING ELDER GOD FROM OUTER SPACE USED THIS AS THEIR MAIN WEAPON.

lies with maintaining your posture immediately after the swing, and planning your next move. This will come with practice. A full-fledged crowbar will require special caution—reckless swinging of the sharp ends could cause injury to yourself or the survivors around you.

PRE-CRISIS TRAINING METHODS

The basic moves are essentially the same as for swinging a bat—aiming for the zombie's head and hitting it as hard as you can should give you the desired result. Concentrate your practice on this technique. To take advantage of the sharpened portions of a crowbar, it's important to emphasize downward swings over sideways attacks. Aside from that, it is imperative that you improve your physical fitness, with special emphasis on the muscles in your lower back, waist, and legs.

OBTAINING THE WEAPON

Crowbars and large wrenches can be found in hardware stores and the offices of contractors, and you may also find them in toolboxes in people's homes. Another possible place you might find large wrenches are in car repair garages and bicycle shops. Bicycle shops might also contain replacement bicycle handlebars, so it may be worth your while to check one of these shops.

Polearms and Two-Handed Weapons
NOT EASY TO USE, BUT PACK A PUNCH

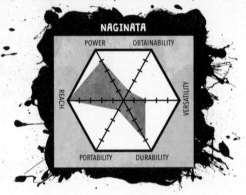

When most people think of two-handed polearm weapons, they think of the spear. However, there are actually a wide variety of them. Among them, the polearm with the greatest anti-zombie power would be the *naginata* (Japanese halberd). Although it would be extremely difficult to get your hands on an actual halberd, the techniques of using a halberd would be extremely useful when fighting zombies. It may be worth your time to consider making one for yourself. Another possibility is to use a laundry pole; it can be used the same way, but its durability is far inferior.

WEAPONS WITH A LONG REACH

 SURE, AND YOU COULD EVEN TAKE DOWN A BOMBER WITH JUST THE STRENGTH OF YOUR WILL... HEY, STOP THAT!!

 I HEAR THAT ONCE JAPAN HAD A "SECRET WEAPON" CALLED "A POINTED STICK" THAT WAS SO EFFECTIVE, ITS USE COULD BE THE DECIDING FACTOR IN BATTLES.

CONCRETE BATTLE TACTICS

The most basic attack method is to swing the polearm down, aiming for the zombie's head with as much strength as possible. If your zombie is one of the kinds that cannot right itself easily after falling, then sweeping its legs can be effective. However, if you are working with a DIY polearm such as a laundry rod, it could possibly break after only a few downward strikes. In that case, the best method is to not bother with downward strikes but to use thrusting attacks at the head instead.

ESSENTIAL PROFICIENCIES

With two-handed polearms, all you really have to do is take a firm stance and wave the weapon around. If you intend to swing downward with the weapon, then you'll need daily practice swinging the polearm to maintain your posture and stance or

your weapon will go to waste. That's a lot of practice! If you intend to use it for thrusting, you will need plenty of practice aiming at the head. It's a very difficult target for beginners to hit.

PRE-CRISIS TRAINING METHODS

Basically, the skill set is the same as for those who use a *naginata*, but the only attack effective on zombies is a heavy blow to the head, so you will need specialized training for that. For this reason, downward blows rather than swinging blows should be emphasized. However, sweeping the legs is also effective, so practice that as well. Aside from that, it is imperative that you improve your physical fitness with special emphasis on the muscles in your lower back, waist, and legs.

OBTAINING THE WEAPON

Obtaining a *naginata* with a sharp blade attached in Japan is extremely difficult, but Shinto shrines and the storage houses of museums are a possibility. But there are a relatively larger number of wooden halberds used in martial arts practice, so those may be found in schools or regional public gyms. Apart from that, you may be able to use thin metal pipes and squared-off lumber to create your own, but be warned—self-made weapons tend to have low durability.

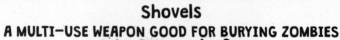

Shovels
A MULTI-USE WEAPON GOOD FOR BURYING ZOMBIES

Usually you think of shovels as being for digging holes or shovelling snow, but they can be reliable weapons for fighting zombies. They're heavy, they pack a punch when wielded two-handed, and since they can be used for thrusting, cutting and bludgeoning, they're handy tools with a wide range of uses. Recently, the military has added martial arts using shovels, teaching how to throw them and to use them one-handed.

CONCRETE BATTLE TACTICS

The basic battle tactics are to swing downwards from above or a sideways slash to the neck. However, there are some shovels with upturned edges to make digging easier; with these, the best attack is a thrusting jab to the throat. Single-handed shovels can be effective when thrown, but you'll need a lot of practice to be able to hit a zombie's head.

ESSENTIAL PROFICIENCIES

A shovel is a very simple tool for its intended purpose, but if you want to use it as a weapon, you will need plenty of training first. This goes double for using it as a weapon against zombies (since you need to hit its head), as you'll be using it for pretty much the opposite of its intended purpose. To be able to utilize its many strengths as a weapon, you will require daily practice. And using it as a throwing weapon will require even more training and practice.

PRE-CRISIS TRAINING METHODS

There is a martial art used by the military that makes use of a shovel, but the number of places where you can practice it are still severely limited. Also, effective learning materials have yet to appear on the market, so you will need to start collecting as much material for self-study as possible (including videos uploaded to the internet). Seek out anything that may be of help to you, and try to copy what you might see.

SHOVELS

AS A WEAPON, SHOVELS ARE GOOD FOR THRUSTING, CUTTING, BLUDGEONING, AND EVEN THROWING. BUT YOU CAN ALSO USE THEM TO DIG OR FILL IN HOLES AND, IN A PINCH, AS A CUTTING BOARD OR FRYING PAN AS WELL!

OBTAINING THE WEAPON

You can find shovels in homes, contracting firms, hardware stores, farms, schools, train stations, and other such facilities. It may even be possible to find them in the storehouse of your city hall. However, the plastic shovels used to clear snow will not work as weapons, so take care when choosing. In pre-crisis times, it may be possible to obtain a military-use, one-handed shovel in army-surplus shops or from online shops. But if the crisis has already started, the best place to check might be the garrison area of military bases.

Hammers
THE PILE DRIVER INTO A ZOMBIE'S HEAD

There are all sorts of hammers, but for anti-zombie action, you will need such hammers as the maul (a two handed, industrial-strength wooden mallet used in martial arts), a sledgehammer, or a pickaxe. But since they are heavy and they need to be swung to be effective, those without prodigious strength may be unable to use them. There are also one-handed pickaxes and ice axes for mountain climbing, which could also possibly be used as weapons.

CONCRETE BATTLE TACTICS

The most basic attack is to aim for the zombie's cranium, bringing the hammer down with as much force as you can muster. However, since very large swings have a tendency to lower your defenses, another way of swinging it is to keep one's dominant hand on the handle nearest the head, while your other hand makes small circling-and-pulling movements as you bring it down on the zombie's head. Also, for the one-handed pickaxe or the mountain climbing ice axe, you do much the same as above—bring the axe down on the top of the head or strike it on either side of the head.

ESSENTIAL PROFICIENCIES

As a tool, its use is pretty simple and obvious, but if you don't

HAMMERS & AXES

 BOTH HAMMERS AND AXES ARE HEAVY AND HARD TO HANDLE, SO IF YOU AREN'T CONFIDENT IN YOUR STRENGTH, I CAN'T RECOMMEND THEM.

have the strength, you won't be able to use it to its fullest. And, of course, any weapon needs training if you want to use it effectively, especially when dealing with zombies. You need to use the basic head attack, which means you will be lifting the heavy weapon very high, so you'll need the physique to do that. Even one-handed pickaxes and mountain-climbing ice axes have plenty of potential as weapons, but you will need daily practice to become proficient with them.

PRE-CRISIS TRAINING METHODS

This author has never heard of any official martial arts school that teaches the systematic use of a hammer, so the only thing to do is learn the basic pile-driver swing of a hammer and practice it. Similarly, the downward swing is also the basic technique for the one-handed pickaxe and the mountain-climbing ice axe.

To approximate a zombie head, try swinging the weapon down into a large-sized lump of dirt or clay, and practice pulling it out again as quickly as you can. It should be effective.

OBTAINING THE WEAPON

Since these tools are used far and wide, you can easily pick one up at any hardware store or contractor's supply. Other possible places include railway offices, emergency shelter supply rooms, farmhouse sheds, or large gardening supply shops. One-handed pickaxes and mountain-climbing ice axes may be available in hardware stores, stonemasons' places of business, and mountaineering shops.

Axes
ONE OF THE BIG THREE ANTI-ZOMBIE WEAPONS

Separating axes into the most general three categories, we have the professional-use two-handed types, the one-handed types, and the military one-handed axe; any of these three would be effective against zombies. However, the two-handed type is heavy and difficult to swing, so you can't get the most out of it without the muscles to match. On the other hand, the military-use one-handed axe is also good for throwing, so it is extremely effective in anti-zombie combat.

CONCRETE BATTLE TACTICS

The basic tactics for this weapon are to slice downward onto the head with as much force as possible, or to swing sideways aiming for the neck.

With the military one-handed axe, there is a spike on the opposite side of the blade, which is used the same way as the mountain-climbing ice axe. Also, throwing the military one-handed axe may be effective on a target, but it will take quite a lot of practice to regularly be able to hit a zombie's head with a thrown axe.

ESSENTIAL PROFICIENCIES

The basic method of using an axe is pretty simple, but since it is heavy, you will not be able to use it to the fullest without some body strength. And you'll need practice to use the military one-handed axe. The base attack against zombies is a blow to the head, so you will need the physique to be able to raise the axe and bring it down for a strike.

PRE-CRISIS TRAINING METHODS

There is a martial art developed by the military which features the use of the military one-handed axe, but the places one can learn this are extremely limited. And since there is no official martial art that features the use of professional-use axes, the best thing to do is gather as much information as possible, as well as download videos on the military's martial arts and try to imitate them.

OBTAINING THE WEAPON

Aside from hardware stores, the businesses of contractors, and farmhouses, one may also find such axes in the storehouses of fire departments. Before the crisis, you might find the military one-handed axe in army surplus stores or on the web. But once the crisis starts, you may have to search a military base that garrisons troops.

Hatchets, Machetes & Wide-Bladed Weapons
ARE YOU REALLY PREPARED TO CLEAVE BOTH FLESH AND BONE?

To divide the category up into its main components, we need to include the square-bladed hatchets, the pointed *kennata*-style outdoor knives, and machete-like woodman's hatchets. Any of these can be used against zombies. However, hatchets have a short reach, so you have to be prepared for the possibility that, in a scuffle with zombies, you run the risk of becoming infected. It is also possible to throw a hatchet, but it takes quite a lot of practice to be able to hit your target.

CONCRETE BATTLE TACTICS
As with axes, the basic tactic is to aim for the zombie's head with a downward stroke, or utilize a sideways swing for the neck. In the case of *kennata* outdoor knives, you can also try to stab, in which case you must aim for the zombie's eye or mouth. Since the reach of a hatchet is very short, you should try to get some distance immediately after making your attack.

ESSENTIAL PROFICIENCIES
It's easy to use this tool, but since this weapon uses its heft as part of the attack, you must have a certain amount of arm strength to use it to its fullest. At the risk of repeating ourselves, this weapon doesn't allow you much distance, so you will have to learn how to avoid being attacked yourself.

JAPANESE HATCHETS & SIMILAR WEAPONS

THIS IS THE TYPE YOU SEE IN MOST ZOMBIE MOVIES-- THE MACHETES MADE IN CENTRAL AND SOUTH AMERICA.

THIS TYPE

ITS SHAPE IS WEIRD, SO IT'S PROBABLY HARD TO USE.

THERE'S A KNIFE CALLED THE KUKRI KNIFE THAT WAS USED BY THE FEARSOME MERCENARIES KNOWN AS THE GURKHAS, AND IT IS RATHER HATCHET-LIKE.

YOU'RE A LIAR!!

GRAARH!!

 SARAH TOLD ME TO SAY IT!

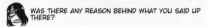 WAS THERE ANY REASON BEHIND WHAT YOU SAID UP THERE?

And since, again, the basic attack against zombies is to the head, you will need physical strength to be able to lift the weapons and slash at the neck time and time again.

PRE-CRISIS TRAINING METHODS

Training for hatchets will follow along the same lines as axes. There are no official schools of martial arts for them, but there is a military martial art for the woodman's hatchet (machete). If you want to learn it, download videos and information on it from the internet and do your best to copy the moves.

OBTAINING THE WEAPON

These can possibly be found in contractors' businesses, hardware stores and farming houses. Other places include the small shops and homes in rural mountain and farming villages.

Pre-crisis, you may be able to purchase the military-use mountain hatchets from army surplus shops and over the internet, but after the crisis happens, you may have to go to a military base or troop garrison to get your hands on one.

Ice Picks
THE OPTIMAL LAST-RESORT WEAPON

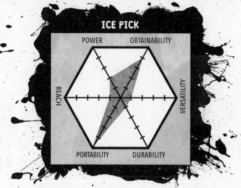

ICE PICK

POWER OBTAINABILITY
REACH VERSATILITY
PORTABILITY DURABILITY

There are two general kinds of ice picks—the type used in food-preparation and the type used for mountain climbing. The latter, known as the ice axe, was covered in the hammer section above. Also, there is a three-pronged type of ice pick used in food preparation, but that type cannot be effectively used as a weapon. These weapons are used in very-close-range combat with almost no reach. This is a weapon of last resort to be used in a scuffle with a zombie, but that is also the time when it is most effective.

CONCRETE BATTLE TACTICS

The basic attack is to stab at the head and gouge. Yes, it is effective to aim for the eye, but that may lead to you getting bitten and infected yourself. An ice pick's reach is extremely short, so the moment after your attack, you will have to put some space between you and the zombie. Since it's easy to carry, it's

ICE PICKS

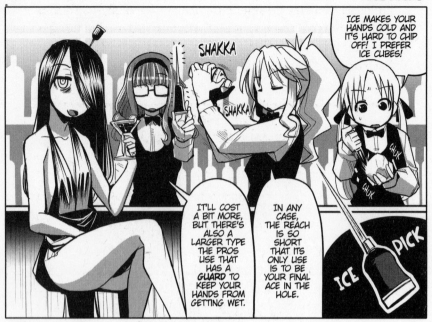

ICE MAKES YOUR HANDS COLD AND IT'S HARD TO CHIP OFF! I PREFER ICE CUBES!

SHAKKA

SHAKKA

IT'LL COST A BIT MORE, BUT THERE'S ALSO A LARGER TYPE THE PROS USE THAT HAS A **GUARD** TO KEEP YOUR HANDS FROM GETTING WET.

IN ANY CASE, THE REACH IS SO SHORT THAT ITS ONLY USE IS TO BE YOUR FINAL ACE IN THE HOLE.

ICE PICK

THE BASIC ATTACK AGAINST A ZOMBIE IS TO AIM FOR THE HEAD, BUT SINCE A HEAD IS ROUND, IT'S DIFFICULT TO PENETRATE. AND SINCE ITS REACH IS ALMOST NON-EXISTENT, IT ISN'T A WEAPON ANYONE SHOULD BE EAGER TO USE.

an ideal weapon for a hand-to-hand scuffle with a zombie. So be sure to keep it in a place that makes it easy to draw quickly.

ESSENTIAL PROFICIENCIES

Its use is quite straightforward, but there's a knack to stabbing through into a skull. Since a stab that relies on force alone may be deflected by sliding along the bone, be sure instead to stab at an angle that is perpendicular to the bone. And because you'll need to be even closer than with a hatchet, you will definitely need to learn techniques for evading a zombie's attacks.

PRE-CRISIS TRAINING METHODS

There is no specific martial art using this as a weapon, but a lump of ice is kind of slippery (like a zombie's head), so simply

breaking ice makes for practice. Get yourself a lot of practice breaking ice apart using strong thrusts at a perpendicular angle.

OBTAINING THE WEAPON

It's possible to find ice picks in hardware stores or restaurants, but the type you'll really want is the large-type chosen by professionals who work with ice.

Be especially careful of the small types with grips shaped like a *biwa*. They can't be used as weapons, as it is hard to get any power into the thrust. If you have a wide selection to choose from, the large-size ice picks with a hand guard that protects against fluids will add that extra power in exchange for its bulkiness.

Chainsaws
THE MOVIE-STAR WEAPON THAT'S ACTUALLY A DISAPPOINTMENT

There is probably no shortage of people who are left with the deep impression that chainsaws are a truly effective weapon to wield, based on what they've seen in movies. Unfortunately, the opposite is true. Chainsaws are heavy and difficult to use, making them perhaps the tool least suited to fighting zombies. To make matters worse, they present many dangers to the wielder as well.

CHAINSAWS & POWER TOOLS

 CHAINSAWS SPRAY FRAGMENTS OF WHATEVER YOU CUT BACK ONTO YOU, SO FROM A MENTAL HEALTH STANDPOINT, I CAN'T REALLY RECOMMEND THEM.

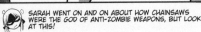 SARAH WENT ON AND ON ABOUT HOW CHAINSAWS WERE THE GOD OF ANTI-ZOMBIE WEAPONS, BUT LOOK AT THIS!

CONCRETE BATTLE TACTICS

The basic attack is to try to cut in the neck or head area, but you must not spin around quickly using them. It is also possible to thrust with them, and when you do, you must make the thrust as deep as possible. The noise of the chainsaw might also draw more zombies to you, so let's figure out an escape route before we begin, shall we?

ESSENTIAL PROFICIENCIES

To gain proficiency, you must master not only the use of the chainsaw but its maintenance as well. For beginners, we would recommend a chainsaw with an engine of 40 cc or less. Also, for practice, you will require a small, electric-powered chainsaw. If you use a gas-powered engine, you will need to know how to mix your fuels, as well as having an excellent grasp on quick refuelling. A mastery of replacing the chain and maintaining the tool is a must.

Additionally, since you will be wielding a machine of between 3-4.5 kg (6.5-10 lbs), you will need plenty of arm strength.

PRE—CRISIS TRAINING METHODS

In Japan, there are special training courses provided by local municipalities, taught by professionals who are versed in chainsaw use. You should become practiced in their basic use from one of these classes, where you may also learn how to obtain the tool. Beyond that, recently an art style of creating pieces though wood sculpture using a chainsaw, called "chainsaw carving," has become popular. It is possible to be trained in a chainsaw's uses and requirements by joining a club that specializes in this kind of art.

OBTAINING THE WEAPON

It's possible to find them in a contractor's places of business, hardware stores, or farmhouses. Other possible places are small stores in mountain or farming villages or even in regular homes with a decent garden. Although you can get them through internet shops during the pre-crisis period, once the crisis is underway your biggest problem will be in recharging the battery for the electric versions or finding fuel for the power-motor types.

Other Types of Power Tools
TO TELL THE TRUTH, THEY AREN'T VERY USEFUL

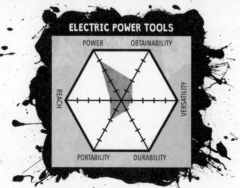

ELECTRIC POWER TOOLS

POWER • OBTAINABILITY • REACH • VERSATILITY • PORTABILITY • DURABILITY

Unfortunately, the vast majority of power tools are not in any way useful as a weapon for fighting zombies. They're heavy and hard to utilize, and since they make loud noises, there is a large possibility that they might draw more zombies toward the noise, putting the wielder into even more danger. Not only that, but since power tools use precious fuel or electric power, the amount of time you can use them is limited.

CONCRETE BATTLE TACTICS

The basic attack is to aim for the head or neck, but the reach on most power tools is very short. You'll have to be very conscious of the space between you and the zombie when you fight. The biggest problem is the engine noise. In the case of zombies who react to sound, you could draw even more attackers towards you. For that reason, you have to be sure you have an escape route planned before you fight.

ESSENTIAL PROFICIENCIES

You will need to practice not only the use of the tools but their maintenance as well. Also, since you won't be using it as a tool but as a weapon, you will need to understand maintenance of the machine (under circumstances that even the manufacturer has never hypothesized). On top of that, you will be lifting the engine, along with its fuel or batteries, so you must build up your arm strength before being able to use it effectively.

PRE—CRISIS TRAINING METHODS

Large power-tool manufacturers have training courses, so there you can learn how to obtain them and get the basics of their use among other information. However, you will only learn use and maintenance of them as tools. You'll have to learn on your own how to use them as weapons.

OBTAINING THE WEAPON

It's possible to get your hands on them from contractors' offices, hardware stores, factories of all kinds, construction firms,

or work sites, among other places. During the pre-crisis time, it's possible to buy them on the internet. But after the crisis starts, the biggest problem will not so much be obtaining the tools themselves but keeping them supplied with battery power or fuel.

Thrown Weapons
SO DISAPPOINTING, YOU'LL WANT TO THROW THEM AWAY

Unfortunately, the vast majority of thrown weapons are completely inadequate to the task of fighting zombies. They have a short range of effectiveness, it is very difficult to hit the target, and they don't have a lot of force behind them. An exception might be the large-type of shuriken or throwing knife with the power to pierce a skull. However, those will be heavy, they still have a short range, and the opportunities to use them will be extremely limited.

CONCRETE BATTLE TACTICS

The basic attack is to aim for the head. However, since nearly all thrown weapons will be unable to penetrate the skull, you'll need the accuracy to bull's-eye the eye socket for your attack to be effective. But even if you do hit the eye socket, there's no guarantee that you'll destroy the brain, so target practice is a

SHURIKEN (THROWING STARS)

THROWING STARS SUCK! COMPLETELY INEFFECTIVE! EEEEEEK!

EVEN IF WE HIT HER, IT WOULDN'T KILL HER! THESE THINGS ARE NO GOOD AT ALL!!

must. A large rock or iron ball might just possibly break a zombie's skull, but that really depends on your physical strength.

ESSENTIAL PROFICIENCIES

You will need an extremely high rate of accuracy and proficiency. You must first have a firm grasp on the posture for throwing weapons, and having the muscles to hit something at range is essential. Not only must you hit an eye socket at range, but you must also pierce all the way through to the brain. Failing that, you'll need the strength to break through a skull, so either way you will need an outstanding physique.

PRE-CRISIS TRAINING METHODS

Individual lovers of shuriken or throwing knives or groups of enthusiasts for such weapons may teach courses covering their

use. Seeking these out might be the best way to learn and practice the techniques for throwing weapons. But their main goal will be practice for martial arts or contests, not to fight zombies. For that, you will need to work on techniques used by the military found in videos, and you should practice by studying these.

OBTAINING THE WEAPON

It should be fairly easy to obtain blunt shuriken or throwing knives either directly from the enthusiast groups or from on-line shops. But if you want versions that are useful for fighting zombies, you will need to fashion them yourself. We strongly urge you to be careful of their razor-sharp edges after they have been honed.

Bows and Arrows
A POSSIBILITY YOU HADN'T THOUGHT ABOUT

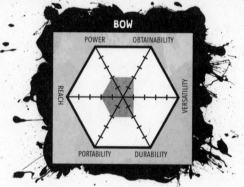

Nearly all archery, both Japanese style and western-style, is unfortunately not very well suited to anti-zombie warfare. Why? Well, even if you manage to penetrate the skull, it's still very difficult to destroy the brain inside it. Even just hitting the skull itself may prove difficult. However, depending on the circumstances, a fire arrow may be effective. Creative use will be an asset.

BOWS & CROSSBOWS

 THIS IS ALSO TRUE OF A FLAMETHROWER, BUT IF FLAME-ENGULFED ZOMBIES START WANDERING AROUND, THE FIRE CAN SPREAD INTO AREAS YOU HAD NOT PLANNED FOR. SO, IT'S SAFE TO SAY THAT FLAME ARROWS ARE ONLY EFFECTIVE DEPENDING ON YOUR AREA.

CONCRETE BATTLE TACTICS

Because most bow-fired arrows cannot penetrate a skull, you will instead need to aim for the eye socket. But even if you hit the eye socket, it will make no difference unless you destroy the brain. Target practice is essential. Fire arrows may be able to engulf the zombie in flames, but there is a danger of spreading the fire to unintended places. And that's assuming you even have the opportunity to use a fire arrow.

ESSENTIAL PROFICIENCIES

You will need a lot of high-level practice. First, you must master the proper stance for archery, and you must train up your muscles to hold the arrow cocked as you aim your shot. Since the head of a fire arrow is heavy and meets a lot of wind resistance, it takes exceptional muscles and marksmanship to get it to fly straight and sure towards a far-off target.

PRE-CRISIS TRAINING METHODS

In Japan, where gun ownership is limited, a crossbow is pretty much the only effective ranged weapon you can own in your fight against zombies. Although the effective range is short, you have a comparatively high rate of accuracy. And not only will it penetrate the skull, it has the power to destroy a zombie's brain as well.

Both Japanese-style archery and western archery have competitive leagues that offer courses, so you can learn proper posture and firing techniques with them, as well as have a place to practice. However, this training is strictly for martial arts or competitions, so any practice with fire arrows will have to be done completely on your own.

OBTAINING THE WEAPON

You can pick up archery equipment for both Japanese style and western-style bows either directly from archery leagues or from online services. You will have to create your own fire arrows, but please be mindful of criminal and fire-prevention laws.

Crossbows
THE ONLY FIREARM YOU CAN OWN WITHOUT A LICENSE!

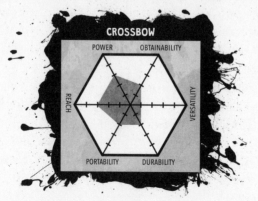

A huge advantage of this weapon is its relative lack of sound when firing, so it is unlikely to attract any noise-sensitive zombies.

CHAPTER 3

CONCRETE BATTLE TACTICS

The basic tactic is to aim for the zombie's head, however if you do not hit it just right, it won't pierce the skull. Do your best to aim for an eye socket or an ear. The biggest drawback to a crossbow is that you have to stand still to reload, and reloading takes time. For that reason, do not take on more than one zombie at a time with the weapon. Once the shot is released, beat a hasty retreat.

ESSENTIAL PROFICIENCIES

You will need practice in firing, reloading, and maintenance. You will need to especially concentrate on the reloading procedures. Learn the mechanisms for drawing and release of the bowstring. You will also need proficiency in adjusting the scope and you will need to become thoroughly versed in how to replace parts, such as the bowstring.

PRE—CRISIS TRAINING METHODS

Amateur crossbowmen, as well as competitive leagues, have courses from which you can learn the basics of shooting, posture, and reloading. You will need at least as much practice in reloading as shooting, and maybe even more. Be extra careful during reloading, as that is the time when accidents are most likely to happen. We encourage you to bring your own crossbow to the courses in crossbow use and safety.

OBTAINING THE WEAPON

You can obtain your crossbow by buying directly from competitive leagues or through online shops, but be extra careful you do not run afoul of local firearms control laws or other, similar rules. Also, pistol-style crossbows tend to be low power, and as such, they are not very suited for anti-zombie combat. Choose your crossbow carefully.

Handguns
GUNS, THE FINAL WEAPON!

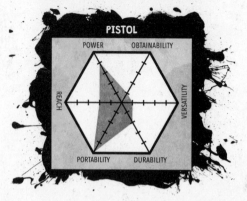

Because Japan has extremely strict limits on the possession of handguns, the odds are almost nonexistent that you might be able to own one (unless you happen to be the type of public servant specially required to carry one). As such, the likelihood of getting your hands on one is unfortunately severely limited. They don't have much range, they aren't very accurate, and they need the power to pierce the skull and destroy the zombie's brain. However, when used at the last moment, a gun can reliably deliver the coup de grace.

CONCRETE BATTLE TACTICS

The tactic is to aim for the head, but if you hit it in a bad spot, you may not be able to pierce the skull. You will need to do your best to aim for the eye sockets, ears, or nose. The very best time to use a gun is during a hand-to-hand scuffle with a zombie; in this instance, we recommend you try to blow its head off at point-blank range. That is the reason we call the gun your final weapon.

ESSENTIAL PROFICIENCIES

You will need to master skills in shooting, reloading, and maintenance. You will need to emphasize reloading procedures,

HANDGUNS

IT ISN'T THE GUN THAT'S CALLED A MAGNUM! IT'S THE AMMUNITION! AND IT'S GOT SUCH A STRONG KICKBACK; IT'S NO WEAPON FOR AN AMATEUR! I'M TELLING YOU, YOU'LL *NEVER* FIND ONE ANYWHERE IN JAPAN!

OKAY THEN! NOW THAT IT'S COME TO THIS, I'LL JUST USE THE GUN THAT I ALWAYS FIND IN THE GAMES! YOU KNOW, THAT GUN THEY CALL A "MAGNUM"?

so you should get in a lot of practice. Of course, it will be very important for you to learn effective firing techniques, both single-handed and two-handed, and if possible, it would be best to learn how to quick-draw as well.

PRE-CRISIS TRAINING METHODS

There are marksmanship tours overseas where you can learn the basics of shooting posture, reloading, and maintenance from an instructor. Also, there are groups who use air guns and laser-based pistols in competitive leagues, and it is possible to practice with them. On top of that, if you obtain level four in air pistol competitions, you will be recognized to join in the handguns division.

OBTAINING THE WEAPON

For average Japanese citizens, gun ownership is illegal. However, once the crisis has started, there are possibilities. Aside from the police and the Japanese Self-Defense Forces, you may find a gun with criminal gangs or other locations where illegal activities occur. It is unlikely but possible that you may come across a hidden cache of firearms.

Assault Rifles and Submachine Guns
NOT RECOMMENDED FOR AMATEURS

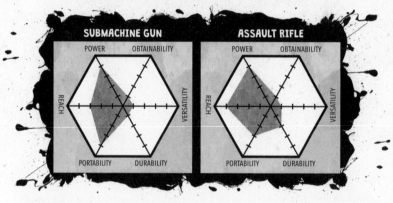

Although it is virtually impossible to obtain an assault rifle or submachine gun legally in Japan, it would be an effective weapon if you could manage to get one. But even if you were to obtain one, using it effectively requires such a high level of training that we would recommend extreme caution. Controlling rapid fire is extremely difficult, so firing at zombies will mean a large expenditure of wasted ammunition. Although it is a highly effective gun for trained users, since amateurs cannot use the weapon to its fullest, using certain hunting rifles (described below) would be the better choice.

ASSAULT RIFLES

LET'S JUST BE GOOD GIRLS AND CHOOSE SOME OTHER WEAPON. THAT'S OUR BEST BET.

AT FIRST GLANCE, MILITARY-USE WEAPONS ARE HIGH-POWERED AND SEEM THE PERFECT CHOICE. BUT SINCE IT'S PRETTY MUCH *IMPOSSIBLE* FOR CIVILIANS TO SHOOT AND MAINTAIN THEM...

ALTHOUGH THE TWO GUNS LOOK COMPLETELY DIFFERENT, THEY USE THE SAME AMMUNITION. CONVENIENT! BUT EVEN SO, THESE ARE SIMPLY FOR EMERGENCY MEASURES. PLEASE BE CAREFUL NOT TO BREAK ANY FIREARMS CONTROL LAWS.

THE RIFLE I'M FIRING IS THE M4 CARBINE USED BY THE AMERICAN MILITARY, AND LINA IS HOLDING THE HOWA TYPE 89 ASSAULT RIFLE USED BY THE JAPANESE SELF-DEFENSE FORCES. IF YOU'RE GOING TO FIND ONE IN JAPAN, IT'LL BE ONE OF THESE TWO.

CONCRETE BATTLE TACTICS

The key to using this gun is to aim at the head, but with assault rifles and submachine guns, it's important to not use the rapid-fire option. Stay as far away from the zombies as possible and aim carefully. The basic tactic is to try to blow off the zombie's head. At the risk of repeating ourselves, we must emphasize that you are not to use the rapid-fire option with these guns. Also, the inner working of assault rifles and submachine guns are complicated, so you mustn't use these guns as a bludgeoning weapon. You could cause damage to the weapon or, at worst, harm or kill yourself.

Remember that the folding gunstocks of these weapons were never meant to be used for attack. An exception might be the Russian-made AK series or the old-type BARs, but it is

extremely unlikely that you would ever be able to obtain one of those in Japan.

ESSENTIAL PROFICIENCIES

You will need to master the skills of shooting, reloading, and maintenance. It is especially important to learn reloading procedures, so be sure you get plenty of practice. Of course, it will be very important for you to learn effective firing techniques, and beyond that, it would be useful if you could take apart and clean the weapon without constantly referring to a manual.

PRE-CRISIS TRAINING METHODS

There are marksmanship tours overseas where you can learn the basics of shooting posture and reloading from an instructor. However, these lessons are aimed at tourists, so in order to learn how to use and maintain one in the heat of battle, you will either have to study on your own or join up with the Japanese Self-Defense Forces (for Japanese citizens).

OBTAINING THE WEAPON

Gun ownership is outlawed in Japan for everyday citizens. However, once the crisis has started, there will be possibilities. Aside from the Japanese Coast Guard and the Japanese Self-Defense Forces, you may find them in the lairs of criminal gangs or at other locations where illegal activities occur. It is possible, but unlikely, that you may come across a hidden cache of firearms that includes assault rifles and submachine guns. But even so, these are simply for emergency measures. Please be careful not to break any firearm control laws.

Heavy Weapons
EXTREMELY POWERFUL BUT DISAPPOINTING WEAPONS

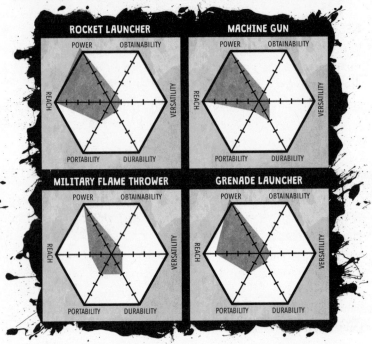

Machine guns are rapid-fire heavy guns for which there are many varieties, such as those supported by bipods or tripods, among others. Flamethrowers are, as the name suggests, weapons that project fire over a distance from a nozzle, and the most basic type use fuel contained in high-pressure tanks carried on one's back. Grenade launchers and rocket launchers tend to be small, hand-held (or shoulder-mounted) devices that fire small ordnance, and rocket launchers range from tripod-mounted devices to huge, wheeled-vehicle-mounted launchers. That is to say, they come in all shapes and sizes.

※ *Although the true meaning of "heavy weapons" is a weapon that cannot be carried by an individual, we are placing the more bulky, unwieldy weapons in this category as a matter of convenience.*

HEAVY WEAPONS

 ALL THAT ASIDE, LET'S BE SERIOUS FOR A MINUTE. EXPLOSIVES CAN HAVE A LOT OF POWER BUT ALSO A HUGE BLAST RADIUS. THEY'RE DANGEROUS, SO AMATEURS SHOULD NEVER EVEN TRY TO TOUCH THEM!

Aside from the fact that these weapons are severely restricted by law and, as such, are nearly impossible for a normal civilian to obtain, their effectiveness in zombie combat is also extremely limited. Aiming, firing procedures, and maintenance are all complicated, and they are difficult to transport. Even if you were able to obtain one, being able to fire this sort of weapon is beyond the scope of any amateur's abilities.

CONCRETE BATTLE TACTICS

First, for the sake of this book, we are calling very big guns "heavy weapons" as a matter of convenience. The basic tactic is to fire several shots at the zombie's head and blow the entire head off. But since a machine gun is basically a rapid-fire weapon, it takes quite a lot of practice to be able to aim while spraying bullets from your gun. An amateur could probably never manage it.

With a grenade launcher and rocket launcher, you aim for the head as well. But these weapons have ordnance meant to hit harder targets than zombie flesh, and that triggers an explosion. So even if you hit the zombie head on, it may still not explode. Also, a grenade launcher's ordnance flies on a parabolic arc, and aligning to your target is extremely difficult. An amateur will probably never hit anything. A flamethrower's basic tactic is to set the zombie on fire, so you may be able to burn down zombies in groups. But because the procedures for firing are complicated, you have to be sure of your posture while using the weapon. If the user were to fall while firing the weapon, you could wind up frying all your nearby allies.

ESSENTIAL PROFICIENCIES

You will need to master skills in shooting, reloading/recharging, maintenance, and, in the case of weapons like machine guns, setup and placement of the bipod or tripod. You will need a firm grasp of reloading procedures, so be sure you get plenty of practice. Of course it will be very important for you to learn effective firing techniques, and beyond that, it would be useful if you could take apart and clean the weapon without constantly referring to a manual.

PRE-CRISIS TRAINING METHODS

Only a tiny fraction of possible foreign "Marksmanship Tours" or individual instructors will be willing to train you in these weapons. So as a general rule, learning to fire and practice with these weapons is impossible for a civilian. If you want to learn battle operations and maintenance of these weapons legally, there is little other choice for a Japanese citizen than to join the Japanese Self-Defense Forces.

OBTAINING THE WEAPON

Pre-crisis, you will find it difficult to legally obtain a firearm. However, once the crisis has started, there are possibilities. You

may be able to stumble upon a cache of Self-Defense Force or American military heavy weapons. That being said, this is only true in a crisis situation. Please be careful not to break any firearms control laws.

Hunting Guns (Rifles, Shotguns, Carbines)
THE MAIN WEAPONS FOR ZOMBIE HUNTING

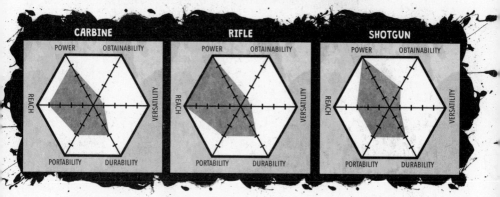

Because of Japan's extremely strict gun regulations, the purchase and ownership of hunting rifles is almost impossible for the average person. However, if you were to come across one, it could become your main weapon in the fight against zombies. Rifles and carbines not only have a long range and accuracy, they also have plenty of power to pierce the zombie's skull and destroy its brain. On the other hand, you must be careful with shotguns as they have a shorter range than rifles or carbines, and the power of their ammunition varies greatly with the shells employed. They use smaller caliber shells than carbines or rifles and their power is inferior, but in exchange, they have less of a kickback. Also, with a rifle, you need to pull the bolt back to load the next bullet in the chamber, but with

---

※ Normally carbines are a rifle (handgun) with the gun barrel shortened for use by cavalry, but here it is used in the hunting gun sense, which means a small-caliber repeating rifle.

HUNTING RIFLES

SLUGS ARE SOMETIMES CALLED "MASTER KEYS," BECAUSE THEY CAN BLOW APART LOCKED DOORS TO OPEN THEM!

THE MOST EFFECTIVE TYPES OF SHOTGUN AMMUNITION AGAINST ZOMBIES ARE SLUGS OR BUCK-SHOT.

ONE OF THE BASIC TOOLS FOR A RIFLE IS TARGETING THROUGH A SNIPER SCOPE. THIS LIMITS YOUR PERIPHERAL VISION, SO YOU'LL ALSO NEED AN OBSERVER WHO CAN KEEP AN EYE ON YOUR SURROUNDINGS. THE MILITARY DOES THIS, TOO.

GRUNCH

GAG! GAG! WAIT! ISN'T THAT MILITARY RIFLE THAT LINA IS AIMING A BARRETT M82?! THAT'S OVERKILL, WOULDN'T YOU SAY?!

a carbine, the chamber is reloaded automatically. So, with a carbine, you can fire repeatedly while keeping your aim. It's probably easier to use in fighting zombies than a rifle.

CONCRETE BATTLE TACTICS

Basically, you aim for the head. With a rifle or carbine, find a safe spot, and bring down the zombies from a distance.

Also, aiming scopes for long-distance marksmanship will cut off your field of vision, so they can be problematic when working alone. Therefore, if you plan to use a rifle with a scope, do your best to team up with someone who has binoculars to act in support of you. And we suggest you do your firing from a shelter of some kind. Depending on the terrain and how well set up your rifle is, you should be able to blow the heads off zombies from a very long distance.

With shotguns as well, the basic tactic is to aim at the head. To steadily bring down zombies, you should position the gun firmly against your shoulder when you fire. The shotgun's barrel, caliber, and choke (the tapered constriction at the end of the barrel's bore) determine the power and effective range of a shotgun, but the kind of ammunition you use is also very important. Depending on the caliber, shells with shot used for birds, small animals, and clay pigeons are pretty much useless. At the very least, you will need slugs or shells filled with buckshot.

ESSENTIAL PROFICIENCIES

You will need to master skills in shooting, reloading, and maintenance. You will need a firm grasp of the procedures for adjusting the sighting scope, so be sure you understand your situation in relation to your target. Of course, it will be very important for you to learn effective firing techniques, and beyond that, it would be of use if you could take apart and clean the weapon without constantly referring to a manual. For shotguns, you should be familiar enough to understand the kind of shot patterns achieved by different barrels, calibers, and chokes.

PRE-CRISIS TRAINING METHODS

There are competitive leagues for marksmanship that have shotgun divisions, so it is possible to train with them. Also, there are colleges that have informal and formal clubs based on clay pigeon shooting, so joining one of those may be a shortcut to proficiency. There are also leagues with divisions for air rifles, and it is possible for even a minor to practice with an air rifle after joining these groups. However, these are for competitions only. For anti-zombie skills, one has to go more into the area of hunting. If you want a hunting license, we suggest you gain a lot of outdoor experience.

Since it is extremely difficult to practice rifle or carbine shooting on Japanese soil, we suggest it is far more efficient

to practice it overseas. There are marksmanship tours overseas where you can, as an option, learn the basics of shooting posture, reloading, and maintenance from an instructor.

OBTAINING THE WEAPON

If you are legally an adult, it is possible for you to obtain a license to possess a shotgun. However, since a licensed gun possessor is licensed for each particular gun one owns, that gun cannot legally be borrowed or loaned out to someone else. Also, if someone has maintained a legal license for a shotgun for more than ten years, he/she is then allowed to possess a rifle. On the other hand, once the crisis has started, it may be possible to more easily obtain one of these weapons. Please be careful not to break any firearms control laws during the pre-crisis period.

Body Armor and Shields
SOFT IS BETTER THAN HARD

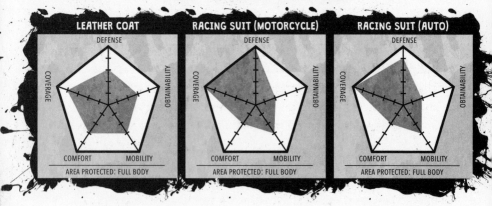

When it comes to defense in a zombie apocalypse, you want something that will not only help protect you against the attacks of zombies but also against accidents in your fight for survival. Setting aside the abnormal zombies, most zombies don't have weapons—they simply use their teeth and fingernails

BODY ARMOR & DEFENSES

BUT THEY CLANK LIKE A METAL-WORKS FACTORY, AND WHERE ARE WE SUPPOSED TO GET ONE, ANYWAY?!

LINA IS WEARING WESTERN-STYLE PLATE ARMOR, WHICH, DEPENDING ON THE TYPE, CAN WEIGH SEVERAL DOZENS OF KILOGRAMS. PUTTING ASIDE THE WEIGHT ISSUE FOR A SECOND, THE TYPE MADE FOR ACTUAL COMBAT CAN BE PRETTY EASY TO MOVE AROUND IN.

as their weapons. So all you need is to prevent penetration, and thus hard defenses are not absolutely necessary. In most cases, softer material like leathers or strengthened fibers will protect you quite comfortably. And when you think of how long you may be wearing them and how fast you must move in them, soft defensive clothing would be the top choice.

RECOMMENDED ITEMS

The most recommended items would be racing suits from motorsports or riding suits from motorcycle competitions, leather racing suits, or even a long leather coat. However, keep in mind that none of these are specifically made for long-term use.

We also recommend such outerwear as the one-piece winter mountain climbing suits or protective suits made for polar

regions, as they are hard to rip even when scraped with rocks and ice. Although a hand-held shield is relatively useless in anti-zombie battles, if you can use something like a bath towel as a matador cape, it may be effective.

CONCERNS WHEN EQUIPPING

These clothes, aside from the leather coat, have a tendency to feel hot and stuffy. During the summertime, in places such as the tropics and the desert, it's probably best to avoid this kind of clothing. Also, wearing these suits can take a toll on your body when worn for long periods of time, so be sure to take breaks. When possible, take them off and air them out period-ically. Racing suits for auto racing have a belt that allows rescue and pit crews to pull the driver out of the car in an emergency, but a zombie might be able to grab hold of such a belt. Be sure to cut the belt off before you wear the suit.

OBTAINING THE EQUIPMENT

During pre-crisis time, you can obtain these items from certain specialty stores or online shops. But after the crisis starts, even though you may be able to find specialty shops for each cat-egory, you still might have difficulty finding a one-piece suit in your size. On the other hand, leather coats are very easy to ob-tain. Depending on the season, they may even be in the back rooms of your common fashion boutique. Another advantage is that it is much easier to find them in your size.

Protective Headgear
NO FULL—FACE HEADGEAR! DON'T EVEN THINK ABOUT IT!

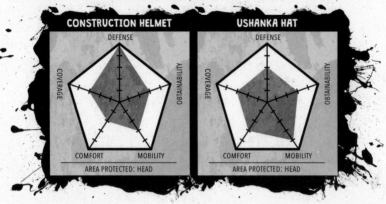

Having something to protect your head is one of the basics of survival. But during a zombie crisis, keeping your vision or hearing unimpeded will protect you much better than any helmet could. Since you will be wearing these for long periods of time, choose a helmet that is lightweight and comfortable. As long as you're standing up, it will be very hard for a zombie to bite your head. Don't wear anything that's easy for a zombie to grab on to, or that might clue a zombie in to your whereabouts. When you think about it, full-face helmets give you protection against accidents but at the cost of limiting your field of vision and impeding your sense of hearing. Overall, they put you at a disadvantage. When fighting zombies, even a normal hat is preferable.

RECOMMENDED ITEMS

Since there is a hunting aspect to battling zombies, we feel you must choose headgear that impedes your senses as little as possible. You might consider bush hats, cowboy hats made with thicker cloth material, ushanka hats (a Russian fur-lined hat), Peruvian-style hats that don't have the ear coverings, or even just a knit cap. We'd recommend the type of construction helmet that leaves your ears exposed, but bicycle helmets are

PROTECTIVE HEADGEAR

 THE MOMENT I SAY IT, THOSE TWO HAVE TO GO OFF AND... WELL, ANYWAY, IF YOU HAVE LONG HAIR, ZOMBIES CAN GRAB HOLD OF IT. SO WHEN YOU'RE ON THE MOVE OR BATTLING ZOMBIES, TRY TO KEEP IT FROM BEING A HINDRANCE BY BRAIDING IT OR WEARING IT UP.

acceptable too. To put it another way, we feel that wearing any type of helmet that limits your field of view, such as full-face helmets, hockey masks, or disaster hoods, would be an act of suicide. We also don't recommend the metal military helmets, as their weight might help to tire you out (and they provide little protection against zombies anyway).

CONCERNS WHEN EQUIPPING

One of the most important considerations for surviving a zombie apocalypse is fatigue prevention. Head protection can be an unexpectedly large factor in that, so do your best to avoid wearing your head protection for long hours. For this reason, we feel you should remove your headgear when taking rests. With that in mind, we suggest you choose head protection that can be easily donned and removed, such as hats. There's also

the possibility that a zombie might grab ear protectors on a winter cap, or straps on a helmet, so we suggest folding in the ear protectors and tightening straps if you have them.

OBTAINING THE EQUIPMENT

Protective headgear is available for purchase at shops that feature clothes for manufacturing, construction, or contracting, as well as hardware stores. Other places include sports specialty stores for such outdoor sports as mountain climbing, and even in various auto specialty stores or in the "emergency equipment" corner of some supermarkets. During pre-crisis times, you can also order them online with ease. After the crisis breaks out, there are construction sites, businesses with stores meant for disasters, and factories. Another place you might want to check out are farm houses. There are all sorts of places where you can procure headgear. However, we cannot emphasize enough that any headgear that limits your sense of hearing or field of vision should be avoided, so even if you find full-face helmets, disaster hoods, or any such headgear, don't use them!

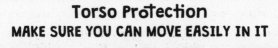

Torso Protection
MAKE SURE YOU CAN MOVE EASILY IN IT

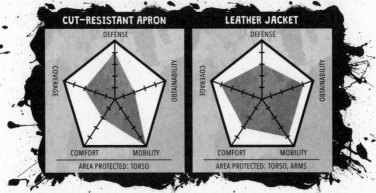

When battling zombies, the priority for protecting your torso is so low that you could pretty much ignore it altogether. Anyone who thinks that a zombie will bite their torso has already made a terrible mistake in their anti-zombie activities; they may as well have been completely caught off guard in a zombie surprise attack or fallen into a position where they have to grapple with a zombie. Because of that, what you're really looking for is some form of coat or clothing that protects against accidents, like a leather jacket, worker's apron, leather apron, or something similar. For your back, look for a normal backpack, hikers' framed backpack, or a Japanese-style *shoiko* wooden frame for carrying loads. Any of these will provide plenty of protection.

RECOMMENDED ITEMS

Basically, if you wear a worker's apron on your front, you will be pretty well protected. Among those, we recommend the cut-and-slash-resistant type. Aside from that, leather or denim jackets work well, and even some of the thicker mountain-climbing jackets have some pretty good protection. If you can get your hands on the cut-and-puncture-resistant jackets or overalls that some industries use, they would be the best. However, the cut-and puncture-resistant clothing only protects a limited amount of places on your body, so if you're ordering it during pre-crisis times, be sure you know which areas are protected and which aren't. On the other hand, meat-processing industries have ring-mail aprons, but they are too heavy relative to the amount of protection they give.

CONCERNS WHEN EQUIPPING

Leather and denim jackets aren't very breathable, so they can take a toll on your body when worn for long periods of time. We recommend ones that can be easily slipped off and on as the occasion permits. The makers of cut- and puncture-resistant protective clothing have given some consideration to breathability, but as these are also first and foremost protective

TORSO PROTECTION

THEY COME IN DIFFERENT SHAPES, SIZES, AND MATERIALS, SO YOU CAN CHOOSE ONE TAILORED TO YOUR PHYSIQUE!

PROFESSIONALS USE CUT-RESISTANT WORK CLOTHES IN PLACES LIKE FISH MARKETS.

WEAR SOME CLOTHES *UNDER THAT*, WILL YA?

HEY... THIS BULLET-PROOF VEST IS PRETTY CONSTRICTIVE IN THE CHEST AREA...

WHAT'S WITH THE "NUDE UNDER THE APRON" LOOK?

CUT-RESISTANT

SQUEEZE

SQUEEZE

WE CAN PROBABLY BUY CUT-PROOF OR BULLET-PROOF VESTS OVER THE INTERNET THESE DAYS, HUH?

COME TO THINK OF IT, ZOMBIES DON'T FIGHT WITH BULLETS, SO WHAT'S THE USE OF A BULLET-PROOF VEST?!

gear, they can also take a toll on your body. We recommend you avoid wearing them for long periods of time. Also, the cut- and puncture-resistant clothing are meant to fit a wide variety of workers doing specific jobs, and therefore they have straps and belts for size adjustment. The problem is that zombies may be able to grab a hold of these straps and belts. After you've made your adjustments, cut excess straps and belts as short as possible.

OBTAINING THE EQUIPMENT

The majority of contractors and hardware stores have a wide range of work-related protective clothing in stock, and if they don't, it's possible to order it. Because these materials are in no way restricted, they can be found easily in brick-and-mortar stores or online. Once the crisis starts, then you can search in

126

construction sites, storage houses for disaster supplies, factories, farms, fish-processing factories, meat-processing factories, and other similar locations all over the country. However, once the cut-and-puncture-resistant clothing winds up torn, it is impossible to repair it. It is best to bring as many spares as you can carry with you.

Hand Protection
NOW THIS IS WHAT YOU SHOULD BE PROTECTING

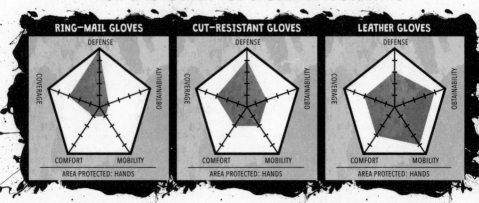

Since the main places you need to protect in anti-zombie combat are your arms and hands, the better your protection there, the higher your survival rate. And since highly-protected arms and hands are useful in accident situations as well, you should protect these areas, even if it seems like a wasted effort. You'll especially need protection for the tips of your fingers, so you should prioritize your choice of gloves above all. Some gloves and all mittens have unseparated fingers, making it difficult to wield tools and weapons, so they should not be used. Still, let's go for worker-use gloves with the fingers separated out and forearm protection whenever possible.

PROTECTION FROM THE FINGERTIPS ON UP

SINCE MY HANDS ARE VERY IMPORTANT, I WANT SOMETHING THAT IS CUT-RESISTANT AND PUNCTURE-RESISTANT-- SOMETHING WHERE I CAN SEPARATE MY FINGERS AND STILL BE PROTECTED *THROUGHOUT* THE ENTIRE GLOVE!
THEY USE RUBBER AND ALL KINDS OF OTHER MATERIALS. THESE CHAINMAIL GLOVES LOOK REALLY STRONG!
DON'T! YOU'LL BREAK IT!
THIS TYPE WITH THE METAL PLATE ON THE BACK OF THE HAND LOOKS LIKE IT COULD BE HANDY IN A FISTFIGHT!
CRUNCH

BUT DOESN'T IT GET HARD TO HOLD A WEAPON WHEN YOU'RE WEARING GLOVES?

WELL, YOU COULD JUST ROLL BACK THE CLOTH ON THE HAND HOLDING IT. ALSO, I THINK THEY SELL GRIP TAPE AND ANTI-SLIP MATERIAL AT HARDWARE STORES AND SPORTS EQUIPMENT STORES.

RECOMMENDED ITEMS

The best hand protection is provided by worker's gloves and mittens that are cut-resistant and puncture-resistant, but depending on the industry, there are those that only protect the palm-side and those that only protect the back-side of the hand. You will want to choose a type that protects the entire hand, reinforced with metal fibers. Aside from those, leather gloves, heavy-denim gloves, and horse-rider's gloves provide quite a bit of protection. Worker's ring-mail gloves are excellent, if you can get them. The very best would be to wear the cut-resistant and puncture-resistant gloves, and over those, a pair of ring-mail gloves, and one more set of cut-resistant and puncture-resistant gloves over that for maximum protection. Other possibilities include the metal gloves worn by riot police, but those will be very difficult to obtain. They also have less

protection for the fingers compared to the rest of the hand, so don't go out of your way searching for them.

CONCERNS WHEN EQUIPPING

The basic problem with protective gloves is that they somewhat lack breathability, so wearing them for long periods can be bad for your hands. When taking a rest, we recommend removing the gloves. Sweaty hands can affect your body by causing a loss of concentration, making you less cautious than you will need to be. People who have sweaty hands should do their best to keep from wearing these gloves for long periods of time. Also, ring-mail gloves and certain varieties of cut-resistant and puncture-resistant gloves require the use of an inner-glove, so before you don them, you should put on some cotton working gloves first.

OBTAINING THE EQUIPMENT

Contractors and hardware stores have all sorts of workman's gloves in stock, and it's also possible to find them at outdoors shops and mountain-climbing specialty shops. Internet shops are also possible, so during the pre-crisis period, they will be pretty easy to obtain. Once the crisis has started, you'll be able to find protective gloves at construction sites, disaster-supplies store houses, factories, farms, fish-processing factories, meat-processing factories, and many other places. You're almost guaranteed to find cut-resistant, puncture-resistant protective gloves anywhere that makes glass items. Other places include butcher shops or fresh meat counters in supermarkets and high-water-pressure cleaning facilities. Garbage men also use cut-resistant, puncture-resistant gloves. It's worth trying to find a pair.

Feet and Legs
OLD, RUSTY NAILS CAN BE SCARIER THAN ZOMBIES!

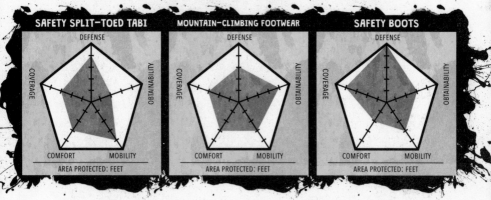

In the fight against zombies, the second most important body parts to protect after the hands and arms are your legs. But here, the fear is less of zombies and more of stepping on wood splinters, sharp rocks, and the like. If you injure your legs or feet, your mobility will sharply drop. In a worst case scenario, you will quite literally find yourself at the end of your rope. The most important part are the soles of your feet, so you will want to prioritize protection on the bottom of your feet. However, if you stress it too much over comfort, you will find you have damaged your feet after long hours of walking.

Look for a balance between protection and walking comfort. You should also consider ankle protection and accident protection in your boots, but try not to get boots that are too heavy for you.

RECOMMENDED ITEMS

The best boots are the safety split-toed *tabi* boots used by Japanese construction workers and foresters, but once the crisis has started, it might be difficult to get your hands on them. Aside from that, there are military boots and the safety boots used by factory workers. The boots used by mountain climbers provide a lot of protection, as do boots worn by horseback

LEG PROTECTION

THE TABI-STYLE ALSO ALLOWS FOR QUIETER FOOTFALLS, MEANING IT HAS AN **ADVANTAGE** AGAINST ZOMBIES.

YA GIVE UP A LITTLE IN DEFENSIVE POWER, BUT WITH THE SAFETY SPLIT-TOED WORK **TABI**, YA GET A LIGHTER BOOT THAT'S EASIER TO WALK IN. GOT IT?

THEY'RE A LITTLE HARDER TO PUT ON THAN REGULAR BOOTS, SO YOU'LL HAVE TO DO SOMETHING TO PREVENT BLISTERS. AND THEY AREN'T VERY **CUTE**, EITHER...

ONE KIND OF FOOTWEAR WITH A HIGH DEFENSIVE FACTOR AND IS COMPARATIVELY EASY TO GET YOUR HANDS ON ARE SAFETY BOOTS. THERE ARE MORE TYPES AVAILABLE ALL THE TIME, INCLUDING TYPES THAT PROTECT YOUR ANKLES.

 STILL, IF A BOOT'S SIZES DON'T FIT YOUR FEET OR OTHER PARTS OF YOUR LEG, IT WILL TAKE A TOLL ON YOUR BODY AND HURT YOUR FOOT SPEED. SO TAKE THAT INTO CONSIDERATION, TOO, WHEN YOU CHOOSE.

 THERE'S LIKELY TO BE A LOT OF BROKEN GLASS AND RUBBLE SCATTERED AROUND IN THE PANIC WHEN ZOMBIES APPEAR, SO YOU WILL WANT WELL-MADE FOOTWEAR.

riders. All are recommended. Also, cut-resistant, puncture-resistant protective overalls and cut-resistant, puncture-resistant protective leggings are good for protecting the legs, but they may be difficult to obtain. You could use sports padding, such as the ones used for soccer and other sports, but depending on the type, they may take a toll on your body if you wear them for long periods of time. Use caution with them.

CONCERNS WHEN EQUIPPING

All safety shoes, especially boots, have low breathability and will take a toll on you when worn for long periods of time. When you have a break, if it's at all possible, take off your footwear and allow both your feet and your footwear to air out. Take special care to prevent blisters. If you're wearing a pair of boots made of hard materials, cover the affected area with a layer of

newspaper or rags between your legs or feet and the boots to reduce the possible damage. Socks are extremely import-ant, so be sure to wear them. Leg fatigue has a big effect on the entire body, as it can bring down your awareness of your surroundings, your decision-making abilities, and even your concentration. You must limit long walks as much as is humanly possible.

OBTAINING THE EQUIPMENT

You can obtain protective footwear at contractors' places of business and hardware stores, but you can also find them in for-est homes and farms. Possible places to find mountain-climb-ing footwear are mountaineering specialty shops and sports equipment stores. You can also buy them online, but you have to be very careful about sizes and what type of footwear fits your feet and legs. We recommend that you find someplace that allows you to try them on. Once the crisis starts, you can check for these at construction sites, storehouses for disas-ter-relief equipment, factories, and lumber yards, to name a few. Forestry stations, offices for forestry operations, and lum-ber mills are also possible places, but they may be difficult to get to. Police departments and Japan Self-Defense Force bases may produce military-style boots, but this is only to be used as an emergency measure after the crisis has started.

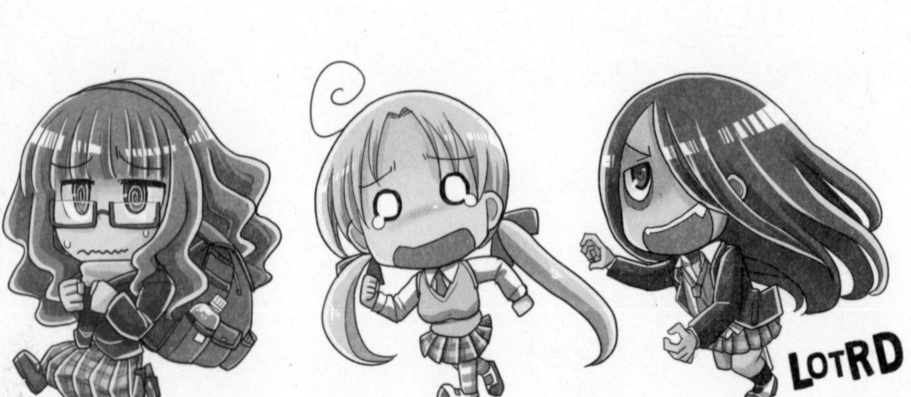
LOTRD

NOW THAT WE'VE LEARNED ABOUT ALL THESE WEAPONS AND DEFENSES, I THINK IT'S ABOUT TIME WE MADE OUR PERSONAL PICKS.

 I THINK I'LL GO WITH A SHOVEL. AND BECAUSE IT'S GOT MEDIUM HEFT, IT'LL HAVE PLENTY OF POWER BEHIND IT, RIGHT?

 NOTHING HEAVY FOR ME! SO MAYBE I'LL FIND A PORTABLE FRYING PAN?

 I'LL GO FOR THE ALL-PURPOSE WEAPON, THE CROWBAR.

 I CAN'T FAULT ANY OF YOU FOR YOUR CHOICES. I *DID* THINK CHRIS WOULD CHOOSE A WEAPON WITH MORE POWER, THOUGH.

 I WAS HOPING THEY'D HAVE A ZANTETSUKEN OR A PILE BUNKER...

 I WANTED TO STAY AS FAR FROM THE ZOMBIES AS POSSIBLE, SO I WANTED A GUN!

 CHRIS, WHO WERE YOU PLANNING TO FIGHT WITH THAT?

 JAPAN HAS VERY RESTRICTIVE REGULATIONS ON GUNS AND BLADED OBJECTS, SO ALL THE ITEMS THAT ARE EXTREMELY EFFECTIVE IN KILLING OR HURTING HUMANS WON'T BE FOUND WHERE CIVILIANS CAN GET THEIR HANDS ON THEM.

 IN AMERICA, YOU CAN GET GUNS AT DEPARTMENT STORES! I CAN'T SAY I LIKE HAVING GUNS EVERYWHERE, BUT IT'D COME IN HANDY AT A TIME LIKE THIS! I'M JEALOUS!

 THIS ISN'T ANYTHING LIKE THE GAMES OR MOVIES!

 EVEN IF YOU HAD A GUN, YOU'D BE OUT OF LUCK THE MINUTE YOU RAN OUT OF BULLETS! THEY'RE TOO DIFFICULT FOR AN AMATEUR TO SHOOT AND MAINTAIN.

 WELL, NO USE CRYING OVER SPILLED MILK. WE JUST GOTTA MAKE DO WITH WHAT WE CAN FIND.

 WHAT SURPRISED ME MOST IS HOW WE COULD GET AWAY WITH LIGHT PROTECTION!

 I'M SO GLAD WE DON'T HAVE TO WEAR THE HEAVY STUFF LIKE SUITS OF ARMOR!

 AS LONG AS WE'RE UP AGAINST SLOW-MOVING PANDEMIC-TYPE ZOMBIES, HUMANS' SPEED IS THEIR BIGGEST ADVANTAGE. SO WE NEED TO KEEP THAT ADVANTAGE.

 THIS IS A CASE OF "NOT BEING HIT IS THE BEST ARMOR," DON'T YOU THINK?

 NOW, IF WE INCLUDE THE STUFF WE CAN EASILY GET OUR HANDS ON THAT STILL HAS REASONABLE PROTECTION, WHAT KINDS OF DEFENSES CAN WE COORDINATE?

 PUT ON A LEATHER COAT...

 A CONSTRUCTION HELMET ON THE PERSON'S HEAD...

 A WORKER'S APRON IN FRONT...

 CHAINMAIL GLOVES ON OUR HANDS...

 AND FINALLY, SAFETY TABI-STYLE BOOTS!

 I WOULDN'T BE CAUGHT DEAD WEARING THIS STUFF, USUALLY. BETTER THAN ZOMBIES, THOUGH...

 IT'S SO YOU CAN STAY ALIVE! GRIT YOUR TEETH AND BEAR IT!

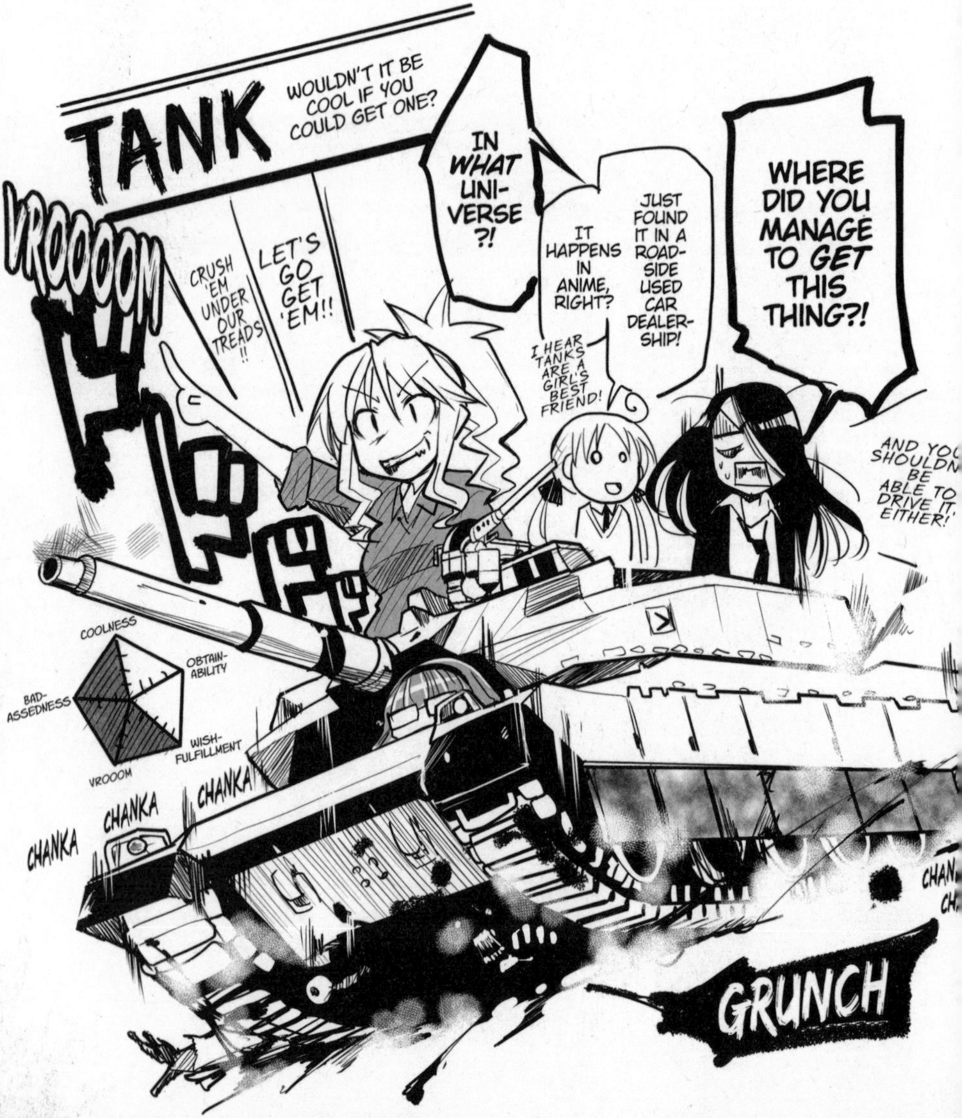
TANK
WOULDN'T IT BE COOL IF YOU COULD GET ONE?
WHERE DID YOU MANAGE TO GET THIS THING?!
JUST FOUND IT IN A ROAD-SIDE USED CAR DEALER-SHIP!
IN WHAT UNI-VERSE?!
IT HAPPENS IN ANIME, RIGHT?
I HEAR TANKS ARE A GIRL'S BEST FRIEND!
AND YOU SHOULDN BE ABLE TO DRIVE IT, EITHER!
LET'S GO GET 'EM!!
CRUSH 'EM UNDER OUR TREADS!!
VROOOOM
COOLNESS
OBTAIN-ABILITY
WISH-FULFILLMENT
VROOOM
BAD-ASSEDNESS
CHANKA
CHANKA
CHANKA
GRUNCH

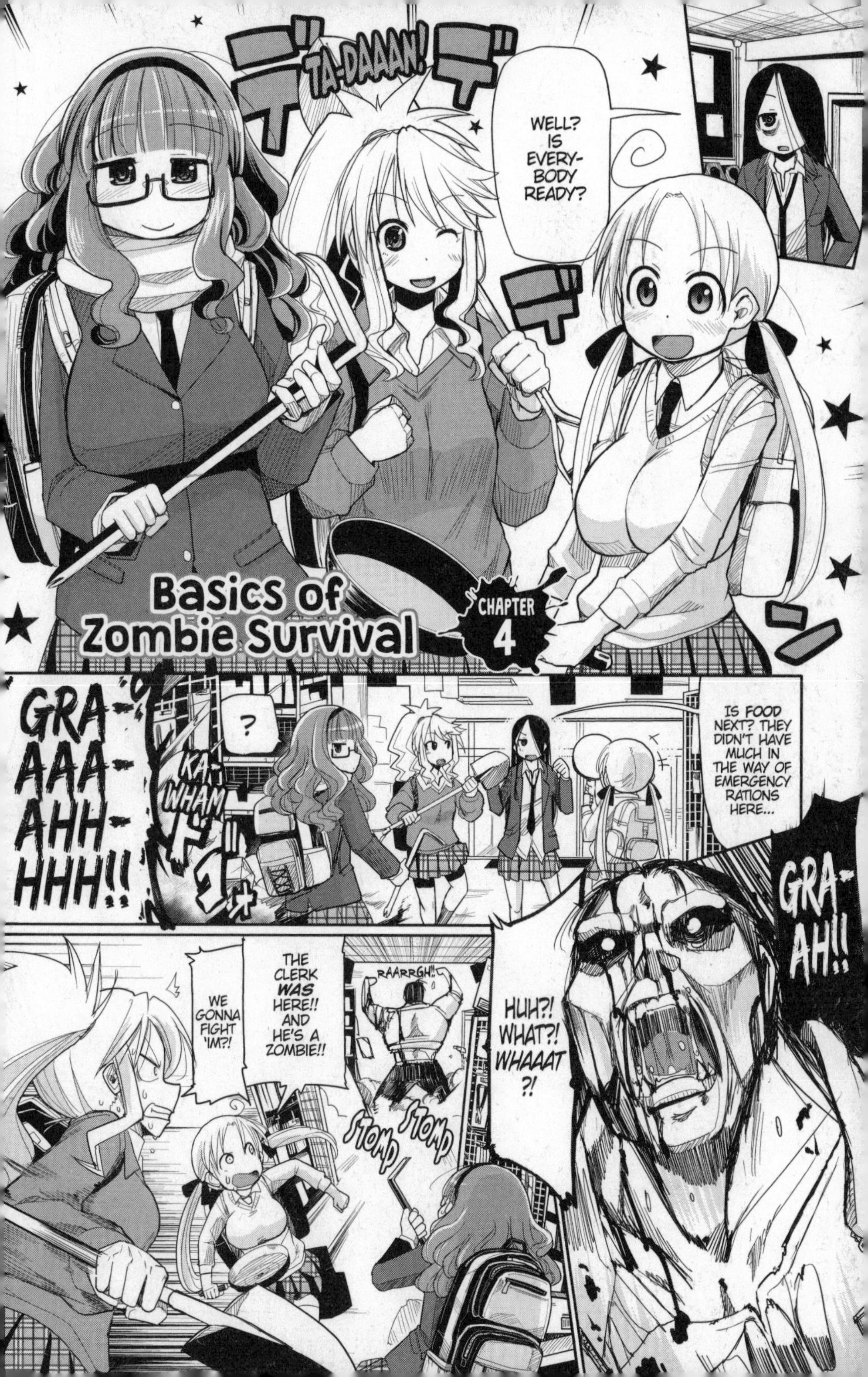
TA-DAAAN!
WELL? IS EVERY-BODY READY?
Basics of Zombie Survival
CHAPTER 4
IS FOOD NEXT? THEY DIDN'T HAVE MUCH IN THE WAY OF EMERGENCY RATIONS HERE...
?
KA-WHAM
GRA-AAAA-AHH-HHH!!
GRA-AH!!
HUH?! WHAT?! WHAAAT?!
RAAARRGH!!
THE CLERK WAS HERE!! AND HE'S A ZOMBIE!!
STOMP
STOMP
WE GONNA FIGHT 'IM?!

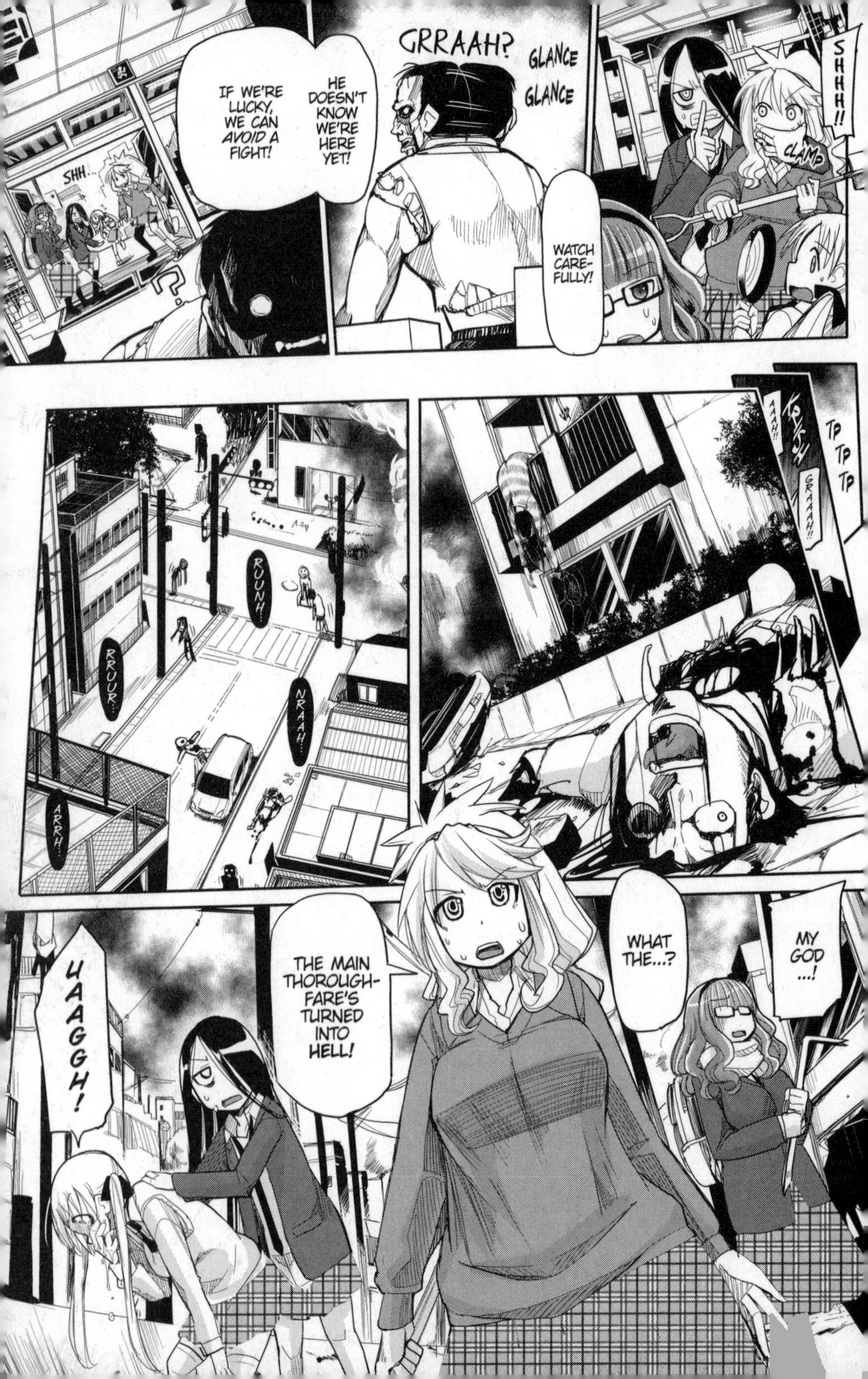
SHHHH!!
CLAMP
WATCH CARE-FULLY!
GRRAAH?
GLANCE
GLANCE
HE DOESN'T KNOW WE'RE HERE YET!
IF WE'RE LUCKY, WE CAN AVOID A FIGHT!
SHH...
?
Tp Tp Tp Tp
KRKSH
AAAH!!
GRAAAAH!!
RUUNH!
RRUUR...
NRAAH...
ARRH...
MY GOD...!
WHAT THE...?
THE MAIN THOROUGH-FARE'S TURNED INTO HELL!
UAAGGH!

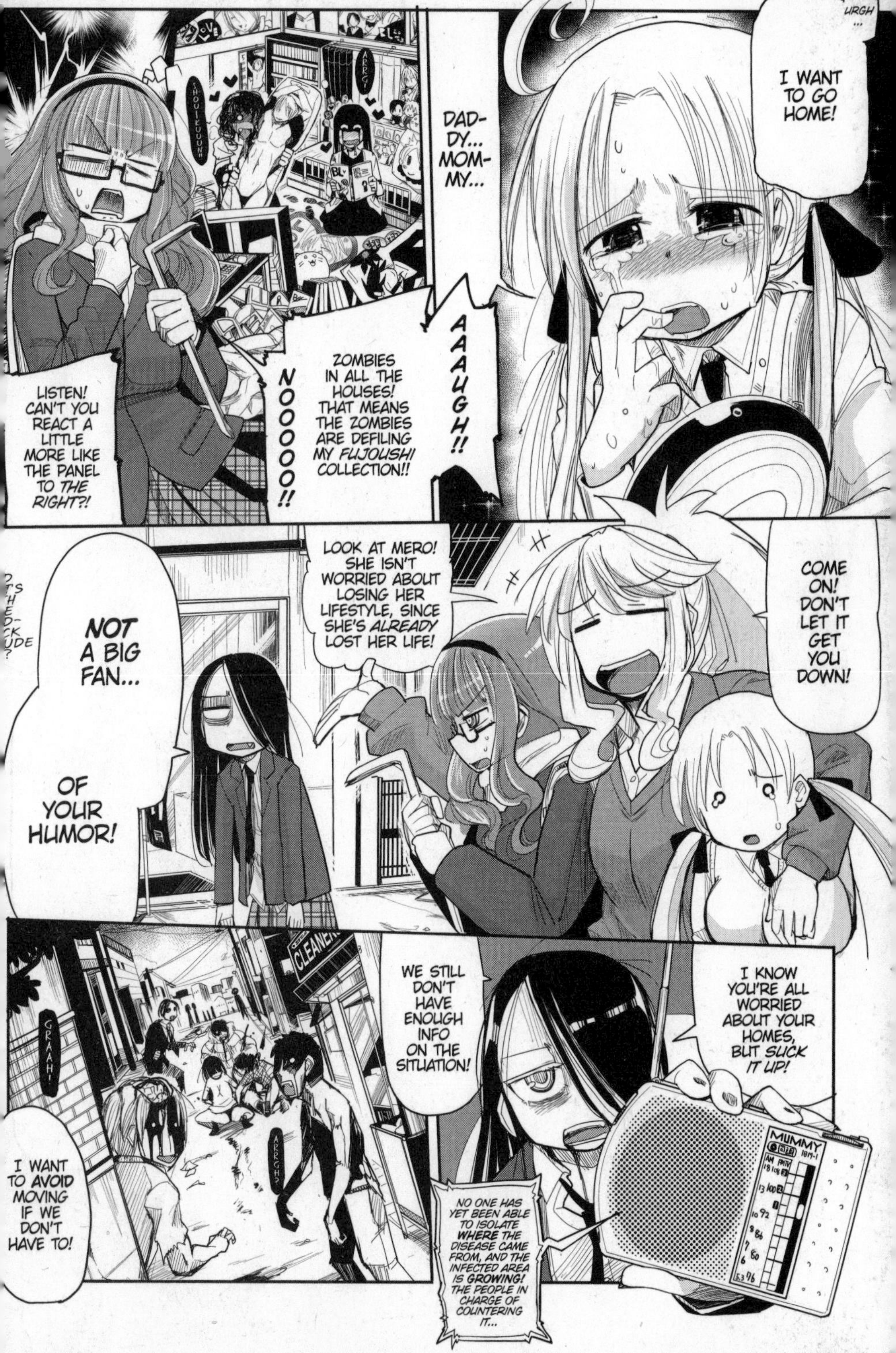
URGH...
I WANT TO GO HOME!
DADDY... MOMMY...
AAAAUGH!!
ZOMBIES IN ALL THE HOUSES! THAT MEANS THE ZOMBIES ARE DEFILING MY *FUJOUSHI* COLLECTION!!
NOOOOOO!!
ARRG!
LISTEN! CAN'T YOU REACT A LITTLE MORE LIKE THE PANEL TO *THE RIGHT*?!
COME ON! DON'T LET IT GET YOU DOWN!
LOOK AT MERO! SHE ISN'T WORRIED ABOUT LOSING HER LIFESTYLE, SINCE SHE'S *ALREADY* LOST HER LIFE!
NOT A BIG FAN...
OF YOUR HUMOR!
I KNOW YOU'RE ALL WORRIED ABOUT YOUR HOMES, BUT *SUCK IT UP!*
WE STILL DON'T HAVE ENOUGH INFO ON THE SITUATION!
NO ONE HAS YET BEEN ABLE TO ISOLATE **WHERE** THE DISEASE CAME FROM, AND THE INFECTED AREA IS **GROWING**! THE PEOPLE IN CHARGE OF COUNTERING IT...
MUMMY
GRAAAH!
ARRGH!
I WANT TO AVOID MOVING IF WE DON'T HAVE TO!

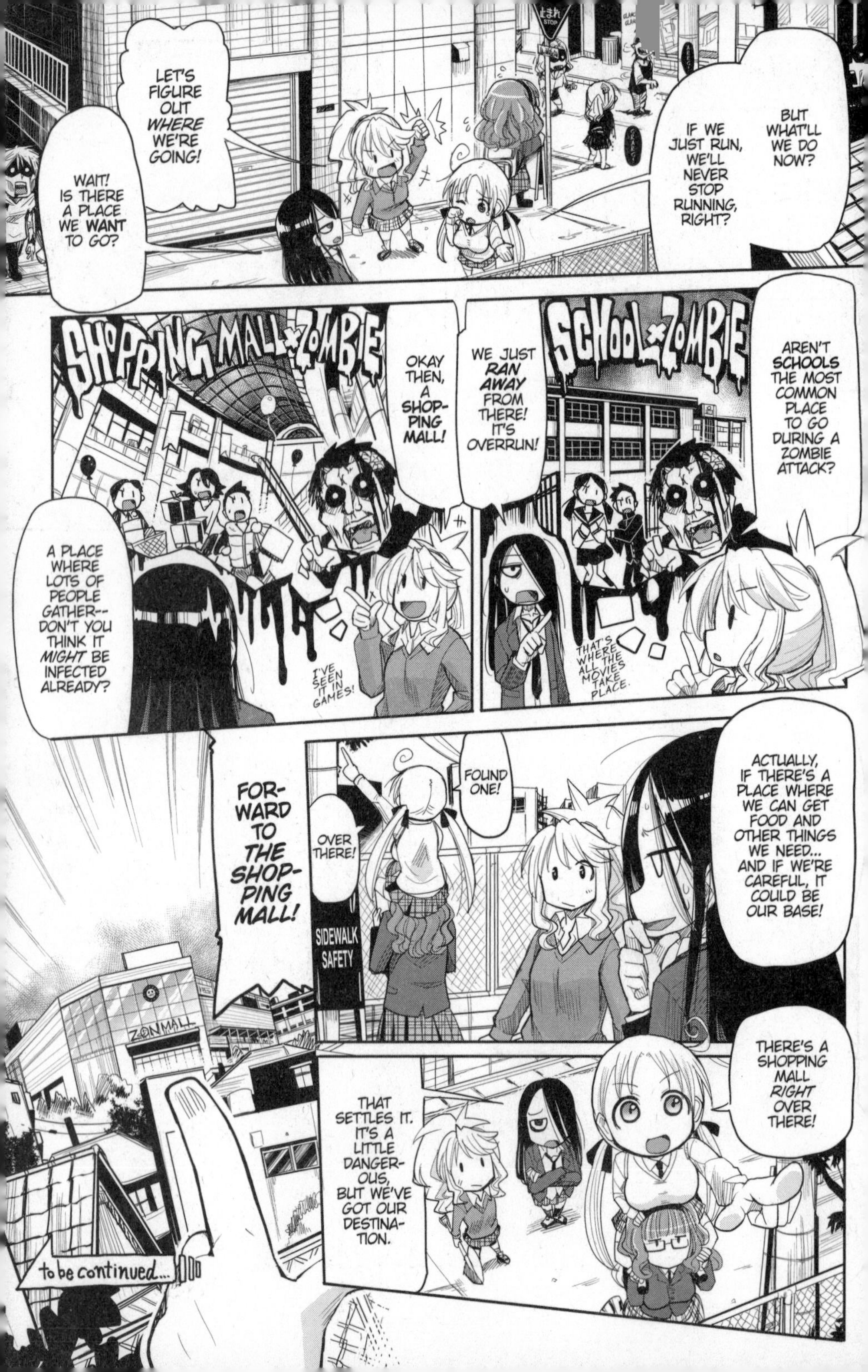
STOP
BUT WHAT'LL WE DO NOW?
IF WE JUST RUN, WE'LL NEVER STOP RUNNING, RIGHT?
LET'S FIGURE OUT WHERE WE'RE GOING!
WAIT! IS THERE A PLACE WE WANT TO GO?
SCHOOL×ZOMBIE
AREN'T SCHOOLS THE MOST COMMON PLACE TO GO DURING A ZOMBIE ATTACK?
THAT'S WHERE ALL THE MOVIES TAKE PLACE.
WE JUST RAN AWAY FROM THERE! IT'S OVERRUN!
SHOPPING MALL×ZOMBIE
OKAY THEN, A SHOPPING MALL!
I'VE SEEN IT IN GAMES!
A PLACE WHERE LOTS OF PEOPLE GATHER-- DON'T YOU THINK IT MIGHT BE INFECTED ALREADY?
ACTUALLY, IF THERE'S A PLACE WHERE WE CAN GET FOOD AND OTHER THINGS WE NEED... AND IF WE'RE CAREFUL, IT COULD BE OUR BASE!
FOUND ONE!
OVER THERE!
SIDEWALK SAFETY
THERE'S A SHOPPING MALL RIGHT OVER THERE!
THAT SETTLES IT. IT'S A LITTLE DANGEROUS, BUT WE'VE GOT OUR DESTINATION.
FORWARD TO THE SHOPPING MALL!
ZONMALL
to be continued...

SO, HERE WE ARE, FINALLY GETTING INTO THE MEAT OF HOW TO SURVIVE. I WAS THINKING MAYBE WE SHOULD DISCUSS SOME OF THE FUNDAMENTAL ASPECTS OF THIS.

 HUH? AFTER ALL THAT, WE HAVE A GOAL, SO LET'S JUST GET GOING!

 I TOO FEEL AVERSE TO REMAINING IN A PLACE WHERE ZOMBIES WANDER! LET'S HIT THE MALL, POST-HASTE!

 I JUST WANT TO CRACK SOME ZOMBIE HEADS OPEN!

 BE NEVER SO FLUSTERED, OH YOUTHFUL LADIES!! WHETHER IT BE MOVEMENT OR BATTLE, PREPARATION AND CAUTIONARY WISDOM WILL INCREASE YOUR CHANCE OF SURVIVING! OH, AND STOP DOING CLICHE STUFF THAT FORESHADOWS YOUR OWN DEATH, OKAY?!

 WHAT PREPARATION? WE GOT OUR WEAPONS. ALL THAT'S LEFT IS TO BASH EVERY ZOMBIE SKULL OUT THERE!

 WHAT'S THE DIFFERENCE, AS LONG AS WE DEAL DEATH TO THE ZOMBIES?

 OR, DO YOU MEAN PREPARATION FOR THE MALL? OH! YEAH, I GET IT! LIKE, WE'RE NOT SUPPOSED TO FORGET OUR WALLETS, RIGHT...?

 CHRIS, WHEN DID YOU CHANGE YOUR GOALS FROM SURVIVING TO ZOMBIE HUNTING? LINA, HAVE YOU CONSIDERED THE SITUATION? AND SARAH, WHAT DID I SAY ABOUT FORESHADOWING YOUR DEATH?

 AND ALL *I'M* DOING IS COMMENTING ON EVERYBODY ELSE'S DUMB LINES. WHAT I'M SAYING IS THAT IN A ZOMBIE SURVIVAL SITUATION, NORMAL DISASTER RULES AND COMMON SENSE WON'T GET YOU THROUGH IT!

 COME TO THINK OF IT, THE VERY PLACES THAT ARE SUPPOSED TO HELP YOU IN A NATURAL DISASTER, LIKE POLICE STATIONS AND HOSPITALS, TEND TO BE THE FIRST TO BE OVERRUN IN A ZOMBIE APOCALYPSE...

 EXACTLY! MISS SPECS JUST NAILED IT!!

 IN OTHER WORDS, A ZOMBIE SURVIVAL SITUATION MEANS YOU NEED TO INTERNALIZE ZOMBIE-SURVIVAL PREPAREDNESS AND KNOWLEDGE. OTHERWISE, YOU'LL FREAK OUT AT A CRUCIAL MOMENT, AND YOU'LL ALL WIND UP AS MINIONS OF THE ZOMBIE ARMY YOURSELVES!

 M-MISS SPECS...?

 YEAH, BUT, HERE YOU'RE TALKING ALL HIGH AND MIGHTY, BUT *WHO* WAS THE FIRST ONE OF US TO GET HERSELF ZOMBIFIED?

 URK...!

 I KNOW! I KNOW! IT WAS MERO, RIGHT?

 ALL RIGHT! FINE! BE THAT WAY! BUT IF *YOU* DON'T WANT TO END UP A ZOMBIE LIKE ME, THEN BEYOND JUST STAYING ALIVE, YOU NEED ESSENTIAL PROVISIONS AND INTELLIGENCE-GATHERING TOOLS!! SO START FIGURING OUT HOW TO MOVE AND FIGHT IN A ZOMBIE WORLD ALL BY YOURSELVES!!

4 The Fundamental Principles of Zombie Survival

By Bakegane

First Things First

Most of the methods of survival in a world affected by a zombie outbreak are very much the same as methods used in the event of the collapse of civilization. Once the area is overrun by zombies, it will be impossible (or at least extremely difficult) to make use of the advantages of civilized life.

Why is that? Most of the amenities of modern life are derived from the fact that labor is divided over a very wide population. If there's something you can't or won't do, then someone else will do it instead. Since this is expanded to a global scale, we have full shelves in our convenience stores; we can get foodstuffs from all over the world to use in the cooking at our local bar and grill; and we can have items ordered from the internet delivered right to our door.

War between human cultures can deprive us of that division of labor, and that's why a war in some far-off land can have an effect on the economics even close to home. The battle with zombies is no exception.

Although this battle is a situation where zombies are the enemy army in wartime, it's closer to guerrilla warfare. Whether zombies are self-aware or not, we still have to look at a person and say to ourselves, "This person may be a zombie. And even if he isn't right now, he may become one eventually." The zombie apocalypse is the beginning of a new society where those doubts have become prevalent.

So, assuming you're in a society overrun by zombies, what kind of methods should you adopt in order to survive?

For the purposes of this chapter, if no particular type of zombie is specified, you may assume we are referring to the Explosive Pandemic-type zombies. Since surviving an infestation of Self-Aware-type zombies requires different methods, those will be summed up at the end of the section.

We are also assuming it's been a few weeks since the zombie contagion began to spread. Further beyond that, the situation will vary depending on the type of zombie involved, the speed of the contagion's spread, and your methods of possible survival. We will go into this in detail in the "simulations" later in the book.

Necessities for Zombie Survival

FOOD

Zombies don't just come out of nowhere. They were humans first, so as the number of zombies increases, the number of humans is necessarily decreasing at least somewhat. That, at least, is one silver lining in the survival thundercloud. Zombies have no need for any of the items that humans need to survive. Not food, nor anything else. They may attack humans, but it is not for the purposes of nutrition.

For this reason, aside from perishable foods that can rot or otherwise go bad, food will not vanish quickly in a world overrun by zombies. Putting aside, for a while, the fact that industry and distribution will be stopped (at least in the beginning), you can rest assured that you will not be starving or dying of thirst any time soon.

However, it is possible that zombies might somehow infect the food or water supplies. This infected food and water should be considered poisonous to surviving humans. For this reason, you should not ingest food or drinks that zombies may have touched.

In a pinch, you may offer zombie-infected food or drink to a living animal to see what happens. In this way, you may be able to verify the safety of the food. Still, it is not a foolproof method, as it may take a matter of hours before any zombifying effects are visible.

Do not put yourself in any unnecessary danger. At the very least, be sure you have at least a day's worth of contagion-free food and water at all times. You may not have access to well-balanced foods, but if you simply have the type of food available to eat on the move as if you were hiking in the mountains, you will be fine. Examples of this in Japan would be items like Calorie Mate (an energy bar-like snack bar), candies, and other similar foods—something that will provide calories and necessary salt content. In other words, light foods for on-the-go snacking should suit you just fine, for now.

Also, until you have positively determined exactly what draws zombies toward humans when they attack, it is best not to eat foods that emit strong odors. Put off eating curry or pot stickers until you have determined that it is safe to eat them.

CLOTHING

Some of this will depend, of course, on the climate conditions of the region in which you live. However, we shouldn't have to tell you that you will need clothing appropriate for cold weather, hot weather, rainy weather, or whatever conditions are likely for your area.

Since this is about survival among zombies, you will want to avoid clothing that is easy to grab, or that might impede you when fleeing zombies. Stay away from frilly or fluffy clothing.

One area of difficulty might be in knowing whether or not zombies will be attracted to bright clothing or apparel that otherwise draws the eye. How do zombified eyes see bright, neon-like colors? If they do see them, will such colors bring zombies to attack the wearer? Or taking the opposite view, will a zombie's eye be tricked by camouflage uniforms or ghillie

suits that allow one to blend into the background? It isn't even known if zombies are able to distinguish between humans and mannequins.

But don't be too quick in the attempt to find answers to these questions. If testing them leads to you finding yourself surrounded by a multitude of zombies, then your zombie survival efforts have ended in failure. And as in determining whether or not zombie-infected food or water carries the contagion, there is no need to put yourself in danger to determine this answer either.

The one aspect in choosing clothing that you should prioritize above all else is clothing that will allow you to move quickly and without impediment. Beyond that, be sure to choose clothes that will be suitable for the temperature and environment around you. Also, make sure that you do not stand out. You can determine later whether subdued, easy-to-overlook colored clothing has the desired effect on zombies when the dust of the crisis has settled somewhat, when you are able to find a method that puts you in as little danger as possible.

REST BREAKS AND SLEEP PERIODS

Since zombie survival requires constant vigilance, a significant problem comes in finding a location in which one can rest or sleep. Every human must sleep, and while sleeping, they are vulnerable. Zombies, on the other hand, don't appear to need anything in the way of sleep or rest.

Like the tale of the tortoise and the hare, even if you are quick-witted and manage to escape a group of zombies with space to spare, eventually you will need to sleep. It is in these hours that the zombies may catch up to you.

It is imperative to find a place to rest or sleep where the zombies will have as difficult a time as possible in trying to reach you. Normal Explosive-Pandemic-type zombies may be unable to climb, so you should be safe on rooftops or even, for the more nimble of us, in the trees. But be sure to camouflage

NECESSITIES OF ZOMBIE SURVIVAL

your spot and have an escape route planned. You may successfully locate a treetop location to sleep, only to wake and find the ground below the tree filled with shambling zombies, with your only route of escape blocked.

If you are managing to band together with several others, your group should be able to take turns sleeping and standing watch so that there is a constant observation of the surroundings. Since you need to trade off rest periods, it will increase the total rest time necessary. However, in exchange, it will also increase the safety and allow quick reaction times when the situation changes.

Japan has turned most of its flat land into urban or suburban areas. Since most zombies are not well adapted to climbing and descending floors, some of the taller buildings might be suitable for finding places to rest or sleep. Especially on the Kanto plain—the greater Tokyo region—there are multitenant buildings where the only access to the upper floors

aside from the elevator is an extremely steep, narrow staircase. If you manage to block the staircase with various types of debris, a regular human would have trouble passing, let alone a zombie. Such buildings are scattered throughout the region. Some buildings, with passageways so narrow that they would be considered firetraps during pre-crisis periods, might unexpectedly turn out to be some of the safer places to rest or sleep during the crisis.

However, trusting your location too much is not advised. There may still be some unfortunate people who thought, as you might, that such places are safe for sleeping. And after having been caught by zombies, they might now be wandering zombified in unexpected places within the building. Were that to happen, the zombies would not descend to the ground floor (most likely, the thought of descending would not even occur to them), so they'd be laying in wait for the next poor victim to fall to their zombie attack. Since fighting hand-to-hand with zombies in tight spaces is about the most dangerous situation possible, you'll want to thoroughly search every floor in the building in advance.

It is conceivable that, depending on the type of zombie, you will want to sleep with earplugs. Some types of zombies put out an incessant, frightening moaning and wailing while loitering in the area. In such cases, it takes someone with true nerves of steel to be able to sleep through it. Other types of zombies give off putrid odors, and in that case, specially treated surgical masks or sleeping in spaces where all cracks are sealed may be a necessity. Weather-stripping tape may be convenient in that case.

Communication and Information

TELEVISION & RADIO

During any kind of crisis or disaster, obtaining new information is essential. In a country like Japan that is under almost constant threat from disasters such as earthquakes and typhoons, the citizens have learned the value of information time and time again.

Twentieth-century technological developments such as TV and radio (especially radio) will likely prove to be extremely useful in a zombie apocalypse. And with the citizen's band radio and power-generation capabilities found even in light trucks, you may be able to broadcast your messages to an entire local region.

There is a great importance to broadcasting on the radio. For example, information can be shared over a broadcast, which is extremely useful, but even just hearing a human voice can cheer someone up. Hearing a song or a joke can give someone the courage to keep on living. It is extremely heartening to have someone talking to you during a time when you are suffering.

With both television and radio, you need a device to pick up the signal. You should carry a small, portable radio when you're on the move in a zombie-survival situation. There are emergency radios that use a crank-handle to recharge, but if you already have it, a normal battery-operated portable radio will be perfect.

INTERNET

Such items such as television and radio only receive signals, and therefore they are simply one-way communication. But an internet-capable device that is connected to the net can both send and receive at the same time.

The internet is made possible by many communications nodes, all interlinked to create multiple paths of communication.

Even if several of the nodes become inaccessible, the rest can still use the remaining active nodes for their communications protocol to send information to their destination. The internet was born from the ARPA Network, a system that was created during a time when the USA and the Soviet Union both lived under constant threat of nuclear warfare. Therefore, the ARPA Network is rumored to have chosen an information protocol that would stand the best chance of surviving an all-out nuclear war.

For this reason, we can reasonably expect the internet to survive for at least a limited time during a zombie apocalypse. Even though the machines that keep the internet running are spread throughout the world, most of the nodes and high-speed data highways are concentrated in metropolitan areas. These nodes would be highly susceptible to failure during a zombie crisis. Also, the internet's infrastructure is dependent upon electric power and access to maintenance. As the zombie contagion spreads, power will eventually go down and main-tenance will no longer be available. At this point, the nodes will shut down.

The question is: when does that shutdown happen? The answer is that it depends on where the zombie outbreak oc-curs, and how quickly it spreads. For the time that the internet remains useful, it would be a good idea to bring along a port-able internet-capable device (and extra batteries), even if it does weigh you down a little.

CELL PHONES

The start of the twenty-first century saw the rapid spread of cell phones throughout all of Japanese society. In the past, a port-able communications gadget that could be carried anywhere by almost anyone was a concept straight out of science fiction. But before we realized it, they became an integral part of daily life. Cell phones would certainly be useful and powerful tools during a zombie apocalypse. That is, as long as the communi-cations infrastructure holds out.

There are plenty of uses to which you can put your cell phone. Let's call it a given that it can be used as a tool for communications, but you can also use the screen to light up very dark places. And if the zombies you are fighting are attracted to the human voice, you can set a trap for them using your phone as bait. Even after the communications infrastructure breaks down, it can still be used for its offline functions, like playing music.

The cell phone is a symbol of daily civilized life that's been lost in the crisis. Surely there are plenty of people with saved photos and voicemail from family, friends, and lovers on their phones. Even if most of the phones don't have an address book full of old contacts, they remain a symbol of the society you would like to rebuild. And even when it's completely useless, you can hang on to your cell phone in the unlikely hope that someday you can go back to the good old days, when you were annoyed at the amount of spam in your cell phone's message center.

But still, the strap can be a liability. Remove it.

CAMERA

Because of the advances in information technology in the modern world, we no longer use film in our cameras. Instead, we can take still pictures and video, transfer them to data, attach them to email, or upload them to the internet. As a result, during times of sudden disasters such as tornados, sudden deluges of rain, earthquakes, and the like, it has become commonplace for images from the scene to be shared on social media and broadcast through the mass media. It has also become possible for specialists to analyze the images from social media. This allows them to come up with conclusions on exactly what happened and to help the situation as a whole.

It's possible that the sharing of images in a zombie outbreak might provide the same boons as with other natural disasters. After all, it is the dead rising and attacking the living.

INFORMATION IS VITAL!

SOME ZOMBIES MAY BE ATTRACTED TO SOUNDS, SO BE SURE OF WHERE YOU ARE AND HOW LOUD YOUR VOLUME IS WHEN YOU LISTEN.

...BUT IT'S *REALLY GREAT* IN A CRISIS, HUH?

I HARDLY EVER LISTEN TO THE RADIO NORMALLY...

WITH ONE SMART PHONE, YOU CAN HAVE A PHONE, INTERNET ACCESS, TV, A CAMERA, A MUSIC PLAYER, AND MORE. IT'S CONVENIENT, BUT... SOMEHOW, I THINK YOUR LIFE ON THE NET IS *VERY DIFFERENT* FROM IRL.

LET'S UPLOAD A PHOTO TO AN INTERNET BULLETIN BOARD, AND GET AS MUCH INFO AS WE CAN.

[Image] Whoa! :D I'm surrounded by zombies! ;)

1. Glasses Girl: 20XX/11/27 (Monday) 5:59:12 ID#Z0
Somebody give me advice, okay?

2. Noname: 20XX/11/27 (Monday) 6:01:02

 LUCKILY, THEY MAKE HAND-CRANK AND SOLAR-POWERED TYPES OF EMERGENCY FLASHLIGHTS AND WEATHER RADIOS NOW THAT HAVE USB PORTS SO YOU CAN KEEP EVEN YOUR CELL PHONE CHARGED.

IT'S TRUE THAT SMART PHONES ARE REALLY CONVENIENT, BUT YOU HAVE TO BE CAREFUL OF THEIR BATTERY LIFE.

At the sites of various zombie outbreaks, there will be people snapping images of the carnage on their mobile phones and uploading them to Twitter or Facebook.

This information being available at the very beginning of a zombie apocalypse may bring about widespread panic. But for those determined to survive the zombie crisis, it may be useful to have access to firsthand, eyewitness experience.

The sight of a zombie shambling toward you will be difficult for anyone without special training to face with a calm, analytical mind. However, that is not necessarily true of someone who is sitting in a safe location, looking at the disturbing images that will certainly flood the internet.

What kinds of stimuli draw a zombie toward the living? How strong are they, and what other physical attributes might they have? What happens to those humans who are attacked?

The answers to those questions will be immediately useful in helping you survive a zombie crisis.

The communications infrastructure will eventually break down, but try to download as much image data as you can possibly manage before that point. You can always analyze it after you've found a new power source.

Being the one who is taking the images and posting them online has its own survival advantages. While the information infrastructure is still in working order, someone with more specialized knowledge and ability may be able to examine your images. Upon analyzing them, they may be able to send you useful survival information based on what they see.

MIRRORS/FLAGS

Modern Japan is a highly computerized society, but it is susceptible to a zombie disaster. When it comes to normal natural catastrophes, there are plenty of opportunities for infrastructure repairs. But in the case of a zombie apocalypse, repairmen and equipment cannot simply be sent into affected areas while zombies are loitering around waiting to attack someone. The Japanese Self-Defense Forces have a certain amount of ability and training to help deal with the situation, but they will be up against an unknown force—the zombies. The initial chaos will only go on longer.

If the information infrastructure fails during these early stages, that's when you and your comrades should start to use mirrors and flags. Mirrors can reflect bright lights, and while the amount of information you can communicate by waving flags is limited, it could be considered heaven compared to the hell of being unable to communicate at all. Also, while the amount of information communicable with flags and mirrors is low, the speed at which the information can be transmitted and the distance at which it carries should not be underestimated!

If you are careful in setting up relay points, you should be able to communicate a message over a distance of a hundred

PRIMITIVE COMMUNICATION METHODS

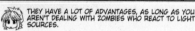

THEY HAVE A LOT OF ADVANTAGES, AS LONG AS YOU AREN'T DEALING WITH ZOMBIES WHO REACT TO LIGHT SOURCES.

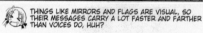

THINGS LIKE MIRRORS AND FLAGS ARE VISUAL, SO THEIR MESSAGES CARRY A LOT FASTER AND FARTHER THAN VOICES DO, HUH?

kilometers (60 miles) or so. With practice, you can set up even more complex codes to communicate over long distances.

The one attribute that will eventually allow humans to defeat the zombies is a person's resourcefulness. And by resourcefulness, we don't simply mean an individual's physical agility; they have to defeat the zombies using information as well.

If humans are reduced to running away every time they see a zombie, humanity will eventually suffer an embarrassing defeat. If someone can reconnoiter where the pack of zombies is, where they're headed, and then effectively relay that info back to the group, the group can then plan its moves accordingly.

Going on the Move

THE GOAL OF MOVEMENT IN A ZOMBIE SURVIVAL SITUATION

One of the surest ways to survive a zombie apocalypse is to avoid fighting the zombies if at all possible.

Zombies are already dead. Living people will flinch away from pain as long as they're alive, and the only way to completely avoid battle wounds is to run from the fight.

Unlike humans, zombies have no fear of pain, nor do they hesitate when faced with otherwise fatal wounds; they're simply out to kill you. The only time you fight such an enemy is when you literally have no other choice.

You're free to fight zombies as long as you like, if you are able to win, but if your win comes at the expense of a zombie bite turning you into a zombie too, any win you might have had suddenly becomes an all-out defeat.

The best way to avoid fighting zombies is to never encounter them in the first place. So, the first rule for moving around in a zombie apocalypse is to go where the zombies aren't.

But this is where the main problem arises.

How can you find a place where there are no zombies? Zombies are reanimated versions of dead human bodies. After the normal Explosive Pandemic-type zombie attacks a human, the human eventually becomes a zombie also. If there is any place where humans are, odds are good that there will be zombies there as well. So if you consider the places that are created for normal natural disasters such as earthquakes or typhoons—places like public evacuation shelters or hospital—odds are they will be the first to be overrun with zombies. They are likely to have quickly become hells on Earth, filled with the agonizing cries of victims.

In any case, no matter where you might think of going, there is no guarantee that it will be a place of safety. Since zombies attack humans, and those humans then become zombies, you'll certainly want to at least try to run away.

BE SURE TO CHECK YOUR ESCAPE ROUTE AT EVERY OPPORTUNITY

No matter where you decide to run in a zombie survival situation, the first thing to consider is how to escape if zombies attack your present location. At that point, you should know where your gear is so that you can grab it at a moment's notice to go on the run. This is much like when you stay at a hotel, where you will also want to check where the emergency exits and evacuation routes are. When you are together with family or friends—people you feel you must protect—then everyone in the group should have some say in the escape route. However, when you are on your own, you may simply use your own judgment. In either case, it's vital that you make your preparations in advance.

The reason for this is that timing is everything when you're desperately fleeing from zombies. You can be sure that you won't have time for a leisurely discussion of your escape options when you're under attack. After all, if a person in that location is attacked by a zombie and becomes a zombie in turn, you will soon have a mob of zombies pressing in on you. No matter how you look at it, it will become a scene of chaos.

So to keep from panicking when that situation happens, you will need to do your planning while you are still in a relatively safe spot. Figure out the timing of when to run, what route to take, and where to meet up, in case you somehow get separated.

PREPARATIONS TO MAKE BEFORE RUNNING

This is true of any disaster situation, but you will not be able to carry everything you will need to survive. This is especially true in a zombie survival situation, when civilization has been attacked by the living dead. The shock to society will be great, and at the beginning of the panic, the roads will become clogged. Packing everything in your car and running will most likely not be an option.

At the same time, in a zombie survival situation, the walking dead will need no food or other necessities. You can probably

expect to be able to loot many of the consumables that humans need while you are on the run. And if that's the case, then all you really need when you're running from any particular place are the items you will need for the escape itself.

First, lighting and sturdy footwear are indispensable. But in zombie survival, you may not have the chance to choose the time of your escape. If someone in your group turns into a zombie or if a mob of zombies attack during a typhoon or while you're asleep, then what can you do?

In nighttime escapes, two items will be essential: a flashlight and well-made footwear that can be worn even in bad weather. But while you're sleeping or when resting up from a hard run, it's best to take off your shoes or boots and put them in a spot where you can don them again in a hurry. Also, a basic rule is to rest or sleep with your footwear off in order to rest your feet as well. However, if you rest in a dangerous spot, you will probably want to sleep with your shoes or boots on. Similarly, you will want rain gear during times of winds and rain or winter gear in locations or seasons when the weather will turn cold.

When deciding what you will constantly need to keep on your person, you will first want to imagine yourself on the run and hiding from zombies for at least a day (or, to be safe, up to a few days). Then, from this imaginary scenario, decide what you think you will need. For example, if you are in a place where fresh spring water rises up from the ground, or if water pipes are still working in your area, then you won't need to carry water with you. Otherwise, you should keep perhaps one to two liters of water with you.

If there are a lot of zombies wandering around in your area, and the odds are better that you'd be hiding in some secret spot for a while, then you will need several meals' worth of food on hand. It will make your eventual escape more difficult if hunger leads you to search for food—zombies may find you while you're looking.

The types of equipment you will need and what other preparations you must make during your zombie survival period will change almost constantly. If you are in the town where you lived as a child, your need for a map will decrease. On the other hand, if you have recently moved into a new residence or if your flight from zombies has led you to unfamiliar areas, then you will want to keep a map handy.

And how is your eyesight? Are you fine running from zombies without eyewear? If not, then you will probably need your glasses or contacts. You will need to carry a strong case for your eyeglasses with you at all times. Then, when you remove your glasses, make sure to place them in the case and keep the case in your pocket until you need them next.

Some medications are also a necessity and, for some, absolutely crucial. You will have very limited chances to get your hands on a fresh supply while on the run. Aside from the medications your doctor prescribes for any chronic condition you might have, you will probably also want to investigate what other medications are available.

Use your imagination!

Chased by zombies, leaving your home or familiar environs behind and going on the run—what may hinder your free movement?

The main thing you should think about isn't really the zombies. Put aside those thoughts of swinging that axe you've never held before or throwing that hard-to-handle knife. Don't even think of fighting the zombies. Your first move is to run! And what you need to pack are the items and information that will help you to do so.

BEWARE OF FIRE HAZARDS

During a zombie apocalypse, the chances of a fire increase dramatically.

First, there are fewer and fewer people to help keep the area fire-safe. Some will have run, and others will have been turned

TRAVEL PREPARATIONS

OKAY, WE'RE GOING TO GO ON THE MOVE SOON. IS EVERYONE PREPARED?

SURE ARE!!!

AND PEOPLE SHOULDN'T FORGET THEIR MEDICINE, OBVIOUSLY.

GOBBLE GOBBLE GOBBLE

DEPENDING ON THE PERSON, THEY MIGHT NEED THEIR GLASSES.

I DON'T LIKE THE LOOK IN YOUR EYES. ARE THOSE REALLY YOUR PRESCRIBED MEDICATIONS?

I'VE GOT THE MAP... BUT HOW ARE WE SUPPOSED TO READ IT AGAIN?

YEAH, I DON'T THINK YOU'LL BE CARRYING THE MAP!

FOOD AND WATER ARE THE BASICS, RIGHT?

FIRST, WE GOT FOOD!

MM! TASTY!

BUT WHY ARE YOU EATING IT NOW?!

POTATO Cookies

DO YOU GUYS *REALLY* WANT TO SURVIVE? YOU DO REALIZE YOU'RE MAKING A *ZOMBIE* WORRY ABOUT YOU, RIGHT...?

into zombies. There will be some people who will have done the right thing and turned off their gas before they ran, among other considerations. But in the confusion and panic, it is likely that most will simply leave without observing any precautions.

There will undoubtedly be people who will want to use the threat of fire in the hopes of scaring off the zombies. After all, it works on wild animals, right? But if you take the time to actually consider what zombies are, you will realize that they have no instinct for self-preservation. As a result, the threat will have no effect. Quite the opposite: in a worst-case scenario, it might bring more zombies to you. Zombies do not fear fire. They don't mind setting themselves ablaze. They will continue to wander around, fully engulfed in flames and unwittingly setting their surroundings on fire as well, until they are completely consumed in the blaze.

Within the early days of the zombie outbreak, you can expect fires to crop up in spots all over your town. At the very beginning, there may be fires that can be put out by home extinguishers, and the fire brigade will be called in for larger fires.

But one of the aspects of zombie survival is the realization that, at some point, the fires will start spreading out of control. One big drawback of fire is that it puts humans at a disadvantage. The most dangerous part of fire is the smoke. Smoke limits your vision, chokes you, and in a worst case, can contain poisonous gases. The threat of suffocation and the hazards caused by gas don't affect zombies, so it's only a danger for humans.

It's no exaggeration to say that the best way to prepare for fire is in your plan to deal with the smoke. As for decrease in visibility caused by smoke, you should have an evacuation route planned out ahead of time. It's best to practice evacuation procedures repeatedly well in advance. To keep from suffocating, do your best to keep low so you do not breathe the smoke. You may also want to practice wrapping a towel around your mouth as you escape.

Preparedness is your best weapon against panicking in the face of a fire, so it's best to understand the importance of diligent practice.

BREAKS WHILE ON THE MOVE

Most people's daily routines in modern Japan do not normally include very much long-distance walking, with some exceptions for certain jobs and hobbies. Also, it's very important to adjust the amount of long-distance walking to match your body type. No matter how much information on walking you amass from magazines or the internet, it's quite another thing to transfer that knowledge to your body.

We suggest you avoid long periods of walking when your body is still not used to it or when wearing footwear that is not broken in. Unless, of course, your area is presently filled with zombies and you must escape long distances in a hurry. This

MOVING THROUGH RURAL AREAS

 ALSO, YOU'LL WANT TO KEEP A CLOSE EYE ON YOUR OWN FOOTING, UNLESS YOU FEEL UP TO MUD-WRESTLING WITH ZOMBIES.

RICE PADDIES WON'T DO MUCH TO SLOW ZOMBIES DOWN IN THE WINTER OR WHEN THE FIELD IS DRAINED.

doesn't just apply to your feet. In a zombie-survival situation, any wounds that keep you from moving quickly are an invitation to be trapped by the zombies. In other natural disasters, you have the choice to survive a debilitating wound by waiting for help, and if you can avoid running out of essential supplies, you may be able to make it. But in a zombie apocalypse, if you can't go on the run, you will be in danger of the zombies finding you before help arrives. If that happens, it's all over for you. For that reason, you need to take even short breaks every one or two hours to keep up your health and physical condition. Overextending yourself should be forbidden!

In an urban or suburban location, the best place to take a break will probably be the upper floors of a building. It'll be hard for the zombies wandering around outside to notice you, and since the number of places for a zombie to hide is limited

inside the building, you should be able to discover and dispatch them quickly. Even if there are zombies on the ground floor, normal Explosive Pandemic-type zombies find it difficult to ascend and descend staircases. In other words, you should be able to run away with time to spare.

In more rural areas, you should aim for rice paddies and farmland. As these are wide-open spaces with long sightlines, it will be easier for zombies to see you. But since rural areas have a much lower population density than urban areas, there will be relatively fewer zombies to face in the first place. The main reason, though, is that footing is slow and difficult when walking across farmland and water-filled rice paddies. You can clearly find the footpaths that farmers leave for people to walk through.

Fortunately, these paths are only clear to humans. Zombies don't distinguish footpaths from the deep mud of rice paddies. Once they see you, they will head in a straight line toward you. At that point, they will enter the mud and hopefully be unable to move farther. So as you lead the zombies into places with terrible footing, you can escape along the footpaths. On the other hand, in some rural locations you might find yourself in areas where you are up to your waist in undergrowth. In such places, not only will your movements be slowed, zombies might be hidden among the foliage there.

CAMPING GROUNDS

There are many rodents and small creatures that move around in the nighttime trying to avoid predators. In zombie-survival situations, the zombies are the predators, so some of the same concepts apply. And conversely, other concepts do *not* apply. Since zombies don't need to rest, they will be making much of the same kind of movements during daylight as nighttime. During nighttime, the chances of being spotted decrease, but this disadvantage applies both ways. If you encounter a zombie at night, you likely won't spot the zombie until you're up close. And if you finally spot the zombie at too close a distance, then

CONDITIONS OF YOUR CAMPGROUND

 OF COURSE, I EXPECT THERE WILL BE PUBLIC RESTROOMS THAT DON'T PASS ALL THE CONDITIONS. SO RELY ON YOUR WISDOM AND PROBLEM-SOLVING ABILITIES WHEN DECIDING.

 ANOTHER REASON FOR THE "NO FOLIAGE" CONDITIONS IS NOT ONLY TO KEEP ZOMBIES FROM HAVING A PLACE TO HIDE, BUT ALSO TO KEEP YOU FROM MAKING NOISE DURING YOUR ESCAPE. STILL, A RESTROOM IS A LITTLE TOO...

there may be no room left to escape. Humans have an edge over zombies, as the speed difference allows humans to put a lot of distance between them. But the darkness places the advantage squarely with the zombies, giving them the ability to launch a sudden and unexpected attack.

When you are on the run in a zombie-survival situation, you will want to begin your camping preparations while the sun is still high. Once the clock hits about three in the afternoon, you should start giving thought to finding your camping ground.

The main things to be careful of when camping are sparks from cooking or heating fires and the lighting that may be visible in the nighttime. Like in wartime, even a small light can be seen from a very long distance away in the dark of night. Depending on what attracts the zombies, your campfire may bring zombies to you.

If you're dealing with the type of zombies that are attracted to light in the nighttime hours, one possible method is to check your camping ground thoroughly, then set up some kind of decoy light a very long way from where you intend to camp. Another is to choose a camping ground with a river or steep gradient between yourself and the zombies. If the place has good sight lines, you should be able to spot the zombies, while also making it difficult for them to get to you. Another possibility is to find some kind of shielding to surround the fire and sparks so that the light from them does not leak outside. If you combine that with the decoy light to lead zombies away from you, then you should be able to camp in peace.

But you should prepare for the possibility that all those zombies you attracted and gathered up in one place with your decoy light might block the very road you planned on traveling the next afternoon. Never forget that your best course of action is to be constantly changing with the situation.

Preparing Yourself for the Zombies

SUPPORT FOR FEAR OF ZOMBIES

One of the most important tasks in a zombie-survival situation is reducing and controlling your own personal fear of the zombies.

One of the reasons why zombies are such a threat to human society is simply that people are afraid of zombies. And, yes, zombies are indeed scary. The very fact that the dead walk inspires a certain horror, and that's even without considering that they also attack the living. Depending on the type of zombies, the victims of zombies can also become zombies themselves. What kind of person would *not* be afraid of that?

Fear can cause the loss of reason and good judgment. Frightened people act on impulse, and this can cause them to do stupid things. A person might run from a zombie who hasn't

even noticed them, only to have that action lead to his or her discovery. Or they might find themselves rooted to the spot in fear, even though they could have easily escaped. Terror can bind up your nerves and muscles, draining you of the power to even move.

And it's not just zombies. Have you ever seen a horror movie or read a horror manga where you thought, "I would have been able to do that so much better"? If you thought that, then you are both right and wrong about it. If you can overcome your fear, you will probably live through it. If you can't conquer your fear, then you will probably do some of the same stupid things that the characters in the movie or manga do, and you will most likely die.

Conquering your fears is not the same thing as never feeling fear; instead, it means putting the reigns upon your fear. However, it is the rare human indeed who can feel the fear he or she was born with, and still be able to chose the correct course of action. The average person would be controlled by his or her fear, and become a slave to it.

The vast majority of humanity will need support in overcoming their fears. If they can stick together when the terror starts, they'll realize that they aren't alone, and they may be able to find ways to counteract their fears. Do not become enslaved by your own feelings! Tame them!

OBSERVATION AND ANALYSIS

Knowledge is the greatest vaccine against fear.

At one time, because of the limits on humanity's knowledge of how plagues spread, people thought that such illnesses were similar to curses. This made them hysterical from fear of the plague. How do plagues spread? Is it from people being infected by bacteria or a virus? Or could it be because of vitamin or nutrition deficiency? It's because they don't know the answer that sometimes people can act rashly.

Along with the advancing knowledge of how illnesses spread, people also slowly conquered their fear of those illnesses. There are still many people who are terrified of illness, but in modern society, people are more skilled at conquering their fears. On the other hand, when a new illness springs up and not enough is known about it, humans tend to give in to their previous fears once again.

Perhaps when more knowledge is collected about zombies, people can conquer their fears of zombies as well. When we know what it is that stimulates the zombies, then we will know what can be used as bait to lure them into a trap. If you know how quickly the zombies move, you will know how much distance between you and them will keep you safe. If you know the conditions by which a person becomes a zombie, you'll know ahead of time how to deal with dead bodies in such a way that they don't become zombies.

It's very much like the civilization, when people would learn what nuts from what trees to gather and how to fish or catch small animals to eat. Primitive man observed and analyzed and learned to survive, going from hunting to thriving. Similarly, modern man can observe and analyze the walking dead to learn how to survive.

BINOCULARS

Just as we explained in the section about cameras, the best way to observe and analyze data in a calm way and to share the knowledge gained from it is through recorded images.

But the most important condition, aside from having a specialist on hand to analyze the data, is to do it from a safe location. Still, in zombie survival, there will be times when you have to observe and analyze from a potentially unsafe location.

At these times, the enlarging capabilities of binoculars come in very handy. With binoculars, you can observe zombies while hiding from them in a far-off distant location.

With the very rare exception that they may give off a

CHAPTER 4

OBSERVING ZOMBIES 1

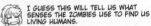

BUT EVEN SO, THEY MAY BE USING MORE THAN ONE SENSE, OR THERE MAY BE DIFFERENCES BETWEEN INDIVIDUAL ZOMBIES! WE WON'T REALLY KNOW UNTIL WE TEST THEM OVER AND OVER AGAIN!

I GUESS THIS WILL TELL US WHAT SENSES THE ZOMBIES USE TO FIND US LIVING HUMANS.

harmful gas, as long as you keep a respectable physical distance, the zombies won't be able to harm you. And when you are in a safe place, it's easy to keep your fear under control.

Of course, you mustn't get complacent! At the very instant that you are looking through the binoculars at zombies far away from you, there may be zombies creeping up on you from behind.

If it is at all possible, you will want to be a part of a team of observers, pairing up one person who is observing the far-off zombies through the binoculars with another guard who is watching the immediate surroundings for possible threats. It would also be beneficial if you had shielding or camouflage to keep you out of sight from the zombies you are observing. And be sure to keep in mind the fact that light may be reflected off of the binoculars' lenses.

WHAT ATTRACTS ZOMBIES

You may not be able to glean all the information you need for analysis based simply on observing zombies as they wander to and fro. The basis for scientific experiments is to observe the subject in a situation where only one factor is varied and all other conditions remain the same. It would be best if your observation of zombies used the same techniques.

▶ **LIGHT:** Do zombies head toward light sources? This is actually fairly easy to discern. Simply put a light in a good place to observe one night, and watch to see if zombies gather around it.

▶ **SOUND/VOICES:** Zombies may be attracted to sounds. This too is fairly easy to test. Record music, nature sounds, people's voices, and other sounds, and use them to see how the zombies react.

▶ **SMELLS:** Do zombies head in the direction of certain smells? This one will be pretty difficult to experiment with. After all, compared to sight and sound, there is a wider variation between individuals' sensitivity to smell. Also, humans have a tendency to get used to smells quickly, to the point where they don't register on a human's consciousness anymore.

Even so, if you can determine what smells zombies seem to like and at what distance they can smell it, it will become easier to keep from attracting zombies toward whatever meal you happen to be cooking.

▶ **THE HUMAN FORM:** Can zombies distinguish between a real human and a mannequin?

As this is another easy item to test, it's something that will probably help in your survival of the zombie apocalypse. Zombies may not have a sense for actual living humans and are instead simply attracted to a human form. Knowing this could be useful in helping to survive the zombies. Let's say that all you needed were ghillie suits with twigs and

OBSERVING ZOMBIES 2

 SO IF THEY'RE DETECTING WHAT HUMANS EXHALE, THEN THAT WOULD BE CO_2, RIGHT? IF SO, THEN WE MAY BE ABLE TO LURE THEM INTO A TRAP USING DRY ICE OR CO_2 FILLED CYLINDERS.

 SOME ZOMBIES MAY HAVE SENSES THAT GO BEYOND THE FIVE SENSES OF HUMANS. THEY MAY HAVE SENSES THAT HUMANS DON'T HAVE, LIKE DETECTING GASES THAT HUMANS EXHALE OR BODY WARMTH.

leaves attached to netting that masks the human contour while providing camouflage at the same time and that you were able to effectively hide from zombies while wearing them; your survival in the outdoors would be practically assured.

Of course, it could also be that these zombies who don't differentiate between humans and non-humans might simply attack just about everything. So trusting too much in this factor would be dangerous.

▶ **ANIMALS:** Do zombies attack animals the way they attack humans? We don't like it, but it's still easy to test. Put an animal in a cage or tie it to something, then observe how the zombies react to it. You should also experiment with non-mammals such as insects and fish as well.

▶ **DO THEY CLIMB OVER BARRIERS?:** Once you have determined what attracts the zombies, you should observe their behavior when you put a barrier between the zombies and what they are attracted to. What happens when there is a fence between the zombies and the object they attack? How about a steep land gradient? Do they try to come straight toward it, or do they look for a way through or around the obstacle?

If they try to head toward the object no matter what obstacles are in their way, then it will be easy to build traps for the zombies. In an extreme case, if there is a crevice in the vicinity, you can lure the zombies to it and destroy them after causing them to fall in.

▶ **INDIVIDUAL DIFFERENCES:** Are there differences between individual zombies? We've previously mentioned zombies who are self-aware, but there may even be differences in the perceptiveness and decision-making capacity of Explosive Pandemic-type zombies (which otherwise act almost exactly alike). There might also be special stimuli or particular locations that will attract one zombie more than others.

If you find a wide gap in individual differences between zombies, then it will be difficult for us to advise you on techniques for battling and trapping zombies. You're in for some dangerous times.

THE TEN-FOOT POLE

A long time ago in role-playing games (RPGs), especially the types where you explore a dungeon, there was an often-used tool called a ten-foot pole. It was a sturdy pole of about three meters in length, with which you tapped walls and the floor searching for traps. You could also attach a mirror to it in order to peer around otherwise blind corners.

And every now and again, you would encounter zombies in those dungeons. In the world of RPGs, zombies weren't exactly

THE TEN-FOOT POLE

IT ISN'T AS LONG OR AS EASY TO GET A HOLD OF AS A CLOTHES ROD, BUT A TREKKING POLE IS LIGHTWEIGHT AND IT COLLAPSES INTO A SMALL SIZE!

THE EXPANDING TYPE ISN'T TOO HARD TO HANDLE. NOT BAD!

ALMOST ANY HOME WILL HAVE ONE OF THESE FOR HANGING LAUNDRY!

AND WHEN YOU ARRIVE AT A PLACE WHERE ZOMBIES COULD BE, YOU CAN CHECK YOUR BLIND SPOTS WITH A MIRROR!

COULD YOU DO SOMETHING ABOUT GETTING AWAY FROM THIS BATTLE LUST OF YOURS...?

YOU CAN USE ANY POLE FOR THIS IF IT'S LONG AND THIN. IT'D BE NICE IF IT HAD ENOUGH STRENGTH THAT YOU COULD HIT A ZOMBIE WITH IT AND DO SOME DAMAGE.

much of a threat. But in real life, *you* aren't nearly as dangerous as the adventurers in the game either.

A zombie-survival scenario also has uses for a ten-foot pole. It is certainly better to stick a ten-foot pole into a room first than to blindly thrust in an arm or leg, and have it be bitten. The worst-case scenario would be to have your ten-foot pole taken from you—zombies don't have the knowledge to use that pole for themselves, so it would be a waste of a perfectly good pole.

There's also no real reason to stick slavishly to a pole of ten actual feet. If ten feet is too long to handle, a pole of one or two meters (1 or 2 yards) will do just as well. Such a pole can also be used to reach things in places too far away for your arms or to support you as a walking stick. When you are on the move and walking is your main method of transportation, having a walking stick of some sort will reduce your fatigue and allow

you to avoid accidents like falling. Since it won't be primarily used to beat up zombies, you are free to choose a lightweight pole as long as it is fairly strong.

PROOF OF HUMANITY

What do you think the most dangerous threat in the world of a zombie apocalypse is? Being surrounded by zombies? Well, that certainly is a menace. Or maybe hiding and slowly watching yourself run out of the necessities you need to live on, such as food or water? That too would be an enormous threat.

But the most dangerous threat would be the prospect of being suspected of being a zombie by other humans. You can try to avoid situations where you run out of food or are surrounded by zombies. You can size up the threat and calculate the risks of the necessary movements according to your own capacity and the situation you are in.

However, unless you are psychic enough to tell what is going on in the mind of the person who suspects you, there is no way to measure the urgency and threat level of someone else's zombie suspicions.

This is especially true of the early stages of the spread of the zombie contagion, when people are frightened, in shock, and suffering emotional insecurities. Someone may shout, "She's a zombie!" with a finger pointing at you. Unfortunately, we can't assure you that a lynch mob won't suddenly form with the intent of trying to execute you. So figuring out the best thing to do in every situation can be tricky.

Of course, when information about what constitutes a zombie is diffused throughout the remaining human society, this scenario is less likely. But the appearance of dead people walking around will cause enormous amounts of stress, and there is no way to prevent people from taking on actions that could lead to their own ruin.

So what can a person do? You can laugh and make others laugh.

We're not kidding here. Jokes and funny stories do have a way of calming frayed nerves. Humor manages to relax nerves that are taut from stress, and dial back a possibly explosive situation. This also depends on the zombies, but one of the areas where the border between zombies and humans can be defined is in the emotions that bring about laughter.

ALLOW THE FUN TO COME BACK INTO YOUR HEART

One of the most important parts of zombie survival is to simply create times when you are not thinking about zombies.

Thinking about zombies means facing high levels of stress head on. If zombies have destroyed the society you have been living in, then thinking about zombies involves imagining all you have lost and all the precious things you'll never be able to replace.

Your school, your job, and your hobbies... Your plans for the future, your life goals... Your family, friends, spouse, or lover... Many who you love and many who love you have been turned into zombies. And since life from here on will be so painful, many people have succumbed to heartsickness long before any real sickness takes their bodies. Others may still be there in the flesh, but their minds have now been zombified.

Such situations can make people as fragile as glass. People fight the zombies and go on the run, and eventually they have reached their destination and are trying to make a new life. Then they may find themselves wondering, "What's the good in living in a world like this?"

If a person is doomed to eventually become a zombie, what is the meaning in living through the pain they now feel? Survival is such a struggle, and if there is nothing left to be enjoyed in life, then what's the use in struggling? The strength of will people need to resist this line of thought varies from person to person, but it can be a dangerous situation.

This is exactly why you need to make time when you are not thinking about zombies. Don't think of this as avoiding the

subject. Think of it more as a necessary "recharge" of the heart that is vital to zombie survival.

The ways you can do this vary from person to person. One way is to work out your muscles and build up a sweat. Others might enjoy cooking up a delicious meal, while others still will look forward to eating that meal. Sing or dance, if you like. Reading a novel or manga is also an idea. But, odds are, a combination of things will work best.

It's true that the human heart is flexible, but this strength isn't always constant. There will always be times when it's weak, and other times when it is strong. So we recommend that you find a way to allow your heart to play a bit, so that the next time your situation gets you down, you'll come out of it all the stronger.

R&R FOR THE HEART

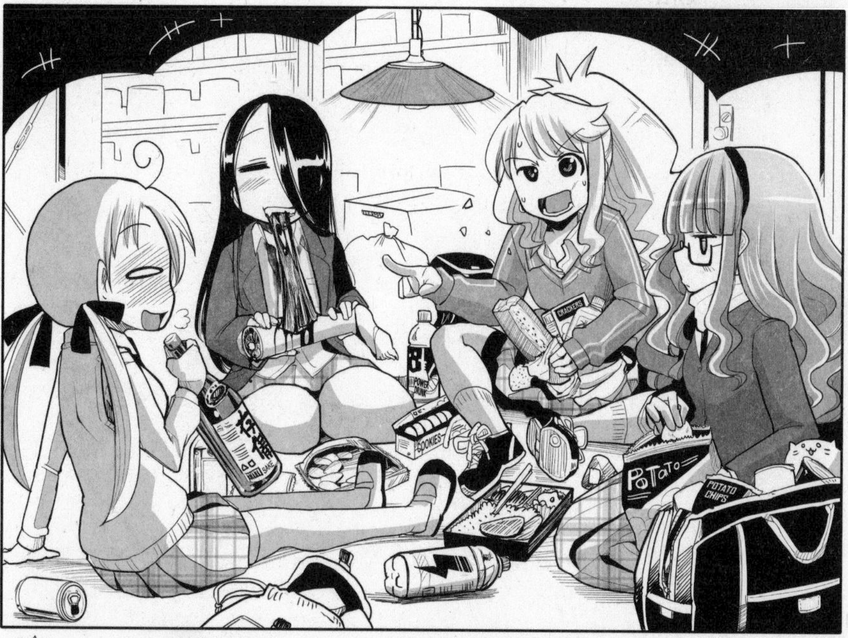
CRACKERS
POWER DRINK
COOKIES
SAKE
POTATO
POTATO CHIPS

ALTHOUGH, IT'S HARD TO FORGET ABOUT ZOMBIES WHEN ONE IS RIGHT HERE WITH US...

IT'S NECESSARY TO DECOMPRESS A LITTLE AFTER BEING UNDER THE CONSTANT THREAT OF ZOMBIE ATTACKS. BUT I DO THINK LINA IS HITTING THE RICE JUICE THERE A BIT HARD.

Anti-Zombie Tactics

TRAITS UNIQUE TO BATTLING ZOMBIES

There are several things that make battling zombies unique. The following is specific to the Explosive Pandemic-type zombies, but many of them will apply to other types as well.

- Zombies engage exclusively in hand-to-hand combat.
- Zombies' physical strength and biting strength is greater than humans'.
- Zombies are slow moving and clumsy.
- Zombies do not use weapons or tools.
- Zombies do not feel pain, nor do they fear being wounded or killed.
- Zombies never suffer low morale.
- Zombies do not possess the ability to learn.
- Zombies have no leader, nor do they fight as a team.
- If a zombie bites a human, that human will almost certainly turn into a zombie.

From this list of traits, we can come up with some specific tactics that are useful in battling zombies.

- Don't allow a zombie's hand or mouth to reach you.
- Try to keep from being wounded in a zombie battle.
- Attempt to deal the zombie a fatal wound (that will destroy the brain).
- The battle with zombies is a battle of extermination.
- Do whatever it takes to avoid losing morale on the human side.

In combat between humans, especially for military people, one of the aims is to destroy the enemy's morale or chain of command. One might attack the enemy commander or communications system—in other words, the point of the battle is not to kill the enemy soldiers, but to damage their ability to fight. For example, a minefield or booby traps might make a human enemy force hesitate before they charge. Also, if a soldier were wounded by anti-personnel mines, a number of other soldiers might be pulled from the front lines in order to rescue that wounded soldier and pull him from the battlefield.

But such tactics have absolutely no effect on an enemy made up of zombies. Zombies have no commander. If you happen to bring down one zombie, the other zombies don't care. Even if they lose their arms or legs, they will still try to creep toward you. And creeping zombies are even harder to snipe at from long distances than standing zombies. Zombies have no lines of communications, and there is no way to attack a zombie army's supply lines to prevent them from getting reinforced.

Another tactic that has been used for centuries is to throw up a smoke screen to reduce the enemy's field of view. But since zombies don't use firearms, you're only putting your fellow humans at a disadvantage. Put simply, you should discard any idea that you're battling human beings. Instead, use the same tactics you might use when trying to exterminate an extremely dangerous animal or insect.

Although they have the advantage of not having a commanding officer or any kind of morale to lose, they also suffer the great disadvantage of having no capacity to learn and they only attack piecemeal without any sort of battle plan.

Meanwhile, how do the humans fare?

The greatest advantage of humans is, more than anything else, the ability to observe, predict, and think. Humans can observe the zombies, predict their movements, and think up a plan to counter them. And when humans communicate with other humans and cooperate, they increase their effectiveness in battle.

But despite these advantages, emotions like fear can dull the thoughts of humans. This can cause them to choose their actions poorly, and this can lead to a loss of advantage. And errors in communications may reduce the possibility of simultaneous action based on cooperation, putting humans in danger of an easy defeat.

Advantages and disadvantages are two sides of the same coin. Before you go into battle, you must know your own strengths and weaknesses as well as the zombies'. Then you can choose your tactics accordingly.

SET TRAPS

When entering a battle with zombies, the most basic battle tactic of all is to set traps for the enemy. Furthermore, since zombies lack any intelligence, even the ability to learn that is found in nearly all wild beasts, they are especially susceptible to traps. Even if you happen to read the zombies' movement pattern incorrectly and your trap fails, it is nothing to be concerned about. Just observe their most recent patterns and improve your traps accordingly. Zombies don't learn, so even if the trap fails to kill it, the zombie won't be any more cautious of traps next time.

▶ **TRAPS USING HEIGHT DIFFERENCES:** It's easy to design and develop traps that make use of ditches, holes, walls and buildings. In fact, most of the ways to fight zombies in Japan will include traps that make use of height differences.

First, observe your surrounding area. Perhaps there is a steep embankment leading down to one of Japan's many fast-flowing rivers. If you can use the narrow area between the embankment and the river, you may be able to attack the zombies from the relative safety of a high place or lead them to where you want them to go.

If your area has one of those samurai-period castles with a moat, then you can use it as a base. It isn't really set

TRAPS THAT USE A HEIGHT DIFFERENCE

OTHER GOOD PLACES ARE CONSTRUCTION SITES OR HIGHWAYS THAT ARE STILL UNDER CONSTRUCTION, SO YOU CAN FIND PLACES FOR TRAPS ALL OVER URBAN AREAS TOO!

RAAH?! NUH! AARH!

BUT EVEN SO, SHE STILL FELL IN.

WHEN YOU'RE DIGGING A PITFALL TRAP FOR ZOMBIES, THERE IS NO REASON WHY YOU NEED TO CAMOUFLAGE IT THE WAY YOU HAVE TO DO WHEN FIGHTING HUMANS.

OWWW! OWCHIE! GET ME OUTTA HERE...!

up for a long siege anymore, but you can stand on the stone walls and safely act as bait while they fall one-by-one into the moat, then throw rocks down on them. This may be an effective tactic against zombies.

You should take a good look at the construction sites that popped up all over Japan before the zombies started to arrive. It's in those places where you'll find the necessary tools and materials to construct your trap. You can use abandoned, still-under-construction bridges, where you can lure zombies up and lead them to a very long fall. Such sites are perfect for traps.

It's also worth a try to see if there is still fuel in some of the heavy construction equipment, even if you don't have a license. In very little time, digging equipment can dig a hole or ditch that would take humans with shovels hours to dig.

But most height-based traps will be ones where zombies fall into them, or ones that will stop the zombies in their

tracks. The kind of traps you see in role-playing games, such as the suspended ceiling trap where heavy objects fall down onto the zombies, require a lot of very heavy rocks or weights in order to be effective. In actuality, it was the job of the guards of the castle to have a good supply of such objects gathered up and ready during peacetime.

Most castles were built during the Japanese Warring States Period (approximately 1467-1603), but afterwards, Japan entered a long period of peacetime where the majority of these fortresses turned into public parks, tourist locations, and spots for public outings and picnics. But with the appearance of zombies, some of these castles may return to the function for which they were originally intended.

▶ **TRAPS THAT IMPEDE FORWARD MOVEMENT**: One of the signifiers of zombies is, despite their increased strength, their athletic abilities are very low. And one of the ways that their lack of athleticism shows is in their shambling walk.

Humans have a highly developed bipedal walk, and because of that, they have a high center of gravity compared to animals that walk on four legs. This makes them comparatively unstable. If you can use that to make your traps, you can slow the zombies' forward movement even more.

Zombies themselves do not use tools or weapons so, by impeding their movement, humans can use their tools and weapons to either gain extra distance from them or to gain an added advantage in battle.

The first thing to do in constructing your movement-impeding trap is to first observe the lay of the land. What is the condition of the roads? What is the height and length of the guardrails? Are there hedges in the vicinity of the buildings? How high have the weeds grown? What locations are paved and which ones are not?

Are you in farmland or rice paddy land? Is the earth plowed into ridges? How are the rivers and creeks? Are they flowing fast and deep? Where are the bridges? Some

TRAPS TO IMPEDE MOVEMENT

SORRY ABOUT THAT. IT WAS OUR FAULT FOR OVERESTIMATING YOUR INTELLIGENCE...

NOBODY TOLD ME OUR TRAPS WOULD BE SO DEVILISH!

traps don't simply inconvenience the zombies but can also improve the movement of the humans. For example, there are a lot of railroads in Japan. Unlike regular roads, railroads tend to have fences running along them, and if they get on the railways the rails and railroad ties will obstruct zombie movements and cause them to fall. Also, since railroads run to places that regular automobile roads don't go, if you can secure a small railroad maintenance car, you will be able to move quickly along the range of the railroad without zombie interference.

After observing the shape of the land, it's time to test the effectiveness of traps you might make to counter the zombies. For example, can that trip-line you made by weaving grasses together actually trip a zombie? It's possible that a zombie could be caught in a trap that even a human child

might not fall for. If it is the winter season, perhaps you can run water on a road so that it freezes. That might be effective. There are also ways to use snow after a heavy snowfall.

So the first thing to do is to test all kinds of traps. You could try a huge project such as diverting water from a river to use it to impede the movements of zombies, much like the water attack that Hideyoshi used at the siege of Takamatsu Castle during Japan's Warring States Period (1582). Or maybe you could use small steel balls found at a hardware store or pachinko parlor, and throw them on the ground to stop the zombies' forward movement. It's certainly worth a try.

A trap isn't something with perfect aim. Instead of spending huge amounts of man-hours building the perfect trap, it'll be more effective to plant several simple traps using personnel and materials on hand.

PREPARE FOR TROUBLE

Humans have far superior mental abilities compared to zombies. So humans can observe the zombies, analyze their movement patterns, and estimate a prediction for how they will move in the future. They can then use those predictions to come up with effective methods of attack, choose battlefields that make full use of those methods, set traps, create battle plans, communicate those plans to others, and finally, commit to battle on those terms.

However, there will be times in the battle against zombies where human intelligence will not be as effective as you had hoped. The reason for this is simple. There will be times when the information gathered on the zombies will be woefully incomplete.

For example, our information on zombies will not be developed to such a high level as our information on hunting animals, catching fish, or exterminating bugs, even though those battles are similar to fighting zombies. Humans have, for

tens of thousands of years, observed these natural creatures, developed tools and techniques, and little by little, through trial and error, gathered the technology and knowledge to accomplish the task.

But we won't have enough information in the battle against zombies. We also won't know what kind of problems other humans have encountered in their battles with zombies. It could be that the zombie you are faced with puts out an incredible stink, has a ghastly or frightening visage, or emits an ear-piercing sound. A human may not be able to hold out against such attributes, which could cause their plans to fall apart.

You can expect that, in your early battles with the zombies, you will have troubles and failures based on a lack of information available to you. So before entering the fray, you should realize the possibility that the unexpected will happen.

So what are the best things you can do to prepare for trouble? First of all, you should prepare escape routes, a means of escape, and a rendezvous point for everyone involved. And as you maintain a place to hide in, you must plan your battles so that you are not fighting within your precious shelter. That would be where you are hiding the women and children, medicine, and other supplies that you can't otherwise easily obtain, so it can't really be abandoned at a moment's notice. You'll regret it if trouble winds up in the same location with those individuals you would protect with your own life.

Therefore, you should gain a lot of experience battling zombies, temper and train your comrades in battle tactics, and do it all outside your main base. Trouble at your school or in your job might be forgivable, but even a little bit of misfortune in a battle against zombies could result in your death and the deaths of others, so you must do your utmost to avoid it.

OFFENSIVE TACTICS

In a battle against zombies, you must take as offensive a posture as you possibly can. This will ensure the fewest casualties, even though it goes against the common sense of other types of warfare.

In human-on-human warfare, there are those on defense and those on offense; and the ones on defense usually have the advantage. After all, those on defense will know the terrain, dig trenches and other defensive fortifications, and fight using them, allowing them to fight from a much safer position than those on offense. And with the advent of the use of such weapons as guns and cannons, this trend only increased, until the introduction of the machine gun cemented the concept.

But in battles against zombies, the zombies don't use the lay of the land, nor do they use guns or other ranged weapons. As such, creating defenses against such weapons is not a factor.

Additionally, there are merits to offensive combat. The attacking side decides when the offensive begins and when to finish up the fighting. There is great value in the taking of the initiative when it comes to deciding when to start and end a fight. Zombies never get exhausted, but humans do. If the human side doesn't determine the start and end of the battle, humans will be fighting zombies day and night until the battle gradually becomes a losing proposition for the humans. Therefore, you have to construct a battle with the zombies in which you never lose the ability to end it on your own terms.

One factor in that construction is arranging the battle so that it can end either when the zombies are exterminated, or when the humans withdraw. And the only way to do that is for the leader to maintain a battle posture that always allows for retreat.

So, prior to the start of battle, you must have your lines of retreat planned, all routes of evacuation secured, and the means of withdrawal ready. This should be prioritized above any other preparations. It's only after this has been prepared that you should take on the zombies.

OFFENSIVE BATTLE TECHNIQUES

YOU CAN ALSO STACK SCHOOL DESKS UP TOGETHER.

FIRST, YOU PREPARE BARRICADES AS YOUR DEFENSIVE FORTIFICATIONS.

AND WHILE YOU'RE KEEPING THE ZOMBIES OUTSIDE THE SQUARE-BLOCK-STYLE SCHOOL GATE, YOU CAN ATTACK THEM THROUGH THE SPACES IN THE BARS.

YOU CAN USE YOUR BARRICADE TO CONTROL THE ZOMBIES' MOVEMENTS. THEN, WHEN THE DEFENSIVE LINE TO WHICH YOU LURED THE ZOMBIES LOOKS LIKE IT CAN BE OVERCOME, YOU FALL BACK.

WE CALL IT OFFENSIVE COMBAT, BUT THE CONCEPT IS CLOSER TO WHAT THE MILITARY CALLS "DEFENSE IN DEPTH."

IT'S VITAL THAT YOU KEEP LURING THEM INTO SITUATIONS WHERE YOU CAN ATTACK, BUT THEY CAN'T ATTACK BACK, AND JUST KEEP DOING THAT.

 YOU'LL WANT TO USE BOTH BARRICADES AND HEIGHT DIFFERENCES. SO, IF YOU CAN, STAND ON THE WALLS OR ON A ROOF TO ATTACK FROM ABOVE. OR YOU CAN DIG DEEP HOLES DEEPER THAN YOUR HEIGHT.

THE IRONCLAD RULE HERE IS FOR THE HUMANS TO ATTACK THE ZOMBIES THROUGH THE BARRICADE CREVICES, OR DOWN ON THEIR HEADS FROM ABOVE--ALL FROM PLACES WHERE THE ZOMBIES CANNOT ATTACK YOU BACK.

After that, you should decide on your battlefield. Zombies close in to do hand-to-hand combat, defeat their human adversaries, and turn those humans into zombies.

So with that danger in mind, the best battlefield is the one where you never allow the zombies to get close enough to fight you. Zombies are easily lured, which gives you an advantage. Prior to the battle, you should choose an area where there are no zombies, but does have some sturdy buildings handy. Dig trenches, construct battlements and other defenses, and use a decoy to lure the zombies in to do battle on your terms.

A famous example out of Japanese history of moving in field fortifications in advance of the battle and then luring the enemy to their ultimate defeat can be found in the Battle of Nagashino (1575) during the Warring States period. In that battle, the combined forces of Oda Nobunaga and Tokugawa

Ieyasu used Nagashino Castle as a decoy to lure the forces of Takeda Katsuyori into a battle on a field of their choosing. And while Nagashino Castle was under siege, they set to building anti-cavalry fortifications on their chosen battlefield. After they had lured the Takeda forces toward them, they used their matchlock rifles to win the day. If you think of the Takeda forces as the zombies, you can use the tactics used in the Battle of Nagashino.

First, you move yourselves from your permanent base, set up the battlefield ahead of time, and when you're done, lure the zombies toward you. This becomes an offensive tactic that will work against zombies. You can also use offensive tactics when fighting in your base. First, lure in a predetermined, fixed number of zombies, then you can use traps and preset defensive fortifications to fight them.

If you use this offensive tactic periodically, it becomes more likely that you can prevent yourselves from being overwhelmed by an enormous pack of zombies attacking your permanent base.

DEFENSIVE TACTICS

There is another way that the outcome of battle can be decided. In a war, both sides will make tactical errors, so it is the side that makes the fewest errors, or the side that copes better with those errors, that will most likely come out victorious in the end.

This is an important rule in the fight against zombies. A number of mistakes or coincidences pile up, and your offensive battle can quickly turn into a defensive battle. It *will* happen! So when it does, do not panic. Just make sure you have defensive tactics lined up to use. For example, zombies may invade your main base, and due to an accident, escape becomes impossible.

The initiative, which is possible using offensive tactics, is something you cannot obtain using defensive tactics. It will all

SECURING THE EMERGENCY ESCAPE ROUTE

YOU CAN SUSPEND A LADDER BETWEEN YOUR BUILDING AND THE NEXT, THEN LET IT FALL AFTER YOU HAVE ESCAPED. THIS IS AN IDEAL ESCAPE ROUTE--IT ALLOWS YOU TO ESCAPE, BUT THE ZOMBIES CAN'T FOLLOW.

be on the zombies' side since they don't give up and they don't sleep. So if you can't exterminate them all, then those humans on defense are in for a rough time. For that reason, when fighting a defensive battle, it is imperative that you somehow steal back the initiative.

There are two ways of doing this. The first is securing an escape route. Even if the zombies take your main base, it isn't like they can use the items you have stored there or use the installation against you. They won't even destroy it on purpose. So, even if you escape, it's possible for you to take it back later. Therefore, at the very least, the goal is to make sure all the humans escape. To allow time for the aged, children, pregnant women, etc. to evacuate, you will want barricades to stop or slow the zombies' advance, and have a passageway prepared. Assuming there is no obvious passageway, you will

want several possible routes, and people with combat abilities to protect them, to get your non-combatants safely away. You will need to practice each of these routes as many times as necessary.

The other is to find a place that is physically cut off from the zombies' attack. In brief, you choose a means to secure a place to take a break, eat, and go to the bathroom. Even if it only means a short while, and even if that place is surrounded by enemies, as long as you can end the fight on your own terms and go someplace safe, it will make your next fight all the more determined. This will take the form of an shelter within your base that you escape to during an emergency evacuation. It should have a several days' worth of water, food, and other necessities. It's best to have several of these prepared ahead of time as you head out to do your reconnaissance or when you go on the attack. So find your possible shelters, and pack each with a few days' worth of bottled water and emergency rations.

You can do both of these things at the same time. If you are on the waterfront of a lake or ocean, and you make a ship your emergency shelter (and have secured an escape route using it), then you can protect yourself with physical distance from the zombies while escaping at the same time.

These are the general rules for defensive tactics. After, you can regroup and go back on the offensive. Remember that, unlike zombies, humans can't fight forever. No matter how spectacularly you are equipped, humans are still the ones using that equipment. Humans need a break.

Now, defensive tactics need a lot more preplanning than offensive tactics do, and of course, you will be doing all this lacking time, necessary materials, and personnel. You won't be able to do everything we advise.

For example, if your base is in a building that is quite close to the building next door, then you can quickly set up a ladder between windows of the two buildings as an escape route.

THE EMERGENCY EVACUATION SHELTER

YOU'LL PROBABLY ALSO WANT A BUILDING THAT'S BEEN MODIFIED INTO A SHELTER AS A BACK-UP EVACUATION DESTINATION.

WHAT WE HAVE HERE IS A DELIVERY TRUCK CONVERTED INTO A MOBILE-TYPE SHELTER.

FOOD, WATER, SIMPLE BEDDING, AND AT LEAST A PLASTIC BUCKET FOR HUMAN WASTE.

YOU WILL NEED TO PREPARE A SPACE THAT ZOMBIES CAN'T GET INTO THAT CONTAINS (AMONG OTHER THINGS)...

BUT FOR THAT, YOU NEED A SHELTER IN WHICH THOSE THINGS CAN TAKE PLACE.

AS LONG AS YOU HAVE THESE THINGS, YOU CAN CONTINUE A DEFENSIVE BATTLE.

UNLIKE ZOMBIES, HUMANS CANNOT DO WITHOUT REST, SLEEP, FOOD, AND BATHROOM BREAKS.

IF YOU ARE NEAR THE WATERFRONT, YOU CAN USE A SHIP OR BOAT.

IN REALITY, IT'LL BE DIFFICULT TO TRANSFORM A TRUCK INTO A SHELTER AS SHOWN IN THE ILLUSTRATION. WHAT'S MORE IMPORTANT IS PREPARING SOMEPLACE WITH FOOD, AS WELL AS A SAFE PLACE TO SLEEP, FOR THE TIMES WHEN YOU BREAK OFF THE BATTLE WITH THE ZOMBIES.

Zombies are too clumsy to use a ladder, and even if a ladder were lying on the ground near them, the zombies wouldn't even think to use it. If, like this example, you can think of things that humans can do but zombies can't, you can start to see ways to break any potential deadlock in your fights.

Think about it. Zombies can't use intelligence, but you can. And the single most important factor in defensive tactics is the cleverness needed to think them up.

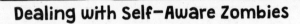

Dealing with Self-Aware Zombies

ZOMBIES MIXED IN WITH HUMANS

Zombies are a nightmare to humans anyway, but if they are self-aware and have intelligence, then you've reached a completely new level of trouble.

We can say they have intelligence and self-awareness, but there can be all kinds of different varieties of mental capacities mixed in here. If they have a certain amount of cunning, then it's possible that zombies may have become mixed in among the human population.

If that happens, as long as there isn't a sure-fire way to distinguish between zombie and human, your life as a human being is in a precarious state.

But hope was always at the bottom of Pandora's box.

For example, self-aware zombies have the sentient-zombie dilemma and probably have worries of their own. Self-aware zombies could, if they wanted to, turn the world into a living hell, but a very different question is this: do the self-aware zombies want that kind of world or not? If those zombies retain some of the underlying values of their humanity, then it may be possible for humans and zombies to coexist. Even from the self-aware zombie's point of view, a world that doesn't treat it as a zombie might be the ideal world.

So with self-aware zombies, it may be possible to negotiate on the basis of common ground. Of course, it's also possible that even with self-aware zombies, you will wind up in a hostile face-off. Humans still wage wars against other humans, despite having the power to reason and sharing many of the same values.

Even so, if you have the ability to talk to the zombies, you should try negotiation. Even if negotiations break down, you will find some new information on these self-aware zombies that you may be able to use later. With this new data, you can learn their mental capacities and their ways of thinking, and

from their movement patterns and their character, you may be able to deduce some weaknesses.

And if you find you have no alternative but to fight them, it's best to know who you are dealing with as well as you can. If the self-aware zombies become your enemies in a fight, your knowledge of them will be your greatest weapon.

Even though humans share a common background and DNA, each one is still an individual with great differences in thought processes and actions. It's possible that self-aware zombies will have similar differences per individual as well.

Just as fellow humans can battle and murder each other, self-aware zombies may also make enemies of other zombies. This division between zombies may provide an opening for gaining zombie allies. You can trust an alliance based on mutual interest far more than an alliance with no such common interest.

COEXISTING WITH SELF—AWARE—TYPE ZOMBIES

In the stories, Self-Aware-type zombies sometimes act as zombies wishing to damage and destroy humanity. At those times, their instincts overcome their reason. For these varieties of Self-Aware-type zombies, how well they control their impulses is a key to knowing whether coexistence is possible or not.

Even if some self-aware zombies have impulses that are hard to abide, it may be possible to get them to control their impulses, or act differently from their instincts for a short time if somehow compensated.

Either way, the first thing is to determine whether or not they have impulses as zombies, and what kind of impulses they are. From this, you can decide if they can be of help to you or not.

Another factor to consider is that from the minute you realize that there are self-aware zombies in the world, it means that eradicating zombies completely and returning to a humans-only world has basically become impossible.

IS IT POSSIBLE TO JOIN IN COMMON CAUSE WITH SELF-AWARE ZOMBIES?

 (A TSUNDERE-TYPE, HUH...?)

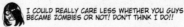 I COULD REALLY CARE LESS WHETHER YOU GUYS BECAME ZOMBIES OR NOT! DON'T THINK I DO!!

The only possible continuation of human history will now be in coexistence with the Self-Aware-type zombies. And if that's the case, then you must analyze what form of damage to humans can be caused by these Self-Aware-type zombies.

If these Self-Aware-type zombies have an impulse to attack humans, then you'll need to know why. Is it because the dead zombies need to absorb a certain amount of life force to keep themselves moving? Can that life force only be obtained by attacking humans? Or is it to substitute for the fact that dead people cannot procreate? And if it's the latter, maybe there is another type of activity that can compensate for it.

For example, imagine that, once a month, certain conditions cause the zombies to lose their reason and start rampaging for a short while. If so, is there something that can be done to make sure those conditions are never met?

Calmly and rationally, think it out.

You could be simply disgusted at the very existence of zombies, and you are presently experiencing the luxury of being in denial. It's all right. Consider it after your society is in a safer place. But your survival is at stake here, so you mustn't allow yourself to be carried away by your emotions.

If you are in danger from self-aware zombies, and you cannot get rid of the problem by exterminating them, then you must consider self-aware zombies the highest existential threat and act accordingly. That's what zombie survival is all about.

Leave Written Records

NOTEBOOKS AND PENS OR PENCILS

If you find yourself in a world infested with zombies and you're trying to survive, there are some things we would like you to do.

The first is to put a small notebook and pencil or pen in your pocket. Take notes—they can be on anything you like. Your experiences, things you've noticed, what you happen to be thinking. You don't need to sum anything up. Just put together a loose record of whatever you want to leave behind.

Why? Well, zombie survival will be something unprecedented in human history, and even things you find not worth talking about at the time may later be considered precious knowledge. Things you would judge to be trivial might contain information that could spell the difference between humanity's survival and their extermination in the war against zombies.

There's something else you might not want to think about, but it's something you should be prepared for. You might find that living in a world with zombies is not something that you can actually survive, and there's the possibility that you might die. On top of this, you might die in a bizarre way, and there is a good chance that ending up as a zombie is your ultimate fate.

Everyone dies at some point, but it would be a shame if all memory of you ended there as well.

That's the whole reason we want you to leave behind records—to provide proof of your life as a human, as a sign that there were people doing their best in a hellish world where zombies spread like wildfire. And even if you do die, as long as you leave a record behind, that can be a tiny, final ray of hope. And hope can become strength.

Finally, what you write in your notebook isn't just a way to remember you after you've died. By simply writing your thoughts into your notebook, you may also bring yourself strength in the here and now.

LET'S LEAVE A WRITTEN RECORD BEHIND

 WE ASK THAT, WITH YOUR NOTES, YOU DON'T LEAVE BEHIND RECORDS THAT WILL MAKE OTHER SURVIVORS CONFUSED OR WITH MISTAKEN IMPRESSIONS, OKAY?

 WHAT'S WRONG WITH IT?! IT TOOK EVERYTHING I HAD TO WRITE IT!!

FOR THE TIME BEING, THESE ARE THE THINGS WE HAVE TO CHECK ON BEFORE MAKING OUR MOVES, RIGHT?

 WE DON'T HAVE TO BRING ALL THAT MUCH FOOD AND WATER WITH US, DO WE?

 WE'LL BE TRAVELLING SHORT DISTANCES IN URBAN AREAS, SO ONE DAY'S WORTH SHOULD BE PLENTY.

 THE PROBLEM IS WHERE CAN WE STOP FOR BREAKS? I'D LIKE TO GET THERE BEFORE NIGHTTIME, SO WE DON'T HAVE TO SLEEP IN A PUBLIC RESTROOM...

 I HOPE YOU HAVEN'T FORGOTTEN THAT WE NEED TO GATHER INFORMATION BEFORE GOING ON THE MOVE.

 WELL, WE CAN STILL USE THE INTERNET, THE RADIO, AND OUR CELL PHONES, SEE?

 THEN WE STILL CAN PLAY ONLINE GAMES!

 HEY, ZOMBIE-BAIT! CONTROL YOURSELF! WE NEED INFO ON THE LOCATION WE'RE GOING TO AND A WAY TO DETERMINE THE ROUTE! ALSO INFO ON WHERE THE ZOMBIES ARE COMING FROM AND THEIR BEHAVIOR. LET'S FIND SOME USEFUL INFO HERE!

 BUT THERE'S SO MUCH INFORMATION ON THE WEB! HOW MUCH OF IT IS TRUE?

 THERE STILL SEEMS TO BE A LOT OF CONFUSION OUT THERE. IF WE WAIT A LITTLE BIT MORE, WE MIGHT GET SOME REAL, HELPFUL INFO.

 THAT ONLY WORKS AS LONG AS WE GET IT BEFORE THE INTERNET GOES DOWN...

 THEN LET'S JUST FIGURE OUT THE NEXT LEG OF THE JOURNEY. WE NEED A MAIN ROUTE, A BACKUP ROUTE IN CASE THE MAIN ONE BECOMES IMPASSABLE, AND A TIME AND PLACE TO MEET UP IF WE GET SEPARATED.

 I GET THE FEELING THAT IF WE CHOOSE A PATH NOT A WHOLE LOT OF PEOPLE TRAVEL, THEN THERE WILL BE LESS ZOMBIES, HUH?

 WELL, FOR THIS LEG, WE'RE STILL IN OUR HOMETOWN NEAR OUR SCHOOL, SO WE'LL HAVE THE MAPS IN OUR HEADS TO RELY ON.

 BUT IF WE GET TO A PLACE WE DON'T KNOW, THEN DECIDING A ROUTE WILL BE MORE DIFFICULT.

 AND LET'S REMEMBER THAT IF WE CHOOSE A VERY NARROW BACK STREET, WE'LL HAVE LESS ROOM TO RUN IF WE'RE SURROUNDED BY ZOMBIES.

 YOU MEAN WE HAVE TO FIGHT THE ZOMBIES AND OBSERVE EVERYTHING?!

 WE HAVE TO SET TRAPS, TOO. I ALREADY KNEW WE'D HAVE TO FIGHT THE ZOMBIES EVENTUALLY. IT'S ALMOST TIME FOR THE BAPTISM OF BLOOD!!

 EVENTUALLY, I'D LIKE TO SHOW YOU WHAT WE CAN DO WHEN WE GET SERIOUS!

 DO WE HAVE TO GO THROUGH THIS AGAIN?!

 THE FIRST THING FOR US TO DO IS TO MOVE TO SOME SAFE PLACE. WE ARE IN NO POSITION RIGHT NOW TO FIGHT ZOMBIES OR EVEN OBSERVE! LET'S GET THE PREP-WORK OUT OF THE WAY!

 THAT MEANS WE'RE HEADING TO THE SHOPPING MALL, RIGHT?!

 I'M ALL FOR THAT! QUIT YER STALLIN', MERO!

 WE HAVE TO HURRY! BECAUSE IF WE DON'T MAKE IT...

 WILL YOU GUYS SHAPE UP...?

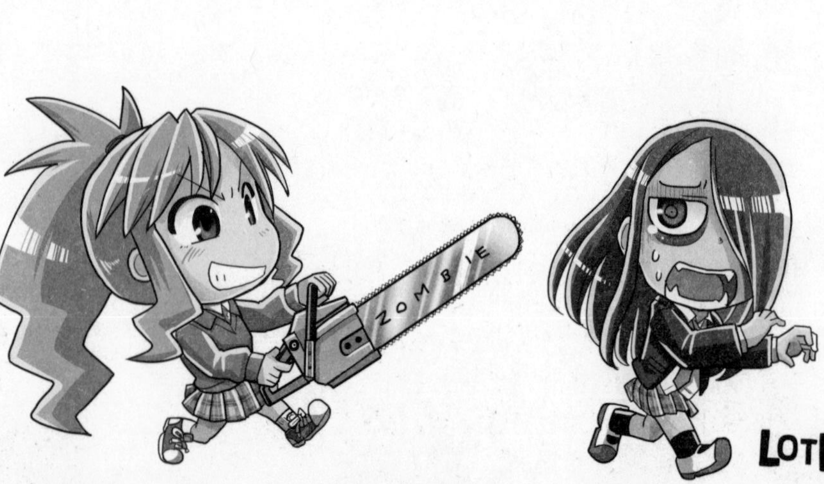
ZOMBIE

LOTRD

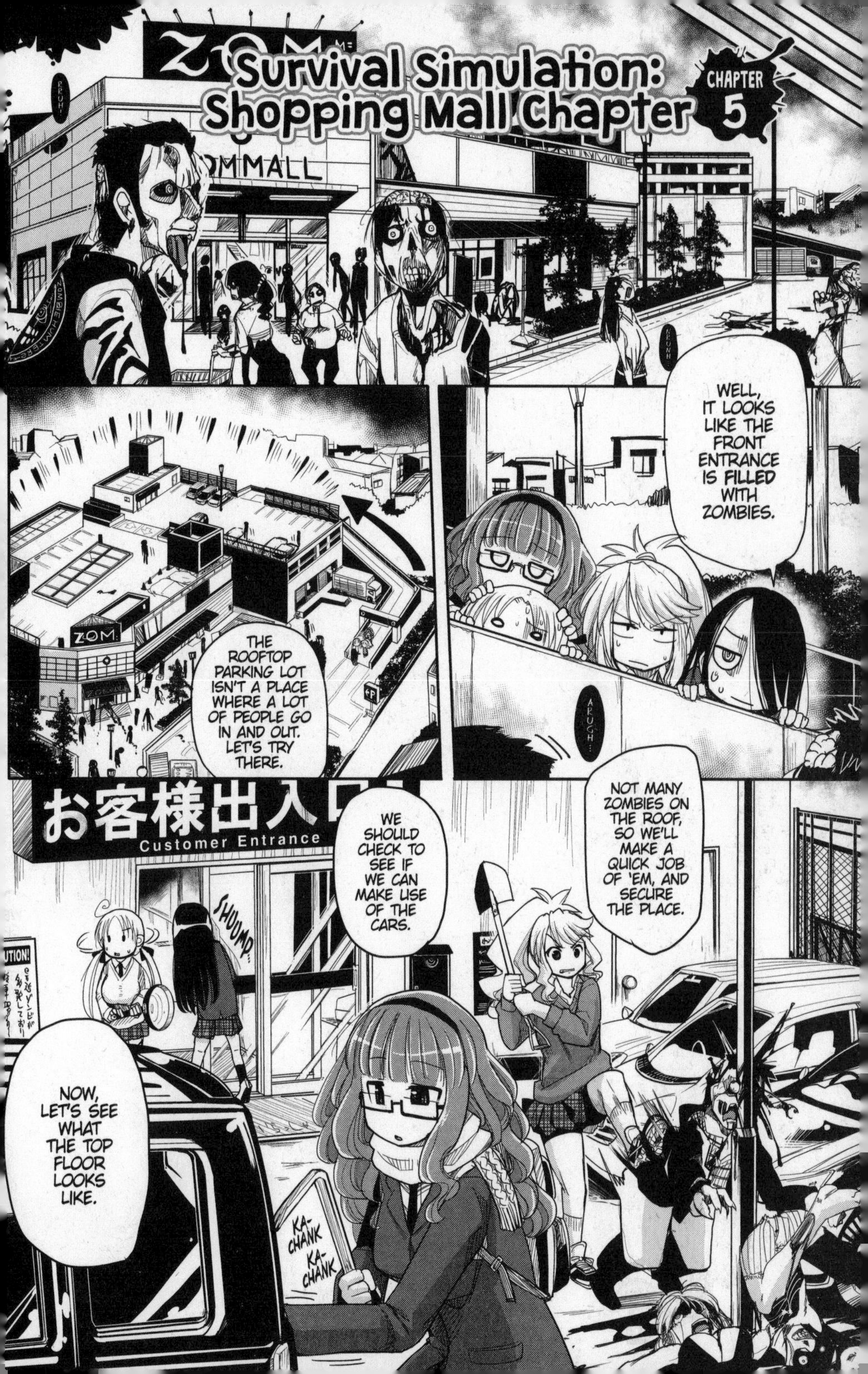
Survival Simulation: Shopping Mall Chapter
CHAPTER 5
RRUH!
NRUNH...
WELL, IT LOOKS LIKE THE FRONT ENTRANCE IS FILLED WITH ZOMBIES.
ARUGH...
THE ROOFTOP PARKING LOT ISN'T A PLACE WHERE A LOT OF PEOPLE GO IN AND OUT. LET'S TRY THERE.
お客様出入口
Customer Entrance
NOT MANY ZOMBIES ON THE ROOF, SO WE'LL MAKE A QUICK JOB OF 'EM, AND SECURE THE PLACE.
WE SHOULD CHECK TO SEE IF WE CAN MAKE USE OF THE CARS.
SHUUMP
NOW, LET'S SEE WHAT THE TOP FLOOR LOOKS LIKE.
KA-CHANK KA-CHANK

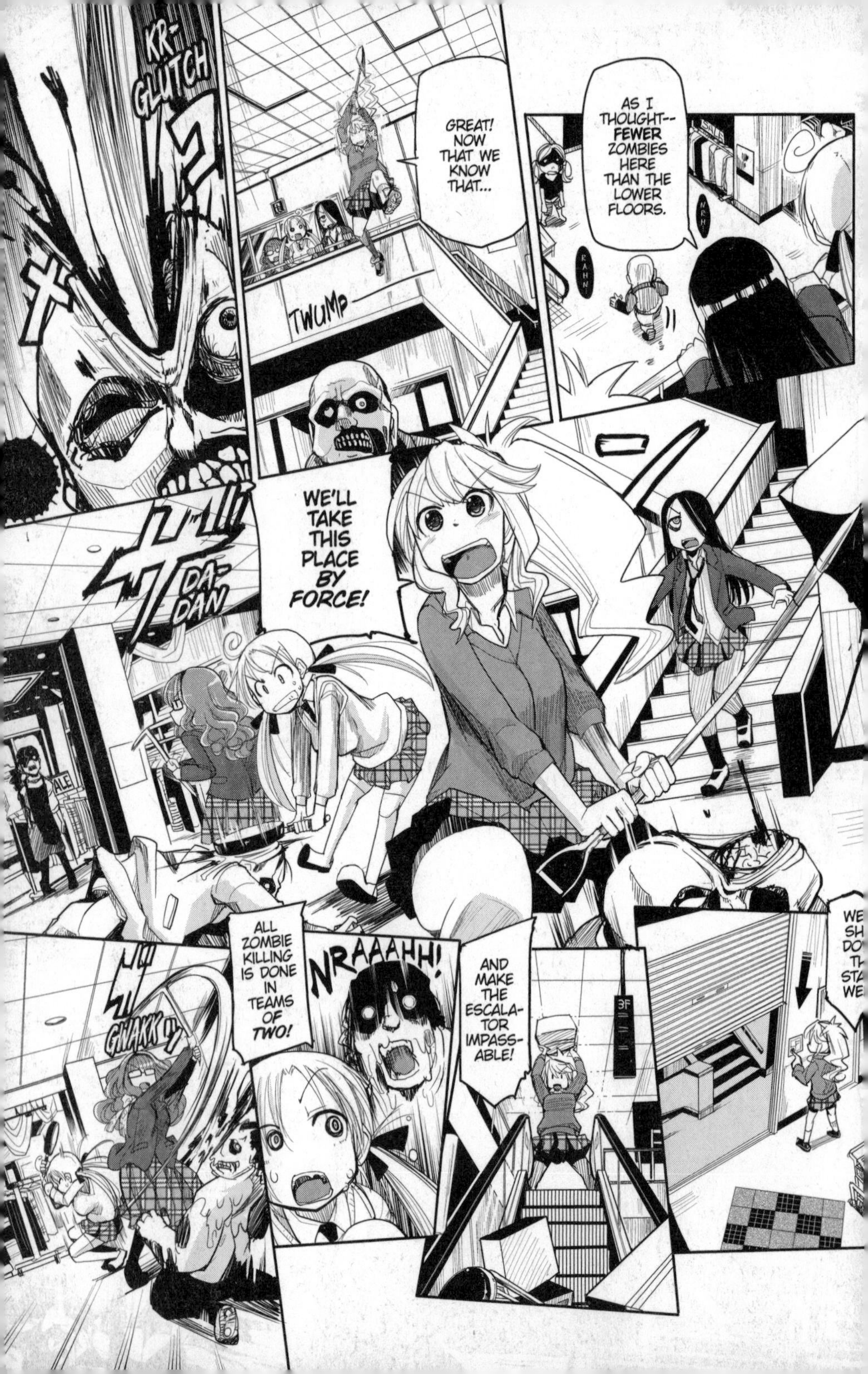
AS I THOUGHT-- FEWER ZOMBIES HERE THAN THE LOWER FLOORS.
RAHN
GREAT! NOW THAT WE KNOW THAT...
TWUMP
KR-GLUTCH
WE'LL TAKE THIS PLACE BY FORCE!
DA-DAN
AND MAKE THE ESCALATOR IMPASSABLE!
NRAAAHH!
ALL ZOMBIE KILLING IS DONE IN TEAMS OF TWO!
GWAKK

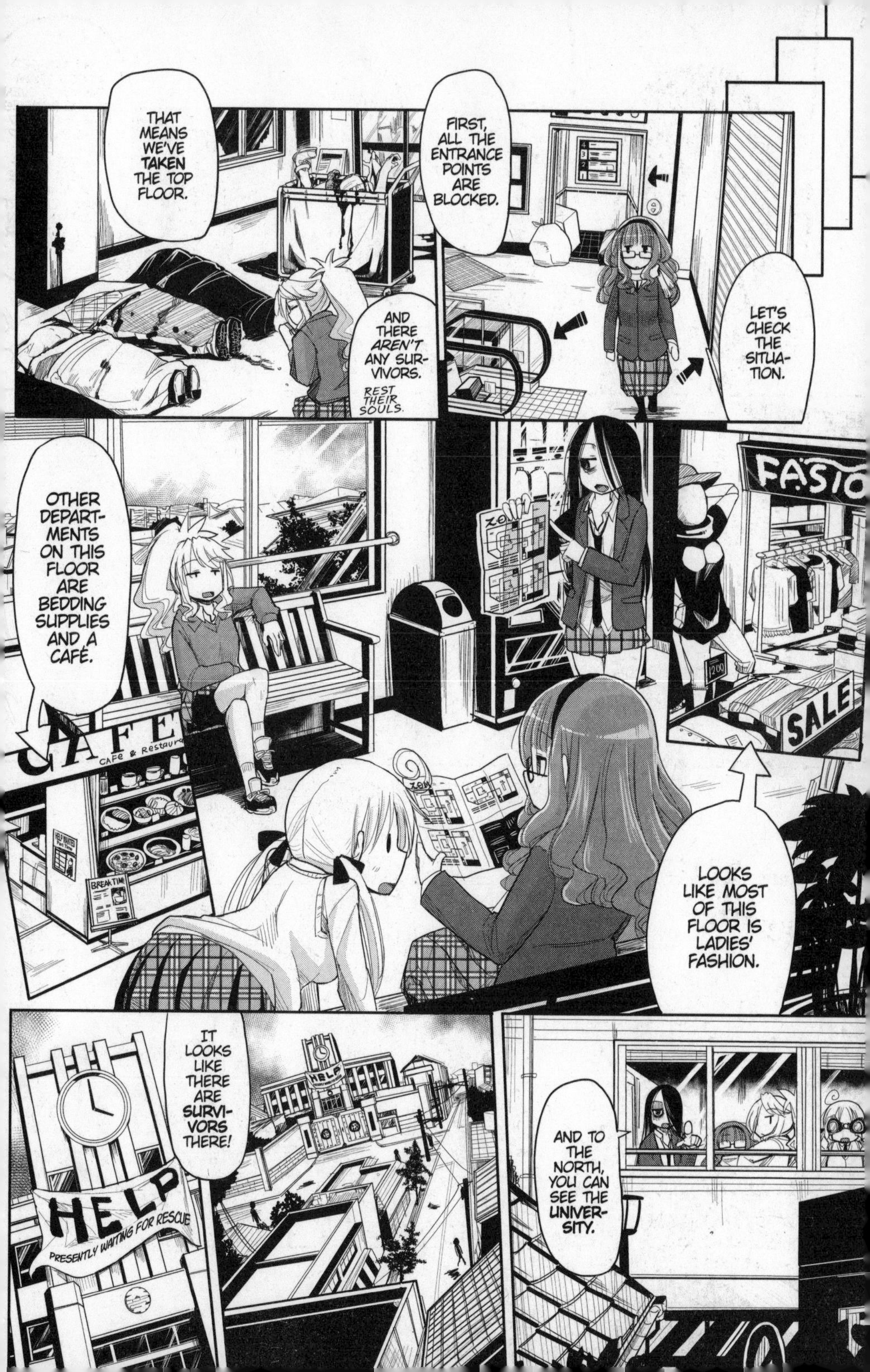
LET'S CHECK THE SITUATION.
FIRST, ALL THE ENTRANCE POINTS ARE BLOCKED.
THAT MEANS WE'VE TAKEN THE TOP FLOOR.
AND THERE AREN'T ANY SURVIVORS.
REST THEIR SOULS.
FASIO
SALE
LOOKS LIKE MOST OF THIS FLOOR IS LADIES' FASHION.
OTHER DEPARTMENTS ON THIS FLOOR ARE BEDDING SUPPLIES AND A CAFÉ.
CAFE
BREAK TIME
AND TO THE NORTH, YOU CAN SEE THE UNIVERSITY.
IT LOOKS LIKE THERE ARE SURVIVORS THERE!
HELP
HELP
PRESENTLY WAITING FOR RESCUE

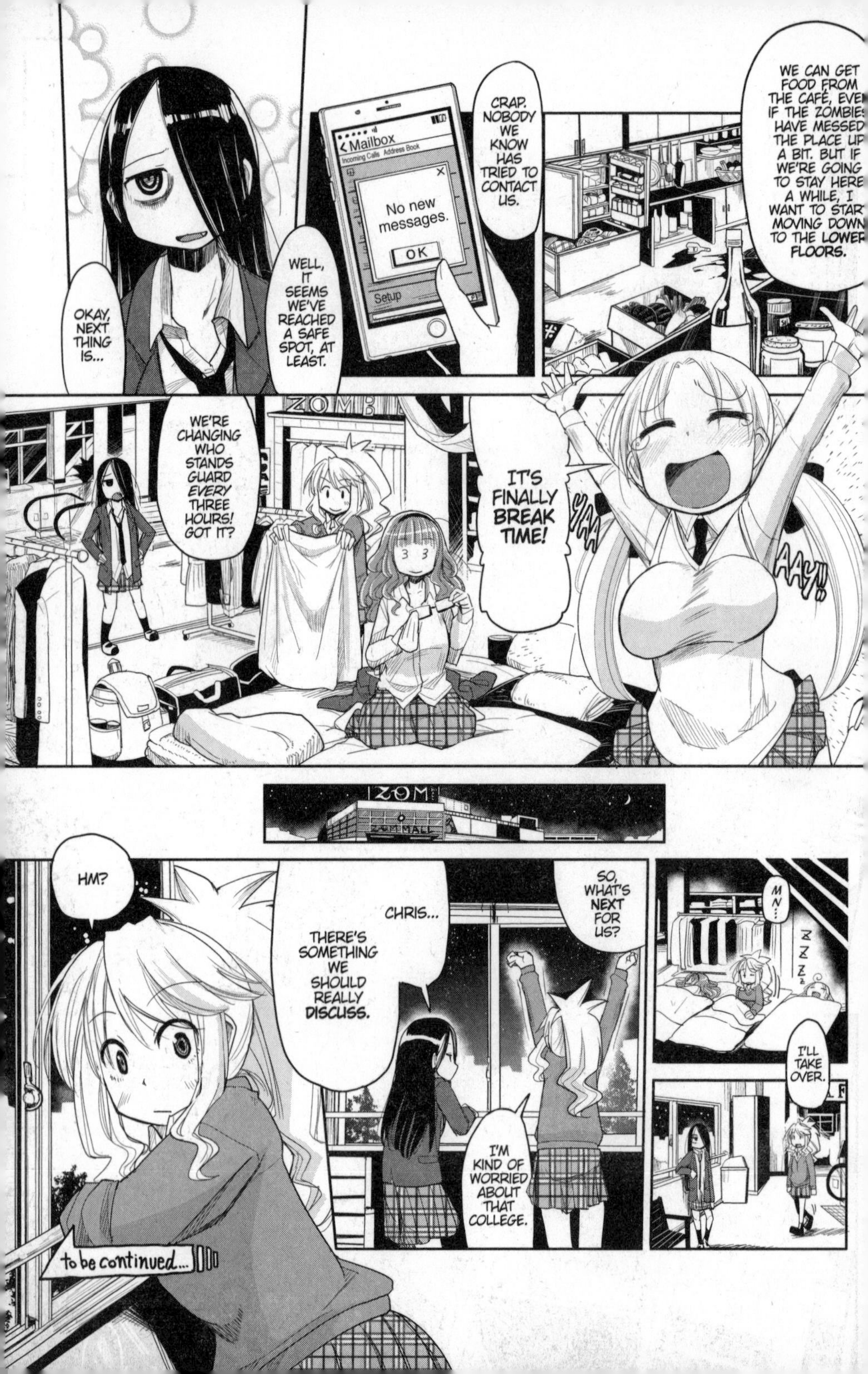
WE CAN GET FOOD FROM THE CAFÉ, EVEN IF THE ZOMBIES HAVE MESSED THE PLACE UP A BIT. BUT IF WE'RE GOING TO STAY HERE A WHILE, I WANT TO START MOVING DOWN TO THE LOWER FLOORS.
CRAP. NOBODY WE KNOW HAS TRIED TO CONTACT US.
Mailbox
Incoming Calls Address Book
No new messages.
OK
Setup
WELL, IT SEEMS WE'VE REACHED A SAFE SPOT, AT LEAST.
OKAY, NEXT THING IS...
YAAAAAY!!
IT'S FINALLY BREAK TIME!
WE'RE CHANGING WHO STANDS GUARD EVERY THREE HOURS! GOT IT?
ZOMB
ZOM
ZOM MALL
MN...
I'LL TAKE OVER.
SO, WHAT'S NEXT FOR US?
CHRIS...
THERE'S SOMETHING WE SHOULD REALLY DISCUSS.
I'M KIND OF WORRIED ABOUT THAT COLLEGE.
HM?
to be continued...

YES! WE'RE FINALLY HERE AT THE SHOPPING MALL!!

 MERO'S REALLY INTO THIS!

 IT'S BEEN A STANDARD ZOMBIE APOCALYPSE LOCATION EVER SINCE ROMERO'S ZOMBIES, HUH?

 BUT CONSIDERING WHAT HAPPENED IN THE MOVIE (AND THE REMAKE), CAN WE REALLY SURVIVE HERE?

 THINGS WERE TOUCH-AND-GO FOR A BIT THERE, BUT WE MANAGED TO TAKE THE TOP FLOOR AND SEAL UP ALL THE ENTRANCES. SO, IT'S A SUCCESS!

 YEAH! NICE TO HAVE A PLACE TO REST!

 BUT IN THE MOVIE, IT'S NOT LONG AFTER THIS THAT THE BIKER GANG COMES WHOOPING IN TO MESS THE WHOLE PLACE UP.

 SUCH FILTH NEEDS STERILIZATION!

 WE CAN'T DO THAT!! AND WHY DO YOU LOOK HAPPY AT THE PROSPECT?

 SO YOU'RE SAYING THAT PEOPLE LIKE THAT WILL COME TO OUR MALL, TOO? WHAT'LL WE DO?!

 HM... IT'S AN EXTREME SITUATION. NO WAY OF KNOWING WHAT'LL HAPPEN. BUT IF IT DOES HAPPEN, I SUPPOSE WE EITHER RUN OR HIDE, AND JUST WAIT FOR THEM TO DO WHAT THEY WANT AND GO.

 HUH? YOU MEAN THEY CAN MESS UP THIS BASE WE JUST TOOK?!

 IT'S EVEN MORE DANGEROUS TO FIGHT HUMANS THAN ZOMBIES. IT'S BETTER THAN DYING, BUT...

 UNLIKE ZOMBIES, WE HAVE NO IDEA WHAT HUMANS ARE THINKING, SO IT'S HARD TO PREDICT HOW THEY'D ACT.

 AND BESIDES, THIS IS REALLY JUST A SPECIALTY BOOK ABOUT HOW TO DEAL WITH ZOMBIES. IF WE ADD IN HOW TO BATTLE HUMAN BEINGS TOO, THEN THIS BOOK WILL NEVER END, RIGHT?

 I CAN'T BELIEVE YOU JUST TOTALLY BROKE THE FOURTH WALL ON US!

 STILL...YOU KNOW, I REALLY THINK IT'S BEST WE DON'T MESS WITH ANYBODY WITH A MOHAWK.

 THEY DON'T ALL HAVE THEIR HAIR STYLED IN MOHAWKS, YOU KNOW... THIS ISN'T MAD MAX.

 I'M ALL FOR SHARING MY FOOD WITH NEEDY PEOPLE AND ALL THAT, BUT I DON'T LIKE HAVING MY STUFF STOLEN BY FORCE!

 IT'D GET ME A LITTLE RILED UP, TOO. BUT THE FACT IS, WE CAN ALWAYS REPLACE OUR STUFF AND FIND A NEW BASE.

 OR IF YOU THINK ABOUT IT FROM THE OPPOSITE ANGLE, THIS IS ALL STUFF WE CAN AFFORD TO GIVE AWAY.

 SO IN THE END, TRYING TO DEAL WITH OTHER HUMANS IS A LOT SCARIER THAN DEALING WITH ZOMBIES. YOU KNOW, I'D REALLY PREFER IF IT DIDN'T COME TO AN OBVIOUS CONCLUSION LIKE THAT!

Shopping
MALL
Survival

5 Survival Simulation

By Bakegane

Before We Start the Simulation

FIRST THINGS FIRST

This chapter will be a simulation in which the Japanese society that you presently live in falls victim to zombies. The zombies here will all be Explosive Pandemic-type zombies. Humans who are attacked by zombies will become zombies themselves and attack others, thereby increasing their numbers.

The next important factor is how much experience the human society has with zombies and how they have prepared. Our society has made some preparations for natural disasters such as earthquakes, typhoons and the spread of infectious diseases. Some of the older readers might remember how to react in the case of a nuclear attack, and the nation is in some way prepared for some of the more unlikely scenarios such as a chemical spill, terrorism using chemical weapons, accidents at nuclear generators, an influx of armed refugees, and the threat of international war.

These are all threats that are already well known, and with the experience gained, we can make a guess of the danger and how to deal with it. Fires and traffic accidents are threats that we have prepared for nationwide with our firefighters, paramedics, and ambulance personnel, and they have daily training and experience with those situations.

But what about zombies?

If our society had dealt with zombies a number of times in the past, then they would have seen zombie-ism spread like an infectious disease. Wouldn't they have recorded it? How would the history of that society have changed? Let's try a hypothetical example. Say that, in the mid-'70s, there was an outbreak of zombies that killed tens of thousands of people.

Your experience of Japanese society in the 21st century would be quite different from the one you enjoy now. It's possible that, as a precaution to prevent another outbreak of zombies, people from the local municipality would probably make daily visits to anyone living alone. Neighborhood associations would probably be pretty vigilant in mutual surveillance of everyone in the area.

There would most likely be security cameras set up all over town and especially in the hospitals. There would also probably be a 24-hour service that checks out anyone who walks like a zombie, or anything that seems at all ominous, to be sure it isn't zombie-related.

Your local government would put out zombie manuals, and they would likely build zombie shelters as well (whether they actually help or not). They may have developed some equipment that will be designed for fighting zombies, or found anti-zombie uses for equipment that isn't quite as useful during other forms of combat.

People will probably invest in anti-zombie items that may cost more and be more trouble to use than they are actually worth. That will truly be a measure of how afraid a society has become after encountering zombies. This is a possibility that would actually distort history.

This aspect changes the simulation considerably. When there are government manuals telling you how to fight zombies, and the entire society is, in certain ways, prepared for the event of a zombie attack, then you have to start by guessing how much and what kind of preparations are in place before beginning your simulation. It requires so many assumptions

that the society represented in the simulation will hardly resemble the society you, dear readers, live in at all.

Therefore, this chapter will present society much like your own everyday life in which, up until now, zombies have only existed in entertainment. In this world, zombies have only been a theoretical concept, and the only place zombies have proliferated are in games, movies, and the like.

It will be a Japanese society that has made no preparations against zombies, and knows nothing about the new disaster they are about to encounter when dead people attack the living and in doing so, increase their numbers. So the question is, can you survive such a disaster?

The Zombie Outbreak!
FROM INITIAL FLEEING TO BUILDING YOUR BASE

It's a Zombie!

We presently live in an information society. When an individual takes a photo or video with his or her cell phone, if that information has value, it will spread far and wide throughout society.

When zombies appear and attack humans, photos or video of the attack will appear on the internet. So what happens next?

In all likelihood, it will spread like wildfire. At first, many will doubt its veracity. They'll think it's a prank, or maybe an advertisement for some movie or game. But when photos and eyewitness accounts start to spread, people will come to realize that the zombie outbreak is real.

At this point, do you run? Or do you find yourself hesitating?

When a danger appears, it doesn't necessarily mean that the danger is anywhere near you.

After all, we're talking about zombies.

If we look at natural disasters such as earthquakes and typhoons—disasters with which we're familiar—are we so frightened that we abandon our schools or workplaces to flee for

INFORMATION AND EVACUATION

SO TO USE THE WEB EFFECTIVELY, YOU HAVE TO BE SKILLED AT DISTINGUISHING FACT FROM LIES.

IT'S TRUE THAT THE INTERNET AND SOCIAL MEDIA ARE A BIG HELP DURING DISASTERS, BUT THEY CAN ALSO SPREAD A LOT OF MISINFORMATION AND FALSE RUMORS, TOO.

our lives? With those natural disasters, we already know what steps to take next, assuming we know where the disaster hit first, how far it is from our position, the effect it can have on us from a distance, and what to do in order to avoid being caught in too much danger. And even if we personally don't know, we can ask someone else who will.

But what happens when it's zombies? The minute someone reports an outbreak in the far-northern island of Hokkaido, does that mean people in Tokyo all simultaneously rise and rush to evacuate? Would it affect the greater Tokyo area at all? And if you wanted to evacuate, where would you go?

NORMALCY BIAS: "FIRST, KEEP AN EYE ON THE SITUATION."

If you've just happened to come across information on the web about zombies, odds are your first reaction will not be to run away. It's more likely you will meet the info with some skepticism, and wait for more details before deciding what to do. And normally, that would be the correct decision.

In modern society, the speed of information being spread from person to person has far outstripped the speed that people can move physically. In our simulation, the zombies will not be intelligent and therefore cannot spread according to anybody's plan—only according to how Explosive Pandemic-type zombies can multiply. At the time of the outbreak, if you are relatively far away from the zombies, then there should be plenty of time to gather enough information.

But there is also one particular mistake that can change the above supposition. That is if the outbreak is happening in the very place that you happen to live. Or maybe the outbreak happens in many places at once. What if every place in the world is simultaneously hit with an explosive outbreak of zombies?

Of the two patterns, the "wait and see" decision might be the mistake. While you are staring at the screen of your internet-capable device, gathering zombie information, and arguing with other commenters about the best way to deal with the zombies, a zombie may be shambling up behind you.

So before you start thinking about how modern society should face the threat, first see if there are any nearby threats to your own life.

Run! But Before You Do...

Where will you be when there's a huge outbreak of Explosive Pandemic-type zombies? If it's during the day, then you will probably be at your workplace or school. If it's at night, then you'll probably be at home—that's what we would consider for a normal Japanese lifestyle. When you're at home, then you need to think over the "running" option a little. Unlike a natural

disaster, you have no idea where a "safe place to run to" might be with Explosive Pandemic-type zombies.

Because zombies are the ruined remains of human beings, there is no safer place to be than a place where there are no humans. If there are a lot people shoved into a confined space, such as one of the evacuation shelters for normal disasters, then that is actually the worst possible place to hide from zombies.

IS IT EVEN POSSIBLE TO NOT RUN?

It's possible to hole up in your own home and wait for rescue, or at least for the situation to get better. That is one option.

And it's an especially good option if you live in a rental apartments that can only be accessed by a narrow, steep staircase that must be climbed and if you have quite a bit of food stashed away there. After all, Explosive Pandemic-type zombies have a very hard time climbing stairs, and that will provide you with a certain measure of safety. While you have electricity, you can charge up your rechargeable batteries, and you can fill plastic bottles with water while the water is still flowing through your pipes. You can also create a barricade for your door, and you may cling to your computer, television, and radio. But there are different threat levels depending on the zombie type. If you still don't have enough data to make a determination on what kind of threat they pose, you won't be able to make an effective decision. So, for the time being, it isn't a bad idea to hole up, close yourself in, and try to gather as much information as you can. It probably won't be too late to run later.

But you should make all the preparations to open the barricades and run at a moment's notice. Why? Well, even if the zombies don't come knocking on your door, their other actions can cause accidents and other disasters. This is something you should be particularly aware of when hiding in your home. It will be impossible for the fire department to come and put out fires with zombies wandering around, especially if you live in a district in a big city that is crowded with buildings. If a fire

breaks out, it could spread into an overwhelming inferno. Also, even if you stay where you are and do nothing, as time passes, your food supplies will run out, and you never know when the infrastructure bringing you water and electric power will break down. It could be that society has learned how to deal with the zombies and has prepared countermeasures, and all things turn out for the best. But if that doesn't happen, you will have to leave your shelter sometime.

If you haven't gone on the run, you should at least choose from your belongings within your home, pick what you will need and what you can use, and set them aside for when/if you need to run. You need to choose clothing to wear on the run. Depending on your climate and season, having clothing that protects against the rain and cold will be convenient. And having a pair of tough-but-comfortable shoes will not only help you move but also increase your morale.

IF I CHOOSE TO RUN, WHAT ABOUT MY FAMILY?

When there is a disaster, the family tends to gather together in their residence. If they're out, they try to go home. When earthquakes or typhoons stop public transportation, the enormous pileup of commuters causes problems in the community. Some family members take their cars to meet their loved ones, and that causes traffic jams. As the zombie outbreak spreads, that problem will become even worse. It's easy to imagine people, in a desperate bid to save their family members, rushing out in their cars onto the streets.

You will have to make your own decisions on what to do about your missing family members, but if they are stuck in school or at their work with zombies wandering around them, it will be extremely dangerous to go and try to rescue them. An accident or traffic jam could cause a second disaster on top of the first. Staying fortified in your home and praying for the safe return of loved ones is a tough option to consider, but you should probably do just that.

Or in the opposite case, where your family is at home and you're the one out and about, the first thing you should do is try and send them a message. "Stay at home! Don't move from there!" That's all you should tell them. From there, whether you decide to go back to the safety of your home or go out and get experience with the Explosive Pandemic-style zombies is something we leave to your own judgment.

But whether you're doing it over the internet or over your cell phone, make sure you get that across to your family members as quickly as possible, even though they think of zombies as just a fantasy. "Infected people are going wild, spreading the disease!" or "There's some drug that been spread throughout town that's stealing away people's sanity and making them go on rampages!" are some excuses you might use, but the main thing to do is convince them to *not* go to an evacuation shelter, but instead stay at home and lock the door. Maybe excuses of that sort will convince them more easily than the truth.

Beyond that, the only thing you can do to help keep them safe is to pray. The more pressing problem is, will *you* be able to survive long enough to join them back at your home?

Where Should I Run?

Whether you decide to venture out or hole up at home, if your choice goes wrong, the only thing left to do is run. But if you run without a goal, you may endanger your very existence. First, you have to think about where to run.

If you're running from Explosive Pandemic-style zombies, the best place to run is where there won't be any other humans around. If there aren't any humans, there won't be anybody to turn into zombies. The problem is that the places where there are absolutely no humans are places that are not suited to human survival: in the polar regions, for example, or deserts. Nobody lives there, so there won't be any zombies. But aside from the difficulties of merely getting there, you will have to bring along all the necessities to keep yourself alive.

The second runner-up would be a place where a zombie might find it hard to get around. Most Explosive Pandemic-style zombies are clumsy and have no intelligence. Once you know the details of the zombie type you're dealing with, then you can choose a place you can run to. But for the time being, let's draw up some criteria.

When your enemy is clumsy, then changes in height are your ally. In urban settings, you will probably want to run to a tall building. You may wish to use the rooftops—in other words, places you can't reach without a ladder—as your emergency evacuation shelter.

DOWN TO THE SEA

If you live along the shore of the Seto Inland Sea or on an island, there's a reasonable chance that you know a bit about sea vessels, and running off to an island may be an option for you. Most zombies can neither swim nor row a boat, so the odds that it will be relatively safe are high. On the Seto Inland Sea, there are many islands that are connected by bridges to the island of Shikoku or the Japanese main island of Honshu. But those bridges will be the zombies' only access, so even those have merits.

But don't feel too safe! Some Explosive Pandemic-type zombies have a very long incubation period post-infection. There may be infected people who have already come to the island who don't realize they're infected. And depending on the zombie, even though zombies can't swim, it's conceivable there may be a type that can walk along the seabed. Common sense says that when you combine the natural buoyancy of the human body with the undulations of the sea, the chances that a zombie can walk on the sea floor and get to your island may be so low as to be insignificant. But what might be an isolated island, could, at low tide, actually be connected to the mainland. So once you've taken refuge there, be sure to ask the locals about the topography of the island.

UP TO THE MOUNTAINS

Or you can go the opposite direction from the sea and head to the mountains. Unfortunately, the mountains of Japan aren't really suited as a place to run to. It depends on the climate, but the vegetation on Japan's mountains is dense, and there are a lot of blind spots even at the top of the mountains. During the Warring States Period (approximately 1467-1603), when they built castles on mountaintops, the first thing they'd do is clear away all the surrounding trees. This provided building supplies, but it also provided a commanding, unblocked view of the surroundings.

Also, zombies don't necessarily have to walk on two legs. If they can't get somewhere by walking, they're not too proud to crawl along on their bellies. And it's hard to detect a zombie on all fours crawling though the underbrush.

But it isn't all bad. For zombies to attack humans, they have to somehow determine a human shape. With their field of view limited and the sounds and smells put out by other animals, it's quite likely that a zombie will never even set foot into the Japanese mountains.

BUT NOT THIS PLACE!

When it comes to the actual decision of where to run to, you may be confused by the zombie outbreak and find it hard to come to a decision.

Consider that, among all 47 Japanese prefectures, the population of one, Tokyo, contains ten percent of the entire Japanese population. If you add in Kanagawa Prefecture (where Yokohama is), Osaka, Aichi Prefecture (where Nagoya is), and Saitama Prefecture on the outskirts of Tokyo, that number adds up to 35.7% of the Japanese population (Stats: Ministry of Internal Affairs as of October 2011). This means that more than one in three Japanese people live in or near high-population-density urban areas.

And high-population-density urban areas are places where

the zombies will have significant amounts of reinforcements handy. Of the well-known threats, the greatest threat from Explosive Pandemic-type zombies is that they spread the contagion from person to person in an epidemic-style fashion. So when thinking about carriers of the contagion, the most dangerous place to be is where people gather. And after all, there is no cure. The minute you are infected, you are fated to an end that is worse than death.

If that's the case, then you must avoid public evacuation shelters. Hospitals and police stations are dangerous, too. To a society that knows nothing of zombies, a zombie might be treated as though they were a drunk or drug-addled person, and they would send those bitten by the zombie to the hospital, wouldn't they? We think you can guess what would happen next.

How Should I Run?

Once you've decided to run, your next choice is what means will you use. Until you know more about the situation, you should consider transport methods such as public transportation to be dangerous, especially trains and airlines. If a zombie becomes mixed up with the passengers, there is no place to escape to. Your escape route becomes a moving coffin. Buses and ferries put you in a similar situation.

But if all you can take is public transportation, when will it become reasonably safe? Only after the society learns how to deal with zombies, and after the government has fully distributed a manual on coping with zombies. In short, it will be safe when the society has accepted that anyone who is bitten by a zombie should have their brains bashed out of their heads, and the public officials have set up stations nation-wide to do just that. And since this simulation only deals with a period long before such an event, let's just accept that we shouldn't ride public transportation.

Avoid buses and trains. At least for the period in which

some people are still trying to treat the zombies as humans, trying to calm the zombie when it goes on a rampage.

ARE CARS ANY GOOD?

In Japan's 47 prefectures, given 100 families, there will be, on average, a vehicle ownership of 108 vehicles (according to a study from the Japan Automotive Manufacturers Association, up through March of 2013). So you can estimate that each household has one car. Although in the huge metropolitan areas such as Tokyo or Osaka where public transportation is highly advanced, there will be fewer cars, and there will be more in the suburban and rural areas. But even though most adults may not have a car of their own, many of them will at least get a driver's license.

So when the crisis comes and the human population realizes they should run, most will first think of escaping by car. But the truth is that there are good reasons to avoid it.

In our modern information society, knowledge about zombies will move much faster than the zombies themselves. And it's fairly easy to imagine that this will cause a panic. People fleeing from the cities will first get into their cars, and flood into the cities to rescue their family members trapped there. In their panic, they will ignore traffic rules, and there will be a sharp rise in accidents. All at once, there will be traffic jams, and the jams themselves will cause further panic. With that, people will probably abandon their cars.

Things will play out differently if you live in a low-population-density area, but if you live in the vicinity of a huge metropolitan area, you cannot place your trust in cars.

Still, there are a lot of plusses to trying to escape in a car. It means you won't be exhausted even when trying to escape over extremely long distances, and they can carry both your luggage and other humans.

Say that you live in a rural area and know the traffic patterns of the area well, so you travel in the dead of night when there

will be fewer other cars on the road. Even if there are zombies wandering around outside your windows, all you need is to do is climb into the car and stomp on the accelerator, and you're off on your escape.

Still, you never know when you will come upon an impassable road where you will have to leave your vehicle. So the minute you grasp the steering wheel, you have to be prepared to abandon your car, and you should consider well what you are going to do when that time comes.

WHAT ABOUT MOTORCYCLES OR BICYCLES?

Well, if four-wheeled cars are a problem, how about the two-wheeled variety? With bicycles and motorcycles, you can expect to be able to move faster than cars, which may get into traffic jams or become abandoned. If you have an off-road motorcycle or mountain bike, then there are ways to use it in this situation.

But with motorcycles and bikes, your body will be exposed, and the zombies won't balk at trying to tackle you. If you were up against living humans or animals, they give a thought to the damage their own bodies may take, and as a result, they will hesitate before acting rashly. But zombies have as much self-regard as a machine. And even if that zombie were destroyed in trying to tackle you, it will still make you fall from your bike which will allow other zombies to feast on you—and which zombie kills you doesn't really matter, does it?

But if you're willing to risk it, there are a lot of advantages to motorcycles and bicycles, including increased mobility and the capacity to carry a certain amount of luggage.

But the most important thing is that, when you are surrounded by zombies and you have to get out of there quickly, it's better to use the bike or motorcycle to flee than to not use it and die. As long as you're still alive later, "later" is when you can decide what to do next.

However, if you have necessities that you cannot live

without, let's not secure them to your vehicle but rather keep them on your person. No matter how much work and love you've put into your bike or motorcycle, there will be a time when you will have no choice but to just leave the thing behind, and there is no guarantee that you will have time to detach your belongings from the bike rack.

ARE THERE ANY WATERWAYS NEAR YOU?

There are quite a lot of rivers in Japan, and most Japanese cities grew around them.

From the Meiji era (1848-1912), when railroads spread all over the country, going well into the Showa era (1918-1989), when the nation became highly motorized, waterways were used in cities such as Osaka and Edo (the old name for Tokyo) to transport men and goods. During the high-growth period, the highway network became more and more developed, and waterways were filled with dirt in an inverse proportion to re-claim the land, burying the waters into subterranean culverts.

If you're trying to escape with children, the elderly, or the disabled, and you cannot use public transportation or your car, then your options suddenly become severely limited. So if you're travelling with someone like that, you might want to consider using a boat instead of a car.

There are far fewer boats in Japan than cars, and there is less of a possibility for a traffic jam of boats on Japanese rivers. Furthermore, the standard version of Explosive Pandemic-type zombies is either bad at swimming, or they can't do it at all. Even simply floating on a boat will be much safer than being on land.

But even so, you mustn't trust in it too much.

Zombies do not need to breathe. Let's say the zombies see you on the boat, jump in the river, and sink to the bottom, they may be able to walk on the riverbed and stretch their hands up to your boat. You will have to be especially careful of the depth of the river in question.

Moreover, boats are hard to manage for someone who is unused to them. They're also vulnerable to heavy rains, especially typhoons. People who have died or gone missing in rivers, channels, etc. in Japan in a recent year numbered 291 (National Police Agency, 2012). And running from zombies only to drown in the river makes the whole running thing pointless.

SO YOU'RE SAYING THAT I'M JUST GOING TO HAVE TO WALK, RIGHT?

Let's face it, the evolution of human beings really started with our ability to walk upright. According to books, walking upright allowed humans to use their hands freely, speeding up their evolution. But on the other hand, when your ancestors lived in the trees, they could use their feet with almost as much dexterity as their hands.

However you feel about that, it was long-distance walking on two legs that allowed Homo erectus (upright man) to become Homo sapiens (modern man). The development of the lower half of our bodies made it possible for us to walk for long distances on two legs, and that in turn led to mankind evolving into highly advanced hunter-gatherers. The fact that mankind's ancestors, with no skills or culture to speak of, spent three million years spreading our living places from Africa throughout nearly every other location on the planet is proof of that advancement.

One thing about zombies is that they don't have a stable center of gravity or the ability to compensate for uneven surfaces and heights when walking on two legs which normal humans have. But they don't feel pain or get exhausted either. Since they're already dead, they have no incentive to maintain their muscles and bodies in any kind of working condition. And that is both a strength and weakness for them. They don't care if their arms get torn off, and since they can't (or don't) swing their arms to help maintain their center of gravity and balance, they tend to be very clumsy in walking.

They don't have the athletic skills that our human ancestors

MEANS OF ESCAPE

IT'LL BE SLOWER THAN OTHER MEANS OF ESCAPE, BUT IF YOU'RE UP AGAINST THE STANDARD ZOMBIES, EVEN A TROTTING PACE CAN OUTDISTANCE THEM.

IF YOU'RE WALKING, YOU DON'T NEED ANY SPECIAL LICENSE, SKILLS, OR FUEL, AND IF YOU CHOOSE YOUR SHOES CAREFULLY, YOU WON'T MAKE MUCH NOISE EITHER. IT'S ALSO PRETTY EASY TO OVERCOME A CERTAIN AMOUNT OF HEIGHT DIFFERENCES, TOO.

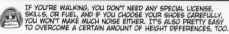

acquired over three million years of evolution. To zombies, the human body is a disappointing, borrowed body that is to be used and thrown away.

But you are quite different. You can use your body better than any other thing in the universe. And that's a big advantage.

There's no need for you to escape by running at full speed all the time. You can observe the situation and think things over. Are the zombies headed your way? Or are they simply wandering aimlessly instead? If you were to run, would the zombies notice you? And if they noticed you, in what way would they start chasing you? Are there sudden changes in height in the immediate surroundings? Is there shelter or cover?

Use all of your five senses, think it over carefully, and you'll probably see that walking is the best after all. Yes, cars and motorcycles and other such human tools can raise your

mobility, but they also don't provide enough time to truly observe your surroundings. There are times when you don't notice the zombie coming at you from off to the side.

Walking is necessarily slow as a means of escape, but you will also have time to observe and think.

Trust yourself. And trust in your ancestors, who managed to survive in a harsh, wild environment for three million years. Your physique and intelligence ensure that you have the potential to survive these dangers.

However, if you have the suspicion you eat and drink too much and get too little exercise, you should probably make some changes to your lifestyle.

Secure Your Base!

Okay, from this point on, we're going to assume that you've managed to flee successfully from the first appearance of zombies, and have managed to secure a relatively safe base (for the time being, at least). That's the premise of this simulation.

For our purposes of the simulation, we're presenting you with two variations.

In the first one, you're in a shopping mall, keeping watch and protecting your base from zombies. A shopping mall is a place where people gather, and as such, it has a lot of drawbacks as a long-term defensive base.

On the other hand, malls are common throughout the nation and a part of people's daily lives. Therefore, it's easy to imagine that you were already in a shopping mall when the zombie disaster occurred. Let's further suppose that it's a shopping mall you are familiar with, so as you read this chapter, it will be easier for you to imagine what you would do if zombies attacked you in this setting.

The second variation is a college campus setting where you are either a student or faculty member. As with the shopping mall in the first variation, let's assume that you were already there when you first encountered zombies.

SIEGE WARFARE

For this chapter, let's imagine that humanity is experiencing the spread of Explosive Pandemic-type zombies—an event that is unprecedented in human history—and that you are trying to survive it.

One way to do so is by holing up in your fortifications. Think of the zombies as a besieging army, and you are trying to protect your castle from them. A number of points in a siege warfare scenario should be considered, since they will also help you survive a prolonged zombie attack. You can't defend your castle if you don't have enough food or drinking water. If you don't take care of your bodily wastes properly, it will lead to the spread of disease. Most importantly, if your castle's defenders lose their morale, you won't be able to hold your castle.

Now, keeping those points in mind, let's look at our two variations.

Simulation 1: The Shopping Mall

Your Emergency Shelter

Shopping malls are better when thought of as a temporary shelter.

They may look like they have a lot of food handy, but much of that food is perishable. It won't last more than a few days. You'll be all right as long as the infrastructure that provides electricity holds up, but once the uproar caused by the zombies begins, it'll only be a matter of time before that infrastructure collapses.

The most important thing about shopping malls is that the people trapped there won't be organized. They'll just be going about their daily lives, at least until the zombies start attacking. Once the walking dead start spreading their contagion, creating a growing zombie army through their infected bites, those daily lives will be thrown into chaos. It will be a major challenge

to unify these people, and inspire them to do the necessary work that will allow a return to some kind of structured society.

From the siege warfare point of view, a shopping mall will only have a few stores of emergency supplies, and not much in the way of possible perimeter defenses. As a result, the people there will already be anxious; in this state, they're capable of losing morale completely and surrendering your fortifications before the attack even begins.

Considering the lack of provisions and the weak defenses, a shopping mall should only be considered as a destination if there are no better options available. In addition, only make a shopping mall your main base if you can reasonably expect rescue before a) you run short of supplies, or a) the morale of the other survivors breaks.

The question is, will you be able to hold out until help comes, or will you have to extricate yourself and make a run for it?

FIRST, HEAD UPWARDS

Explosive Pandemic-type zombies make for awkward walkers. They're stronger than humans, but they have a very difficult time with any changes in height (like a staircase). If you have to choose between downstairs or upstairs, the latter is the only sensible choice. Zombies may not have the mental capacity to handle stairs, but like Winnie the Pooh, they can still "come down the stairs now, bump, bump, bump, on the back of their heads."

Still, you can't be absolutely sure of safety on the high ground either. For a little while at the beginning of the crisis, the elevators and escalators will still probably be working. Quite a lot of the Japanese suburban shopping malls have a rooftop parking lot with a sloping driveway leading to it. If it's a gentle slope, it will be easier for zombies to climb than a staircase.

Even so, if the choice is between going up or down, then up is the answer.

NEXT, SET UP BLOCKADES

Once you're up on the top floor, you will need to press the emergency-stop buttons on the elevators and escalators so that nothing can come up from the lower floors. You'll also need to barricade or otherwise block off the stairwells. And if there's a parking lot adjacent to your base, you'll need to barricade that, too.

Most shopping malls have some kind of floor map. By consulting that, you can find and barricade most of the entrances. However, entrances and passageways that are meant for employees are not usually noted on the maps. You'll want to check the backs of every non-barricaded store. If the mall has offices for the mall administration, they might also have their own entrances, passageways, and elevators. Those will have to be blocked off as well.

BLOCKADING YOUR FLOOR

 OF COURSE, SINCE THE MALL WE'RE IN HAS A ROOFTOP PARKING LOT, WE'LL HAVE TO BARRICADE THAT AS WELL. NOT JUST THE ENTRANCE DOOR TO THE MALL, BUT THE RAMP THAT WAS BUILT FOR CARS TO COME UP TO THE LOT HAS TO BE MADE IMPASSABLE, TOO. WE HAVE TO MAKE SURE THERE ARE NO ZOMBIES ON THE ROOF AT ALL.

IF YOU MEET ZOMBIES...

What do you do if you are in the midst of blockading a floor and you come across a zombie?

If it comes up from a lower floor while you are setting up your barricades, try to hold it back with a pole while the rest of your members help to set up the barricade.

If you happen to see it on what you had thought was a secure floor, you must first run away. A shopping mall will have shelves to hold the different types of items on sale in its many stores. If the shelves can be moved, they could be used to construct a barricade. Everyone who is able to should pitch in to try and impede the zombie's movements. Once this has been done, you can stand outside of its reach and bash in its head with a pole or other similar object.

Explosive Pandemic-type zombies turn their victims into zombies with a bite, but the zombifying contagion—be it a virus, a curse, or a poison—seems to be in their fingernails as well. Make sure they never touch you, and make sure to stop them from moving so you can destroy their brains.

If you crush its head and the zombie is still moving, then your work isn't finished yet. After the head has been destroyed, target its legs next to stop it from walking. If possible, try to toss it down the stairs.

This is the most dangerous point in the operation. Nobody—not you, or anybody else—knows what these zombies are capable of. And anyone who thinks that rampaging zombies are still human beings will think you are cruel for trying to destroy the creatures. It'll be even worse if the zombie is someone's friend or, worst of all, someone's child. But hesitation or fear could cause you to lose the fight and die or even become a zombie yourself.

On the other hand, nobody can be blamed for mistakes at this stage, either. In any dangerous situation, a lack of knowledge is the greatest danger. You're going from your daily life into a nightmare world where the dead walk. Do you actually think the transition from one way of thinking to the next would

be a smooth one? The fact is, you'll never know until it's actually happening to you. No matter how much training and thought you put into it in advance, the question of whether you are equipped with the necessary faculties to handle it can only be answered in a trial by fire.

Therefore, if you manage to survive your first encounter with a zombie, you should obtain some degree of self-confidence after that. You'll need it if you're going to survive!

CHECKING FOR SURVIVORS

The danger is over for the time being. There are no zombies left on your floor. Your barricades are all in place, and you've managed to win yourself a little time until the zombies decide to attack your floor again. So, aside from yourself, who else is with you?

The fact that you are in a shopping mall probably means that there are other shoppers still left alive somewhere. There may be old people. There may be children. Friends or families might have come to the shopping mall together. If they were separated, they'll want to meet up again quickly. There will be some who just want to leave the mall and go home.

At this point, it's going to be difficult to keep the entire group under control. You need a leader to maintain order. And the leader has to take responsibility for the lives and safety of everyone. Can you handle such a responsibility? Even if you want the position, do you have the ability to encourage others to follow your orders as a leader? In this simulation, you can't even guess whether you have the potential to be a leader until you try to be one and see the results.

But for that very same reason, you may have the potential to convince a disorganized group to work together to build barricades and support each other in a fight when a zombie does appear. But since it's likely that you won't be able to gain control over a diverse group of survivors, this simulation will presuppose that you cannot.

Either way, you will have to deal with the other survivors. It's possible that there is someone else in the group who will notice the need to become a team. But you can't count on it. Check among the survivors to see if anyone has been bitten. With any luck, no one has been infected.

But if someone *has* been bitten, then you are faced with a difficult decision. Do you leave things as they are and see what happens, or do you do everything you can to lessen the potential danger to yourself and everyone else?

WHAT TO DO WITH SOMEONE WHO IS ABOUT TO BECOME A ZOMBIE?

If this were a video game, you wouldn't worry about it too much.

Someone who has been bitten by a zombie can't be saved. You blow their brains out and let them die a human. It's the only compassionate thing to do.

WHAT IF YOU'VE BEEN BITTEN BY A ZOMBIE?

IT'S REALLY JUST A STOP-GAP MEASURE.

IN THE ZOMBIE MOVIES, THEY **AMPUTATE** THE ARM ONCE THEY'VE BEEN BITTEN. IT SAVES THEM IN THE MOVIES, BUT IN REAL LIFE IT'S BASICALLY *SUICIDE.*

I DON'T GET IT, WHAT AM I SUPPOSED TO DO? I'M STILL HUMAN, AREN'T I?

EVEN IF SHE BECAME A ZOMBIE, THE ONLY THING WE REALLY CAN DO IS ISOLATE HER IN A SAFE PLACE...

YOU BETTER ACT QUICKLY BEFORE YOU TURN INTO A ZOMBIE YOURSELF... IT WON'T BE EASY, BUT YOU DON'T HAVE MUCH CHOICE!

CAN'T I JUST RUN IT UNDER A COLD TAP?!

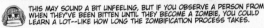
THIS MAY SOUND A BIT UNFEELING, BUT IF YOU OBSERVE A PERSON FROM WHEN THEY'VE BEEN BITTEN UNTIL THEY BECOME A ZOMBIE, YOU COULD LEARN A LOT--LIKE HOW LONG THE ZOMBIFICATION PROCESS TAKES.

But in real life, if you're faced with that situation and you aren't prepared for it, it's a different story.

For the purposes of this simulation, we are assuming that you are being attacked by Explosive Pandemic-type zombies. When you are bitten by one of those types, you cannot be saved. But if you were actually thrust into the situation, you may find yourself reluctant to jump to any immediate conclusions. After all, might it be possible that there is some special medicine for it?

Eventually, this person will become fully zombified and attack you. For now, though, that person still has the consciousness of a human being. Killing or isolating them will be a hard thing for you to do.

It'd probably be best to quarantine the person off from the rest of your group. However, if the person's family is part of the group, odds are they won't be very supportive of that idea. Still, if you do nothing, the person might become a zombie and endanger everyone's lives. There really are no good options in this situation. Therefore, for the purposes of this simulation, let's just imagine that you find the courage to do what needs to be done and move on.

As a member of modern-day society, it isn't always easy to put the needs of the many ahead of the needs of the one. Decisions like these are always going to be tough. That being said, if the family and friends of the bitten person can't be convinced to go along with your choice, then you will have to get as far away from them as you can. Then be ready to act accordingly when the time comes. Just make sure you're carrying a long pole when it does. You might also want to make preparations for a barricade.

There may be other unavoidable tragedies to overcome, and you'd better be ready to deal with them.

MONITOR EVERYONE'S STATE OF MIND

Friends, family, and neighbors will become zombies before your eyes, and this bizarre situation will put a strain on

everybody's psyche. It's one thing to see it unfold in the movies, but in real life, the enormous amounts of stress will likely create problems such as post-traumatic stress disorder (PTSD) and acute stress disorder (ASD), among others. As a survivor, this is something to be wary of. The survival of your body is nothing if your sanity doesn't survive with it.

So for the time being, you've secured a safe spot. That doesn't mean you should let your guard down. Yes, you're more or less secure, but this is no time to celebrate. After all, there are zombies wandering around on the floor right below you.

Your first step is to quench your thirst and hunger and hit the bathroom too. These actions are linked to the health of your rational mind and your nerves as well. As you satisfy your physical needs, your stress will be reduced by a certain amount. So maybe you shouldn't hit the liquor cabinet just yet, but satisfying your sweet tooth may give you extra energy. Go ahead and eat what you like to eat best.

Whatever you do eat, though, be extra careful when you go to the bathroom. Zombie movies often have a scene where a person who has been bitten by a zombie feels sick and heads toward the bathroom. This is where they usually turn into a zombie themselves. After all, when a person is "doing their business" in the bathroom, they are at their most vulnerable.

Preparing to Escape

As we stated earlier, a shopping mall is, at best, a temporary spot to take shelter in an emergency. If rescue can reasonably be expected within a few days, then you put up your barricades, take care of all those who have been infected with the zombie contagion, and wait it out.

Unfortunately, it's very likely that this emergency will last longer than just a few days.

The speed with which the horde of Explosive Pandemic-type zombies grows will depend on how the contagion is being spread. If it has a very long incubation period, what begins as

only a few zombies at the beginning may suddenly become a huge army of zombies in a short time. Zombies will crop up more or less simultaneously in every corner of the nation, and after that, it will take a long time for the government to come up with ways of dealing with the situation.

So for this piece, we will assume that, even though several days may have passed, help is not coming any time soon.

UNDERSTANDING YOUR SITUATION

In modern Japan, it would take a certain amount of time for the populace to see the zombies for what they truly are. At first, the zombies will most likely be perceived as people with a sickness that makes them go on a rampage.

And when you talk to the people around you, you should probably go along with the idea that this is all the product of some disease, rather than something more sinister or fantastical.

At a time like this, the public's familiarity with zombies could likely bring about a disaster on its own. People who have no interest in horror movies would probably snort with disgust or doubt your sanity the moment they hear you talk seriously about zombies. And that's precisely *because* they have heard of zombies already.

In Japan, a better name for the condition might be "Ghoul Disease," since *ghoul* is a word that most Japanese have not heard of. As such, they might be more willing to hear it with an open mind.

So, for the time being, you might simply say that a ghoul is a creature out of North American and European legend, one that gnaws on human flesh. Since those who catch this disease try to bite other humans, it makes sense that you would choose this name for those who suffer from this condition.

As the crisis worsens, society will begin to break down. While the infrastructure is still in working order, make sure you monitor the internet closely for information that could help you survive.

Just where is the problem at its worst? And where are the safest spots to wait it out? Does it look as though help might be coming? Or is that being unrealistic?

Make sure not to put too much trust in the information you're seeing. There will still be a lot of fraud, misinterpretation, and confusion mixed in with the truth. If the government controls the media broadcasts, they may be downplaying the seriousness of the crisis to avoid widespread panic.

WHAT YOU SHOULD PREPARE AHEAD OF TIME

You should be preparing certain things in case you do need to escape. Most of them are things you wouldn't be carrying with you into a shopping mall on a normal day, so you'll have to search through the mall to find what you need.

- Emergency rations (3 days' worth)
- A Thermos
- A flashlight
- A portable radio
- Batteries
- Rain gear
- Insulated aluminum blankets
- A backpack that can hold it all

For the present simulation, you don't need to think about running for an extended period of time. Even if the zombies have destroyed everything in the vicinity, there should still be several shelters around—such as the college campus setting that we'll get into later. Plan your escape with a place like that in mind.

For the escape, you will want clothes that won't impede your movement. Search with that in mind. The expandable-style backpack is something the zombies can grab and use to pull you down, so you should think about limiting the amount of clothes you bring.

ESCAPE PREPARATIONS

 SURE, WHAT YOU BRING ON YOUR ESCAPE IS IMPORTANT, BUT MORE IMPORTANT THAN THAT IS WHERE YOU'RE PLANNING TO ESCAPE TO. YOU SHOULD PLAN SEVERAL POSSIBLE DESTINATIONS AND SEVERAL ESCAPE ROUTES FOR EACH DESTINATION.

OTHER THINGS TO DO IN PREPARATION

What kind of shoes do you normally wear? If you didn't wear anything suitable for running, then you might want to search the shopping mall for a tough pair of shoes you can run in. Get shoes that are slightly bigger than you usually wear, and put on several pairs of very thick socks that can provide shock absorption. Also, you should be sure to break in the footwear you chose, by walking around and around in your safe zone.

Your life may depend on how well you've broken in your shoes when the time comes to make your escape. Plus, the physical exercise will be good for reducing your stress.

TAG WITH ZOMBIES

This simulation assumes that you are somewhere between your late teens and your thirties, with the physique and physical

strength of the average Japanese person. It also assumes that you have no combat experience or martial arts training.

As such, we will not be touching on the best ways to kill zombies, or which weapons to choose for your battles. If you happen to be someone that doesn't have a typical Japanese physique or battle experience of any kind, we suggest you consider your skills while you read over Chapter Three of this book and make your own decisions.

Once you have abandoned the safety of your barricades to make your escape, it's inevitable that zombies will block your way. Trying to engage in hand-to-hand combat with a zombie would leave the average Japanese person far too vulnerable. And even if you do your best to learn how to use unfamiliar weapons, those very hasty preparations will actually put you in more danger.

Instead, what we recommend is for you to get together in a group and learn how to keep your distance from zombies.

To put it simply, you will be playing a game of tag. It's a game in which one or more players act as the zombies. The rest play the roles of the escapees. The "zombies" will walk at a speed that is comparable to the zombies you will be facing, and they chase after the escapees. If an escapee is touched by a zombie, that escapee is out of the game.

Zombies are very frightening creatures, but their reach is the same as a human's. They don't use firearms or any weapons, and their movements are clumsy. As long as you can maintain a distance that will keep them from catching you, you should be able to outpace even a large number of zombies together.

But if and when you find yourself surrounded by zombies, your fear will reach you before they do. After all, they are walking dead people who want to eat you. If you fall victim to your own panic, you'll fall victim to the zombies shortly after. So, before that time comes, you will want to train your body to move in such a way that can help you to keep your distance

from the zombies, and Zombie Tag is the best way to train your body to do so.

Take turns playing Zombie Tag. During the game, some of the zombies should make sure to hide in the shadows, appearing suddenly when an escapee gets too close. Try to think of as many potential scenarios as you can, and as many ways to get out of those scenarios as possible. If you do this, your game will be a good preparation for the real thing.

Zombies can't practice like this. They don't have the imagination for it. As a human, your imagination gives you a distinct advantage.

GETTING YOUR CLOTHES IN ORDER

As you play your games of Zombie Tag, you will probably notice something important about your appearance and how it affects your success in the game.

Those with long hair will find that zombies can grab it, which makes them an easy target. In the same way, clothes with extra material hanging from your body can be grasped easily. When trying to run from zombies in narrow spots, these can become caught on things and slow you down as well. So be sure to wear your hair short, and choose clothing that is relatively form-fitting.

Gaining Total Control of the Shopping Mall

This may depend on when the need to escape arises, but while preparations are taking place, it's time to gain full control of the shopping mall. It's possible that there may be other survivors holed up in some corner of the place. Another possibility is that stores on other floors of the mall may contain food or other necessities, so gaining control of those floors is a good idea as well.

But the most important thing is to observe the zombies, and learn from their behavior. There will be more detail on zombie observations in the upcoming College Campus version

of the simulation. But at the very least, your aim is to learn about their perceptivity and their decision-making capabilities.

Do zombies react to sounds? Light? Smells? Do zombie eyes see? Can they tell the difference between a human and a mannequin? You should be able to learn the answers to these questions during your confrontations with the zombies in the shopping mall.

STUDY THE STRUCTURE OF THE SHOPPING MALL

Before you try to infiltrate any new floor, make sure you memorize its layout, identify any potential obstacles, the places where a zombie can hide, and any possible escape paths. Commit the structure to memory as best you can.

In most cases, only the interiors of the stores are different on each floor, so the width of the passageways and the ways they connect should be the same. In many cases, all you need to do is take control of one floor and memorize its layout. Doing so will help you to build up a mental map of how most of the floors are laid out.

Also, like we said back in the section about Zombie Tag, it's important that you gain experience in evading zombies when you do encounter them.

DO RECONNAISSANCE

First, you will want to establish how many zombies are on each floor. You'll also want to watch for any signs of other survivors, determine if the power has been turned off, and see which stores are accessible.

If you have a camera that can record video, you should strap it to a helmet or something similar and record your journey continuously. For reconnaissance purposes, you will want to run quickly through the floor, even if it doesn't seem like there are any zombies. The zombies might react to something, and you'll want to know what it is.

Once you've established that they react to stimuli like

sound or light, then you'll probably find a lot of things in the toy or party-goods section that can help lure them into places you want them to go. But we suggest you stay away from fireworks, no matter how effective they may be. When it comes to anything that creates fire, the smoke and flames could kill survivors just as easily as any zombie could, if not more easily.

CONSIDER HOW YOU CAN GAIN CONTROL OVER THE ZOMBIES

If you're up against the standard Explosive Pandemic-type zombies, a crushing blow to the head will stop them. And for the purposes of this simulation, those are the types we're assuming you will be facing. However, within the simulation, there is no way that you or your comrades will be able to know that they are this type. All the zombies you've encountered so far *seem* to be that type, but you don't have any definitive proof.

As you take control of each floor, learn the ways to battle the zombies. This is your best chance to gain experience.

First, think of the battle as hunting. And think of zombies as poisonous beasts in human form. It isn't something that you challenge to a one-on-one test of strength. And if there are several zombies at once, then you shouldn't fight—you should run.

So right from the start, you will want several of you facing just a single zombie. You will also want to secure a route to run if things go wrong, so you will need at least one person on sentry duty watching for threats.

There's no need to worry about fighting fair with a zombie. If you happen to have found a ranged weapon such as a gun or bow, let's leave testing it out in combat for later. What you will need to fight are sturdy poles, cloth, and/or rope.

First, throw the cloth or rope to trip up the zombie and stop its movement. And just in case the cloth tears or the rope snaps, be sure to have two or three more handy in reserve. Once the zombie's movement is halted, hit it with the pole, a shovel, or whatever long-reach weapon you have access to.

After several days of this, you should be able to overcome

CHAPTER 5

TAKE CONTROL OF THE SHOPPING MALL!

IN ZOMBIE MOVIES, THE INSTANT SOMEONE SAYS, "WE'VE MADE IT THIS FAR, SO NOW WE'RE COMPLETELY SAFE," EVERYONE IN THE AUDIENCE KNOWS THAT THEY'RE ALL DOOMED.

THE MOMENT YOU LET YOUR GUARD DOWN, YOU'RE IN DANGER! THERE MAY BE CRAWLING ZOMBIES HIDING BELOW THE SHELVES. CHECK THOROUGHLY TO MAKE SURE THERE ARE NO ROOMS OR CLOSETS YOU'VE OVERLOOKED!

any initial reluctance to committing acts of violence against these human-like creatures. And as you repeat this, you'll learn how to gain mastery over the zombies. In the simplest terms, you will find a way to make them unable to attack you.

TAKE ONE FLOOR AT A TIME

Let's take control of the shopping mall one floor at a time. If there are areas that are well populated with zombies, think hard before you act. Try to figure out some way to separate them and lure them away.

At this point, if you have figured out the zombies' behavior, you should be able to set some traps. After you've taken down all the zombies on the floor, set up barricades and block off the zombies from other floors. Next, do a detailed check of the floor to be sure that there aren't any zombies hiding, or any

additional survivors. Be thorough!

Always travel in groups. Someone should always be watching your back, and you should also be making sure nothing is creeping up behind them, either. And don't forget to look up and down! Zombies aren't alive. A dismembered zombie might have its head left somewhere on top of a showcase or below the floorboards.

The methods for taking control of each floor would probably match the methods found in a how-to book on urban warfare. If there's a bookstore in your mall, go to the military section, open one such book if it is available, and do some research.

As we have already written in this book, your survival will largely consist of clearing an area of all zombies, and gradually expanding that territory.

WHERE DO YOU ESCAPE TO?

So assuming you have escaped from the shopping mall to the outside, then where should you go next?

If the information infrastructure still works, you can consult the internet to learn more about the situation. During the several days that you and your fellow survivors have been in the shopping mall, it's likely that the entire world has succumbed to panic.

It's possible that you had particularly bad luck and happened to be in the place where the pandemic began. However, it's more likely that this phenomenon has occurred simultaneously all over the world.

It's likely that the information you receive from other people will waver between hope and despair, and this will be reflected in the news as well. Some news will be so bad you won't want to believe it, while there will be other news you'll want to believe so bad it hurts.

To avoid both of these traps, you should seek out information that isn't based on human opinions or feelings. Live camera feeds and the like will be a good resource. There are live camera

feeds being streamed from tourist locations all over the world, so search out as many as you can so you can determine if zombies can be seen in any of them. If you do happen to see zombies there, cancel your vacation plans for that spot indefinitely.

In any event, you won't know how well the infrastructure is working until you go and see for yourself. The internet will be filled with false rumors and wild speculation, but it also contains crucial information that you could never gather on your own. The ability to discern between the two, especially in a world that is now filled with zombies, is not a skill that can be obtained overnight. You will want to work on developing this skill on a daily basis, as you'll no doubt find it useful even if a zombie apocalypse never comes to pass.

LET'S BUILD A RECONNAISSANCE TEAM

The best place to escape to will preferably be within walking distance. If you happen to have a lot of survivors in your shopping mall, consider building a reconnaissance team from them. You'll want physically healthy team members who can remain cool and collected under pressure.

They have to recon the area, gather intelligence, and come back to report their findings. The very best way to do this is to go out and experience it firsthand. And, using the information gathered by your reconnaissance team, find an escape route. They will need to locate places to hide, assuming that the destination cannot be arrived at quickly.

Make sure they know that their aim is to find places that can act as shelter on the way for a short while. If possible, they should take photos of the interior spaces. Send your team out a number of times. This will be dangerous for them, but it's preferable to have a small team map out a safe route rather than having everyone in your group meet with some disaster along the way.

Besides, there won't be an inexhaustible number of zombies outside, either. In 2012, the population density of Japan

was estimated at 335 people per square kilometer. That number will be higher in the cities, but that's the average number. And not all of them will have become zombies yet. Many of them will have managed to escape, just like you did.

It depends on the behavior of the type of zombies you're facing, but let's assume that they don't attack other zombies, and that they don't run in packs. When humans aren't around, zombies will likely scatter like particles in Brownian motion. So, during the several days that you and your fellow survivors have been holed up in the shopping mall, the zombies will have scattered themselves about the area.

To a certain extent, this will be simply wishful thinking. In a worst-case scenario, the Explosive Pandemic-type zombies are the eyes and ears of some living human with occult powers. If this is the case, the minute you leave the shopping mall, zombies from dozens of kilometers around will be sent to converge upon you.

In any event, you will have to confirm it. If you need to, you can indulge in despair later.

MAKE YOUR ESCAPE!

It's time to start your escape. Make maps made based on the reconnaissance team's observations, and distribute them to everyone. But even as you leave the shopping mall behind, don't go breaking down your barricades. If your escape attempt fails, you might have to come back.

When you depart, leave from the second floor using ladders. Once you are done with the ladders, toss them somewhere in the vicinity. Explosive Pandemic-type zombies lack even the most basic understanding of human tools and how to use them. A chimpanzee would be more likely to use a ladder to reach a banana hanging from the ceiling. Even if you threw the ladder at them, a zombie couldn't possibly come up with the idea of standing the ladder up and climbing up to an open second-floor window.

CHAPTER 5

THE RECONNAISSANCE TEAM SECURES AN ESCAPE ROUTE

With all those preparations that need to be made, the reconnaissance team will surely have to be sent out a number of times.

↑ What I'm doing there is looking for a safe route; finding places to take breaks, stocking them with food and water, and making sure they're clearly marked; and creating new routes by removing barriers for us; and making height differences for the zombies.

Besides, you escaped from it for a reason—shopping malls aren't the ideal spot to wait out a zombie pandemic. But the few days or weeks you spent in the shopping mall did not go to waste. That's where you, and hopefully your friends as well, took your first steps in learning what to do in the face of a zombie threat.

In the meantime, the world has changed completely. Zombies, which used to exist only in stories, are now wandering around your world. And even if you manage to exterminate all the zombies, what will become your daily life will likely be completely different from what you once knew.

However, the fact that you survived your experience in the shopping mall is proof that you can handle those changes. Humans can learn and adapt. And that is something that zombies can never do.

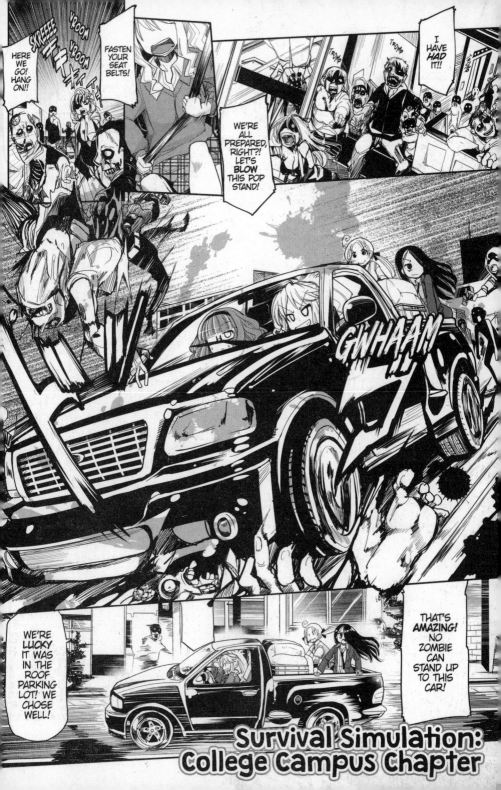

Survival Simulation: College Campus Chapter

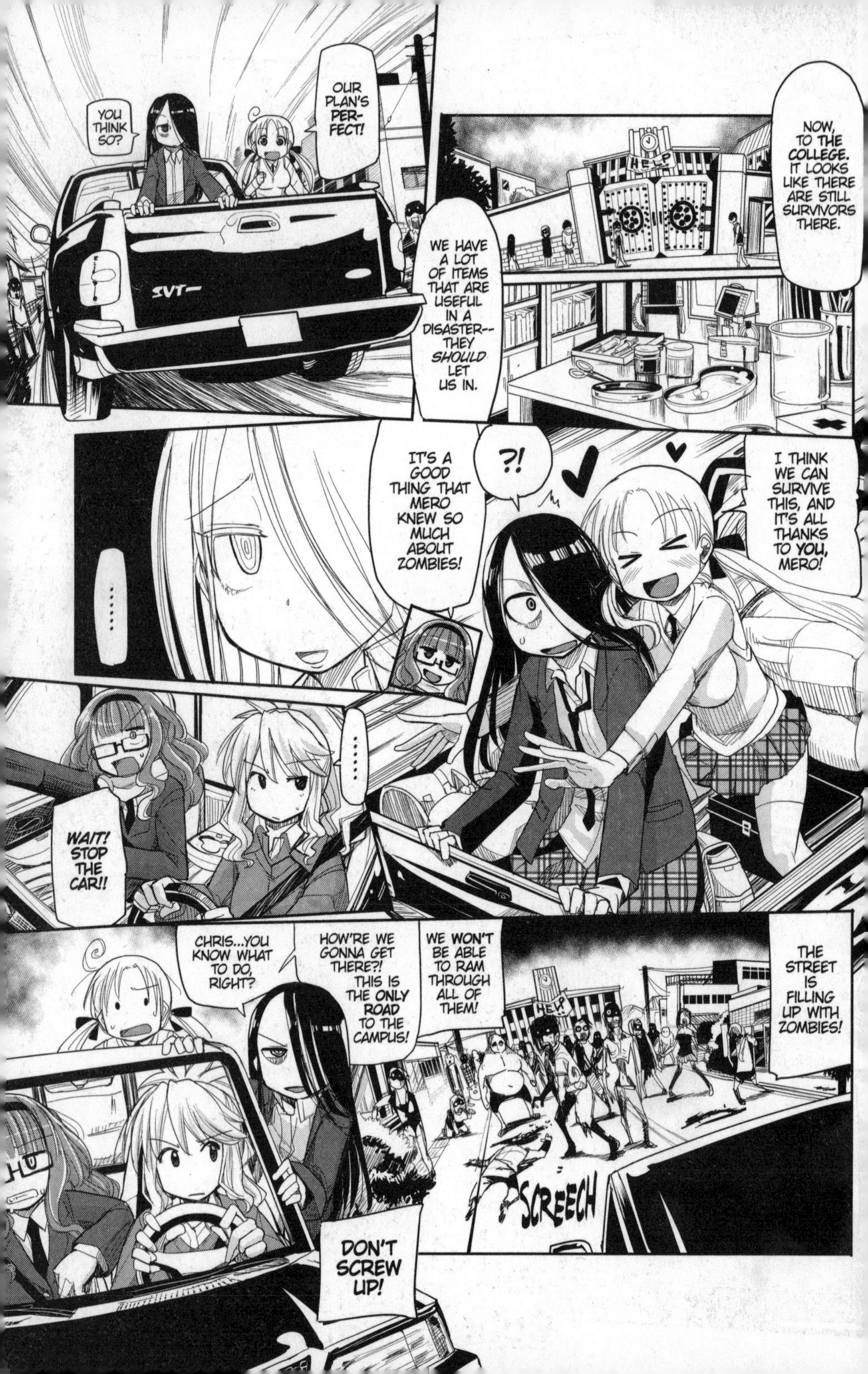
NOW, TO THE COLLEGE. IT LOOKS LIKE THERE ARE STILL SURVIVORS THERE.
HELP
WE HAVE A LOT OF ITEMS THAT ARE USEFUL IN A DISASTER-- THEY SHOULD LET US IN.
OUR PLAN'S PER-FECT!
YOU THINK SO?
I THINK WE CAN SURVIVE THIS, AND IT'S ALL THANKS TO YOU, MERO!
?!
IT'S A GOOD THING THAT MERO KNEW SO MUCH ABOUT ZOMBIES!
......
......
WAIT! STOP THE CAR!!
THE STREET IS FILLING UP WITH ZOMBIES!
WE WON'T BE ABLE TO RAM THROUGH ALL OF THEM!
HOW'RE WE GONNA GET THERE?! THIS IS THE ONLY ROAD TO THE CAMPUS!
CHRIS...YOU KNOW WHAT TO DO, RIGHT?
SCREECH
DON'T SCREW UP!

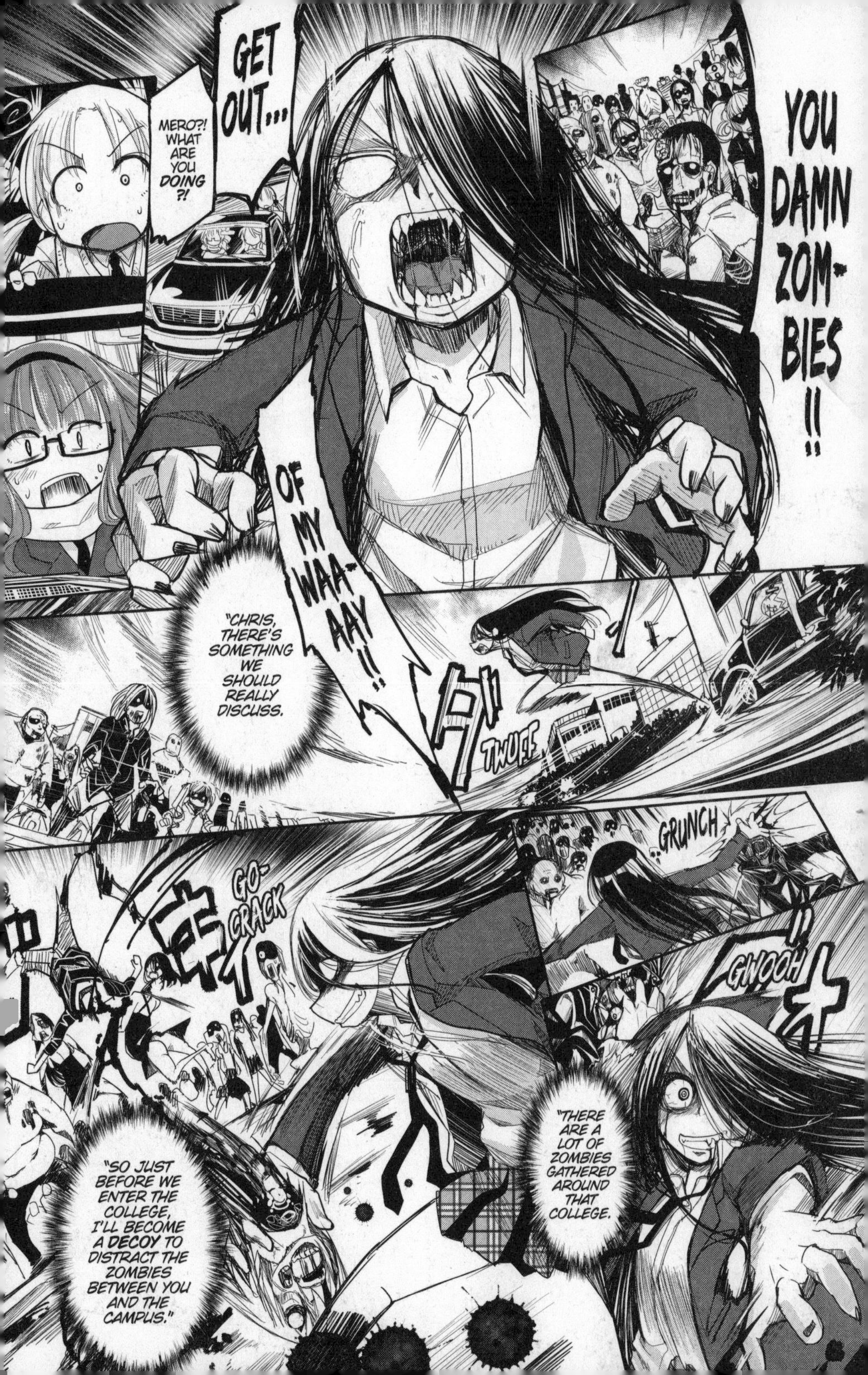
YOU DAMN ZOM-BIES!!
GET OUT...
MERO?! WHAT ARE YOU DOING?!
OF MY WAA-AAY!!
TWUFF
"CHRIS, THERE'S SOMETHING WE SHOULD REALLY DISCUSS.
GRUNCH
GWOOH
"THERE ARE A LOT OF ZOMBIES GATHERED AROUND THAT COLLEGE.
GO-CRACK
"SO JUST BEFORE WE ENTER THE COLLEGE, I'LL BECOME A DECOY TO DISTRACT THE ZOMBIES BETWEEN YOU AND THE CAMPUS."

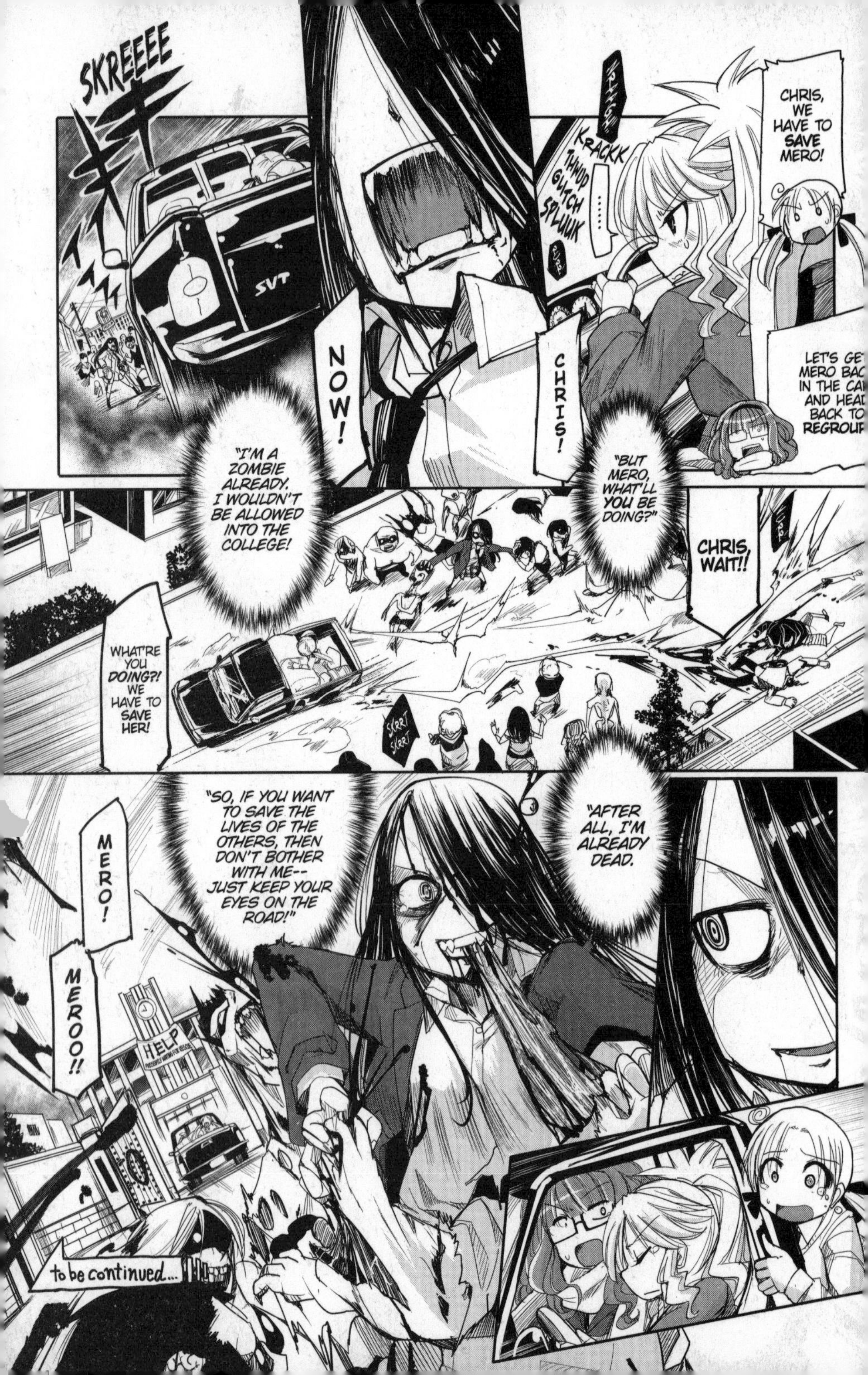

CHRIS, WE HAVE TO SAVE MERO!
LET'S GET MERO BACK IN THE CAR AND HEAD BACK TO REGROUP
KRACKK
THNUD
GLITCH
SPLUUK
......
CHRIS!
NOW!
SKREEEE
"BUT MERO, WHAT'LL YOU BE DOING?"
"I'M A ZOMBIE ALREADY. I WOULDN'T BE ALLOWED INTO THE COLLEGE!
CHRIS, WAIT!!
WHAT'RE YOU DOING?! WE HAVE TO SAVE HER!
SKRRT SKRRT
"AFTER ALL, I'M ALREADY DEAD.
"SO, IF YOU WANT TO SAVE THE LIVES OF THE OTHERS, THEN DON'T BOTHER WITH ME-- JUST KEEP YOUR EYES ON THE ROAD!"
MERO!
MEROO!!
HELP
to be continued...

MERO...! WHY DID YOU HAVE TO GO...?!

 OKAY, SO NEXT IS THE LONG SIEGE ON THE COLLEGE CAMPUS, HUH?

 ?!

 MERO! YOU'RE STILL ALIVE?!

 NO, I'M DEAD, OF COURSE. WHAT DID YOU EXPECT? I *AM* A ZOMBIE, AFTER ALL.

 THEN WHAT WAS WITH ALL THAT TEAR-JERKING FLASHBACK DIALOGUE A PAGE AGO?!

 WELL, THERE'S A MANGA PORTION AND A PROSE/EXPLANATION PORTION. AND THEY EXIST IN A DIFFERENT WORLD, OR TIMELINE, OR...WELL, WHATEVER IS CONVENIENT FOR THE AUTHORS.

 SO HERE, WE CAN SIMPLY PROCEED AS IF YOU'RE JUST THE NORMAL MERO?

 WELL, IF I *WASN'T* HERE, WHO WOULD EXPLAIN EVERYTHING AND PLAY STRAIGHT MAN TO ALL YOUR DUMB REMARKS?

 I SUPPOSE SO...BUT STILL, SOMETHING HERE DOESN'T MAKE SENSE!

 WELL, I'VE GOT COMPLAINTS, TOO! AFTER ALL MY HARD WORK STOCKPILING WEAPONS AND SUPPLIES, NOW I'M OUT OF THE STORY?!

 ANYWAY, WE'VE GOT MERO BACK SAFE AND SOUND!

 OR AT LEAST, ZOMBIFIED AND SOUND.

 BUT BACK TO THE SUBJECT AT HAND--HERE WE HAVE A SITUATION WHERE WE'RE IN FOR A LONG SIEGE AT THE COLLEGE.

 HOW'S THAT ANY DIFFERENT FROM THE MALL?

 FIRST, THERE'S A LOT MORE ROOM ON THE GROUNDS.

 BUT WITH MORE GROUND, WON'T THAT MAKE IT HARDER TO PROTECT?

 IT DEPENDS ON THE UNIVERSITY, BUT MOST JAPANESE COLLEGES ARE SURROUNDED BY HIGH WALLS, LIKE A FORTRESS. THAT GIVES US THE HIGH GROUND, AND IT ALSO HAS SEVERAL GATES WE COULD VENTURE OUT FROM. THAT MIGHT MAKE IT EASIER TO PROTECT.

 IT *IS* A UNIVERSITY, SO WE CAN ASSUME IT WILL HAVE ALL SORTS OF EXPERTS AND FACILITIES.

 OH, I GET IT! LIKE THE MEDICAL COLLEGE SHOULD HAVE, LIKE, DOCTORS AND STUFF?

 IF THERE'S AN AGRICULTURE MAJOR, THEN WE MAY BE ABLE TO DO SOME FARMING.

 IF IT HAS STRONG SCIENCE, TECH, OR LIT DEPARTMENTS, THEN THERE WILL BE A LOT OF OTAKU CLUBS.

 WHOEVER THEY HAVE, WE SHOULD HAVE A LOT MORE SURVIVORS ADDED TO OUR RANKS IN ONE GO!

 WITH MORE PEOPLE, THERE'S BETTER DIVISION OF LABOR. *PRO:* WE COULD TRY SOME BIG PROJECTS. *CONS:* WE'LL NEED LAW AND ORDER, AND WE MAY HAVE TO DEAL WITH PEOPLE WE MIGHT NOT LIKE.

BUT IF A GUY DOESN'T GET ALONG WITH THE OTHER SURVIVORS IN A ZOMBIE MOVIE, THAT USUALLY MEANS HE'LL DIE A TERRIBLE DEATH!

ANOTHER DOOMED TYPE IS THE TYRANNICAL LEADER WHO RULES THROUGH HATE AND OPPRESSION. HE USUALLY GETS STABBED IN THE BACK BY AN ALLY!

ON THE OTHER HAND, THE NICE-GUY SURVIVOR USUALLY GETS A COOL DEATH IN THE FINAL BATTLE, HUH?

RIGHT! SO YOU MEAN ALL THE BAD GUYS WILL DIE FIRST, RIGHT?

I KNOW WHAT YOU'RE TRYING TO SAY, LINA, BUT REMEMBER: THERE'S A PERSON WHO DIED OFF FIRST RIGHT HERE WITH YOU...!

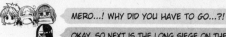 Preparing FOR THE Long Siege

240

Simulation 2: The College Campus

Long-Term Siege Warfare

The second half of our Zombie Survival Simulation will take place on a college campus.

The previous shopping mall simulation assumed that you would be there for no more than a few weeks. This second college campus variation will take place over a somewhat longer period of time. Instead of a few weeks, this simulation assumes you will be there for a few months.

During a period of long-term siege warfare, you will be faced with a more complicated series of obstacles to your survival. How do you deal with depleted food stores, and how will you replenish dwindling supplies? What can be recycled, and how do you recycle it? What items can be refurbished for new purposes? What do you use for fuel and energy? And finally, what happens when you don't have enough medical supplies or medicine?

The biggest problem will be the potential threat posed by large groups of zombies. Depending on the situation, you might find yourself facing several hundred of them at a time.

OUR ASSUMPTIONS ABOUT THE COLLEGE CAMPUS

For this zombie survival situation, we're assuming you are in a good-sized college campus located in a suburb that is some distance from a city's downtown area. By the end of the Showa era (1926-1989), most colleges had moved themselves out from the downtown districts of the big cities to the outskirts of urban areas.

There are quite a few reasons why we chose a college campus on the outskirts of a big city as the stage for our simulation of mid-to-long-term siege warfare and zombie survival.

First, it can accommodate quite a large number of humans. Because of that, there may be a large number of humans with

CHARACTERISTICS OF A COLLEGE CAMPUS

COLLEGE CAMPUSES COME IN ALL SHAPES AND SIZES. WE'RE IMAGINING A SCHOOL BIG ENOUGH TO HOUSE MANY DEPARTMENTS. IDEALLY, THERE'D BE SPECIALISTS WITH EXTENSIVE KNOWLEDGE AND A WIDE RANGE OF EQUIPMENT--PERFECT FOR A LONG-SEIGE SITUATION.

 THEY MIGHT, DEPENDING ON THE SCHOOL, BUT CONSIDERING THAT WE STARTED THIS WHOLE SCENARIO BY RUNNING FROM A HIGH SCHOOL...

 BUT COULDN'T A JUNIOR HIGH OR HIGH SCHOOL SERVE JUST AS WELL?

all sorts of abilities taking refuge there. This will increase your chances of survival. It will have a variety of facilities, which will come in handy at the beginning of a survival situation.

But the most important reason is that the layout of the campus can aid in your defense against zombies. Once the interior of the campus has been cleared of zombies, its wide area and its surrounding fences and walls can be used to keep more zombies out.

In this simulation, humanity's information on zombies was woefully insufficient. As a result, when the zombie outbreak occurred, human society suffered significant damage. Amid the sea of zombies, there are individuals and small groups who are isolated and unable to help one another. That's the situation at the start—humans were disorganized and confused, so zombies were able to crush humanity easily.

Now for this simulation, we're assuming several hundred humans are still alive within the campus.

Defense Against the Zombies

The thing you should prioritize above all else is securing your safety. If you can't defend yourself against zombies, your other survival skills will be meaningless. The most important thing to know is not how to kill zombies, but how to keep zombies from noticing you in the first place.

This simulation is based on Explosive Pandemic-type zombies that are not intelligent. Within the simulation itself, the humans aren't aware of this. However, once a survivor encounters a zombie, they will probably notice their simple, robotic movements, making them aware of the zombies' limited intelligence.

This means that the very first rule of zombie defense is to hide humans—and all traces of human activity—from the zombies' eyes. We mean this quite literally. If there is a fence that blocks a zombie's sight of you, the zombie won't be trying to overcome any obstacles to get to you, since they won't even know you're there.

This is where the large area of land that is a college campus becomes an advantage. If there are no humans near the fences and no human smell that the zombies can detect, then the danger is greatly reduced.

You need to check on any damage to the fence, and you will also need people to watch the fence to be sure that no zombies can breach it. For example, if you use security cameras, you can observe the zombies without them having any knowledge of a human presence.

HOW DO YOU START?

The first thing you'll need to do is confirm any sightings of zombies or people who are at risk of turning into zombies. If you have any zombies on the grounds, you must erect as perfect a defense system around your perimeter as possible. After that,

any zombies remaining on the grounds must be destroyed. The top priority is to check all the humans on the grounds and place any zombified humans in isolation.

In many local disaster-preparedness plans, colleges are often designated as evacuation shelters. It's very likely that quite a lot of people, including the area residents, have gathered together in the local evacuation shelters. And among them, there were almost certainly zombies, or infected people who were about to turn into zombies.

Since we've already covered how to fight zombies during the earliest days of the zombie apocalypse in the Shopping Mall section, we won't repeat any of it here.

Isolating the zombified humans might sound like a half-hearted attempt. It is true that leaving zombies alive on the grounds is a potentially dangerous idea. After all, one of them might get loose or infect one of the people tasked with keeping watch over it. That would be the worst possible outcome. But at this point in a long-term survival situation, it's a necessary risk.

Any human bitten by a zombie will become a zombie. But until that truth has been accepted by all the human survivors, you will need zombified humans as examples.

When you observe an infected person as they become a zombie, you learn how the zombie infection works. It's vital to everyone's survival that they know what zombies really are. And your biggest challenge will be changing what is held inside your fellow humans' hearts.

When people are fighting a desperate, life-or-death battle, the option that provides the greatest chance of survival must be chosen, even if it hurts people's feelings.

But that should only be as a final resort. You should be gathering as much evidence as possible to help convince people of what is really going on. And you need to give them time and space to come to terms with it. This could take a while.

Unlike the shopping mall simulation, there are a lot of

people still alive on the college campus. In the early period of the outbreak, when the nature of the zombies is not yet fully understood, you can't just start mercilessly bashing zombie heads in. This will only engender fear and resistance among the human population, which could lead to infighting within your survivors. There is a very real danger of an insurrection among the members of your group, and this is the worst threat facing survivors during long-term siege warfare.

Of course, a leader who is too indulgent leaves the opportunity for individuals to break off and act on their own, creating a lack of cohesion. On the other hand, controlling through fear is not optimal either, since your people are already afraid of the zombie horde. Their fear of the zombies will be greater than their fear of you.

That's why, until the other survivors can develop a sense of what zombies are, you should simply isolate those humans who turn into zombies. Then, after you've tried doing everything in your power to save them, you dispose of them.

CHECK ON YOUR SUPPLIES

While all of this is important, you should also be keeping careful track of your supplies and equipment. Ask around among the students and faculty to find out where everything is, draw up a map, and take control of the supplies.

A cautionary note at this point: even if it means printing out a hard copy later, you will definitely want these records on paper and kept in a safe place. If you rely on electronic records, you will not be able to access important information when the electricity finally does go out.

Among the things you will want to write down and put safely away are the names of all the survivors within the campus, as well as any pertinent details about people's health and personal attributes. But the most important part of your inventory check is to see what kind of medications you have at your disposal.

Next up is fuel. When gasoline, diesel oil, kerosene, and other fuels run out, you will no longer be able to use any emergency power generators or automobiles. It's possible that the electricity will stay running for a while, but since this particular simulation is concentrating on mid-to-long-term survival, we have to presuppose that the period will come to an end.

And, of course, you have to confirm your stores of food and other emergency supplies. Just how much in the way of stores you will need depends on how many people managed to evacuate to the college campus. If there are a lot of people, then your food will run out quickly. However, food is a comparatively easy commodity to resupply. We'll talk later about resupplying provisions that have run short.

And since this is a siege situation, you can't allow yourself to run out of water. Find out how the city water supply is being delivered. Try to also learn whether you have a supply of fresh water and what condition the storage tanks are in. History teaches us that no matter how strong a castle's walls may be, that castle will fall when the water runs out. The sanitary conditions will deteriorate quickly, making it even more difficult to defend the castle.

You should probably also check out how the infrastructure for the electricity, the city's water supply, and sewers are connected to the areas outside the campus, especially any underground pipes and cables. Be sure to check them thoroughly. It may be possible for zombies to enter the grounds using pipes that have been buried underground, but it also might prove to be your final escape route if the campus is overrun. And if you aren't thorough enough in your investigation, it could lead to ruptured pipes or cut cables when you are trying to dig traps or pitfalls for the zombies.

When the local community uses college facilities as public emergency evacuation shelters, the college campus should have emergency electricity generators and a supply of fuel stored there. You should be able to take advantage of these

energy sources when the infrastructure does break down. Also, many colleges and universities these days are equipped with solar panels for electricity generation.

Even so, they won't be equipped to provide these services for more than a few days. They will have been built on the assumption that help and relief supplies will be delivered quickly after a natural disaster has struck.

It's not a stretch to imagine that people within the evacuation shelter will become zombified, and the electricity generators will be damaged by fire and the like. Repairs will be necessary. Make a list of all the parts you'll to need to repair them.

CONSTRUCTING YOUR FENCE

You will need to build fences to keep the zombies out as soon as you possibly can.

In zombie movies and other entertainment, zombies tend to mass around the very spot where the humans take shelter, led by human sounds or smells. No matter how many zombies the humans kill, they keep coming and pushing forward. In the end, the walls cannot handle the pressure; they will inevitably be breached, and the zombies will come flooding in. Every zombie story ends this way.

However, consider the movement of zombies. If there weren't already hordes of zombies in that location in the first place, there is no way that tens of thousands of zombies would be trying to push those walls down.

This could only work if, as the Explosive Pandemic-type zombies were laying waste to human civilization, the zombies were able to somehow gather all nearby zombies to them whenever they met with human resistance. In Japan, there are mountain passes, tunnels, or even bridges that can serve as lines of resistance.

The zombies would have to gather more zombies to attack the line of resistance until it could not hold out any longer,

allowing them to eventually break through. At this point, if they are unable to bring down the tunnel or collapse the bridge, then the zombies move on to the next place that humans are defending, travelling en masse in search of any place where humans are still holding out.

The concept behind this simulation is that you are holed up on a college campus, and you still have some time until the horde of zombies arrive.

It's possible that there isn't much time before the zombies come, or that there was a large outbreak of zombies in the evacuation shelters, or even that the college itself was the origin of the zombie outbreak in the first place. In any of these scenarios, the odds are overwhelmingly high that the college will fall to the zombies. In any of these cases, any chance of survival will already be lost. You would have to evacuate the campus immediately and find some other place where you could try and survive.

Since you have some time, you will need to build some fences. That might seem easy, but it isn't. Even though there won't yet be a massive numbers of zombies, the zombies that *are* there will be on the attack, and you'll have to construct the fences while fending them off.

The top priority is to set up the fence so that the zombies are unable to sense the humans they are so compelled to attack. It will need to appear that there are no humans left on campus. If all you need to do is obstruct their vision, this can be achieved by hanging canvas sheets over the gate, the fences, and any other places one can see through. That should be plenty.

But time is not on your side here. As you fight off or drive away the sporadic zombies, the main force of the gathered zombies will be on their way. You'll need to isolate the campus long before they arrive.

If you've done the necessary isolation work properly, the main force of zombies should not even notice your campus

CONSTRUCTING THE FENCE

IF WE'RE GOING TO LIVE HERE A LONG TIME, I *DON'T* WANT TO SEE THOSE SCARY ZOMBIES! IT MAKES IT SO MUCH EASIER WHEN I DON'T HAVE TO DEAL WITH THE IDEA THAT ZOMBIES MAY BE *LOOKING* AT ME!

BUT YOU'LL NEED TO CHECK ON THE FENCE REGULARLY AFTER YOU'VE BUILT IT. THE FACT THAT THEY CAN'T SEE YOU ALSO MEANS THAT *YOU* CAN'T SEE ANY NEARBY ZOMBIES, EITHER, SO BE CAREFUL!

IF YOU'VE SEEN ZOMBIES BEING ATTRACTED BY THE SIGHT OF HUMANS, YOU SHOULD ERECT *FENCES* TO KEEP THEM FROM GETTING CLOSE.

TO BLOCK THEIR VIEW OF THE CAMPUS GROUNDS, YOU CAN COVER THE FENCE WITH CANVAS SHEETS OR LARGE WOODEN BOARDS. BLACKOUT CURTAINS ARE ANOTHER OPTION-- YOU CAN FIND THOSE IN MANY COLLEGE BUILDINGS.

TRUE, BUT NOT HAVING TO LOOK AT ZOMBIES IS GOOD FOR A HUMAN SURVIVOR'S MENTAL HEALTH. BUT THAT DOESN'T MEAN THEY SHOULD LET THEIR GUARD DOWN.

IT WON'T PREVENT ZOMBIES FROM AMASSING IF THEY'RE ATTRACTED TO SOUNDS OR SMELLS THOUGH, RIGHT?

grounds. The main zombie force should simply walk around the campus without even trying to enter it, as long as there isn't anything to draw them there. They should just move on to the next spot that is occupied by humans.

Of course, even if the zombie horde does move on, not all of the zombies will necessarily move along with it. And a sudden gust of wind can topple a fence. You must always be vigilant.

PARTIES

By putting up fences, you will have already secured a certain amount of physical safety for the time being. But there will still be psychological dangers. There will be men and women of all ages gathered in a disorganized group inside the college, and some will eventually break under the mental stress.

After all, zombies were once humans. These humans have now become monsters, and begun to attack other people. Family, friends, and loved ones have become monsters and attacked you. And, in the end, you might become a monster yourself.

When humans are confronted with such awful thoughts, they can become nihilistic. This can lead to self-destruction.

Even if you have managed to secure a temporary safety, the anxieties will start to creep in again after the major work has been done. At that point, the thoughts that they were too busy to entertain earlier will come crashing in, and they will start thinking about their lack of a future.

During the Age of Discovery, this was what led to so many attempted mutinies during extended-term voyages on seafaring vessels. The length of the voyages meant there was plenty of time for the sailors to turn those worries over and over in their heads. Also, squabbles and hurt feelings can fester, leading to a larger build-up of anxieties that could culminate in violent action being taken.

In a certain sense, some tension and arguments are unavoidable. But by the time someone points at someone else and falsely accuses them of being a zombie, it may already be too late.

After going through all the effort of creating a fence that hides you from zombie eyes (and ears and noses), all that effort will be rendered meaningless if someone suddenly bursts out and tries to make a run for it.

One thing we suggest is to find time to get people together and celebrate, so they can be thanked for all their hard work and cooperation. This would be a good opportunity to take perishable foods and distribute them liberally. It's also important to have music. Have everyone sing together, and perhaps play party games. If you can create a bit of fun during these parties, it will allow people to endure a little while longer.

Tactics for Survival

Early on, around the time that you and your group are building your defenses, you will begin to see who would make a good leader. You will also see who comprises the group that will be in support of that leader. And if nature is allowed to take its course, this group might eventually develop into an organization of some kind. But if it is at all possible, we suggest that you quickly push for an organization centered around a leader.

Unlike the shopping mall, there will be a lot more survivors on the college campus. But if they aren't structured into some sort of organization, there will be frequent outbreaks of trouble based on the interpersonal relationships within the group. Those can result in splits that may eventually lead to the group's collapse.

ORGANIZING

This will be different depending on the nature of the collection of people that are with you, but if your group is made up of people with a diverse range of age and genders, the first thing to do will be to establish the person with the highest authority on top: someone like a college professor, a politician, or someone else who had a degree of clout before the crisis.

You will want someone at the top who has experience representing people and making leadership decisions. However, if there is no one around with both authority and ability, you will have to resort to watching for someone to display leadership abilities within the group.

But whether a leader starts at the top or rises up from the crowd, having an able leader in the first stages is extremely important. You don't just need authority to be organized; you will also need a force to back it up. A security force will need to be formed.

Our present society crumbled beneath the swarms of zombies. Even so, it doesn't mean that it will suddenly degenerate into a Mad Max-style lawless age. It will likely be something in

between. There will be people who will publicly show no resistance to the rules, while secretly committing thefts or acts of violence towards children, the elderly, and other weaker survivors.

You will need to stop the slide into immorality and restore order to the group, and a security force will be indispensible for that. Your security force should consist of a collection of young, robust people. Their mission will be to maintain order among the survivors and to drive off zombies. If someone in your group was a police officer or security guard before the crisis, then that person should be the force's leader and instructor.

It's best to equip your security force with uniforms of some kind. The best kind is a uniform that includes a characteristic style that is recognizable as a security force member, even in silhouette. A distinctive hat will also help the uniform to stand out. If it looks imposing at even just a glance, then it will be easier to maintain order. Those who may otherwise be prone to violence will hopefully be inclined to resolve their problems peacefully instead.

Train your security force in patrolling the campus and in anti-zombie battle methods. It's a duty that will bring with it physical demands and dangers, so the security force should receive priority access to food and other supplies.

Once you have a security force patrolling the area, you must start creating a list of survivors. Check the list carefully for those who have medical licenses, licenses to operate heavy equipment, or experience in handling hazardous materials. Also, make sure to check for those who have special skills, like electricians.

Take special note of the health conditions of all the survivors. Of course, there will be some who are stricken with chronic illnesses, but there should be others who are experiencing physical problems related to the stress of the situation.

Ask all the evacuees if they have friends or family who are missing, and record their responses. Society will still be in the process of breaking down, so it's important to preserve and

increase the smallest units of society, and that is family.

Much like your list of supplies, make sure this is all recorded physically on paper. Don't forget to keep it in a safe place.

MAINTAINING A DAILY EXISTENCE

When you are isolated, humans under stress will start fighting among each other. Because of that, this small society will be in constant danger of crumbling. To keep this from happening, you will want to create a routine that mimics everyday life. If children and the elderly have order and routine in their new lives, this can help their will to keep up the struggle.

On the other hand, if their new lives are lacking this kind of structure, then they may become disheartened and lose any sort of ambition. There will be few people who will last long under the strain of living in a world surrounded by zombies, if they have no sense of purpose in their lives.

So how can you give them that sense of purpose?

▶ **PATROL:** When we say "patrol," we don't mean patrolling the outer walls where the zombies are. That job belongs to the security force.

The civilians will patrol the campus interior. Has anything broken down? Has anything happened that will make people's lives more difficult? Patrolling and checking on these things is an important task. While this situation lasts, it will be up to the people who are now on campus to do everything for themselves. For this, you will need to have detailed information coming in.

▶ **CLEANING AND TRASH REMOVAL:** Cleaning is vital to everyone's health and hygiene. Not just cleaning, mind you: you will need a well-planned and well-maintained place to dispose of your trash, and you mustn't forget to have it carried there on a regular basis. When trash builds up to a point where it can be seen by the rest of the community, it's a sure sign that morale is low.

► **STUDIES:** It's best to educate the children as well as possible. One of the problems with long-term survival is that the zombie apocalypse will have drastically decreased the human population, and many of the necessary people with the skills and knowledge that helped the culture to thrive will now be gone. The future will require as many reasonably well-educated people as it can get.

Even in the short term, providing the children with an education will help to maintain the regularity of their daily lives. The education of the young is an investment in the future. As such, it will have the added benefit of showing that you, as a society, believe that you have a future.

Even if that future won't be anything like the recent past, it's still extremely important to maintain a feeling that

ORGANIZING & DAILY LIFE

ONWARD AND UPWARD!

ONCE THINGS HAVE CALMED DOWN A BIT, YOU SHOULD START WORKING ON CHOOSING A LEADER AND GETTING THE SURVIVORS ORGANIZED.

ONE THING THAT IS VITAL TO DAILY LIFE IS TO MAKE SURE EACH PERSON HAS SOME KIND OF JOB TO DO. THE WORK ITSELF WILL GIVE *PURPOSE* TO THE WORKERS.

WHEN YOU'RE PREPARING FOOD FOR EVERYBODY, YOU FORGET THAT YOU'RE LIVING AMONG GROSS ZOMBIES, HUH?

SECURITY

A SECURITY FORCE WILL BE NEEDED TO FIGHT THE ZOMBIES AND MAINTAIN ORDER, BUT COOKING AND CLEANING DETAILS WILL BE NEEDED AS WELL.

 WELL, IF YOU THINK OF THE LEADER AS THE MONARCH AND THE SECURITY FORCES AS BOTH THE ARMY AND THE POLICE, IT IS A LOT LIKE BUILDING A SMALL COUNTRY. WE DON'T WANT THIS DESCENDING INTO AN END-OF-THE-WORLD DICTATORSHIP SCENARIO, SO THIS IS NECESSARY.

IT'S KIND OF LIKE PLAYING *RISK* OR PRETENDING YOU'RE THE PRESIDENT OR SOMETHING!

your people can return to some semblance of a normal life through study and testing.

▶ **FOOD PRODUCTION:** In this simulation, we don't have any special hypotheses regarding what happened before the collapse of civilization. We're figuring that the siege warfare on the college campus involves a time period of maybe six months to a year.

But food production is extremely important, even a few months in. Your food stores will gradually dwindle, and if all you do is watch it lessen, then you're bound to feel enormous stress over it. Even if you aren't able to grow as much food as you actually need, the fact that you are successfully growing any food at all will provide a big boost to morale.

Besides, since the amount of perishable food and vegetables you would have been able to eat would be either eaten or rotted early on in the crisis, it would have been easy to grow tired of the food stores that were left. Then, when the green veggies from a vegetable garden (which can be harvested in a relatively short time) can be added to the dinner plate, they will bring with them a bit of emotional satisfaction. Even adding the slightest coloring to a monotonous mealtime can bring a richness to the spirit.

MAINTAINING HEALTH AND HYGIENE

Properly dealing with bathing, laundry, and bodily wastes is not only hygienic, but can also reduce stress. Also, bathing and doing laundry reduce body odors, which can be a big advantage. If zombies are attracted by human smells, then bathing and washing your clothes will attract much less zombie attention. Consider it a necessary act for your continued survival.

Since the water system itself is relatively robust and able to better withstand the collapse of civilization caused by the zombie contagion, you can expect the water infrastructure to last quite a ways into your long-term survival.

However, if a zombie falls into one of the locations that provide your local district with water, drinking that water could turn you into a zombie. It might be difficult to find a way to check the water quality, but check it periodically if you are able.

If you have no machines to test the water and no chemical methods of purifying it, you may try testing it with freshwater fish such as goldfish. Have the children tend them, and if there are some problems with the fishes' health, have the children report it to you immediately.

But for the reasons above, it's vital to store water. Ideally, you would have water tanks specifically made for storing water, but other options include filling a pool or other similar installation with water and covering it with panels and the like to prevent contamination. And, apart from drinking water, you will want water for use in bathing and washing your clothes.

For bodily waste, use the sewers if they are still functioning. If the sewers aren't working, then disposing of bodily waste is a problem that must be prioritized on the level of food and water. If the college campus has a spot to dump waste set aside, use that spot until it becomes full. Once it is full, choose a spot as far away as possible from the places where people live and work, and dig a hole. Then bring your garbage there, and throw it in the hole.

After that, you will have to be careful near that spot because of the smells it will give off. Just like trash, you will have to carefully dispose of bodily waste as well, because living within smelling distance of human waste will cause morale to sharply drop. If zombies are attracted to strong smells, then you will have to fill up the trash hole you've just dug immediately after you've put your trash into it.

The longer your siege lasts, the more important it will be for you to be able to take showers. If you are in a location like Japan where the summer climate is extremely hot and humid, the ability to bathe will become an essential component in maintaining your health.

For decent baths, you will need a way to create large amounts of warm water. And in those facilities, your supplies of electricity or gas will be indispensable. In the short term, you can cut down trees and shrubbery both inside the campus and out to provide some extra fuel. But in the long term, you will need to come up with a sustainable supply of electricity or gas.

CONSTRUCTING YOUR DEFENSIVE LINE AND TRAINING

The integrity of your defensive line is one of your highest priorities. In the early days of your survival on campus, you will have constructed fences to isolate the campus from the outside and to prevent zombies from noticing human activity. That was one form of defensive line.

From now on, the foundation of your defenses will take the form of continuing to keep the zombies from being aware of you. But, at some point the massive horde of zombies will come. If they realize humans are on the campus, that fence will not hold them back.

The human form, the human smell, the sounds emitted by humans—you should do your best to make sure that these things do not escape beyond the campus fences. If the zombies realize humans are there, they will start to gather near your campus.

If a zombie happens to come across the campus gate and finds it shut tight, then the zombie will probably just turn around and find a new direction in which to shamble. But in long-term siege warfare, there will be some time when reconnaissance inevitably comes up short. At some point when somebody is either coming in or going out of the gate on a supply run, a zombie will be there.

That's when you will have attracted the zombie's attention, and suddenly a group of between several dozen and several hundred zombies will try to break through your fences. They will try over and over, and you have to assume that at some point they will breach your walls.

CONSTRUCTING LINES OF DEFENSE

That's why you have to strengthen your defensive line.

The first thing you need to do is clear the lines of sight all over campus. You should cut down all the trees and shrubberies on the campus.

Set up an observation post on the roofs of certain buildings and observe how the zombies in the vicinity move around. Make sure that no human form can be seen directly, even from the observation post. Use camouflage or eye slits to observe.

With that preparation done, you can now set traps in the main traffic lanes that the zombies will likely follow.

You will also need obstacles for the zombies, but when we say "obstacles," we don't mean huge barricades. Use wire entanglements and the like. You only need to make them high enough to prevent the zombies from getting over them.

Those obstacles will restrict the zombie's movement, so the zombies have no choice but to shamble down the open pathway toward the interior of the campus. And as the zombies

are guided down that path, they will find your traps waiting for them.

The most basic trap is the pitfall. Dig a large number of holes in advance, and guide the zombies down that lane. It will cause problems if one trap becomes so full of zombies that they overflow, so use obstacles to guide zombies to different holes. Keep count of how many fall in each hole. When one hole fills up, use the obstacles to guide them to the next pitfall. For that purpose, you will need some movable barricades.

You can also use block and tackle and move things along rails. You can drop large obstacles from upper floors to close off certain paths. Figure out what barricades you can make in each location from the materials on hand. It's also very important to thoroughly train and drill the people who will be moving the obstacles.

If you're going to do battle within the campus, you will need a safe place to hide the non-combatants, as well as having routes for the battling security forces and messengers to go through without ever having to encounter a zombie on the way. Be sure to construct safe passages specifically for these purposes. Connect the second floors of two buildings with things like ladders, and make them safe enough so that people can move through them.

Also, you need to thoroughly train your battle participants so that they can still move quickly through the passages at night with no illumination.

More important than any battle with a zombie is establishing that, when things start to go wrong, you know where to go and to whom to report. Or, if it's necessary, each individual must be prepared to break formation and follow a pre-arranged escape route.

Everyone should know what to do in times of battle, and be trained so thoroughly that their bodies know what to do even before they have a chance to think about it.

OBSERVING AND ANALYZING ZOMBIES

Before you can figure out the correct defensive plan and the proper methods of training, you need comprehensive knowledge of the zombies and their behavior.

Assuming it's been several weeks since you first holed up on the campus, and that public television, radio, and other aspects of the information infrastructure are still holding up, then you can learn a lot of useful information from that area.

From here on out, we will explain what to do when you cannot collect any information from the outside world. The most important thing to learn from your observations is the movement patterns and physical capabilities of the zombies.

In a defensive battle against zombies, the most important thing is to not engage in combat with them. Rather, you should focus on leading them into traps. To do that, you need to check their reactions to see which external stimuli they are attracted to:

- Light
- Sound
- Smell

You should devote top priority to investigating what senses will trigger a zombie's attack reaction, and whether those senses can be used to lure them in. You should also try other methods such as mannequins, photos, reflections, recorded human voices, and any other sounds or stimuli you can think of that will attract a zombie's attention the way a human does, only without an actual human presence.

Once you have a definite method of attracting zombies, you should try to capture one. Dress a mannequin in human clothes, and have the zombie attack it from within a cage. Take a video of it to see just how quickly the zombie movies, and estimate the power and ferocity of the zombie's attack on its prey.

After it's over, check out the mannequin to see how much pressure the zombie's jaw has in its biting force, how much strength is in the zombie's hand as it

CHAPTER 5

OBSERVING ZOMBIES

 SO, THE POINT IS TO LEARN THE BEHAVIOR AND ABILITIES OF ZOMBIES, AND THEN BUILD TRAPS AND CONSTRUCT OUR DEFENSIVE TACTICS ACCORDINGLY.

 WE TOUCHED ON ZOMBIE SENSES IN CHAPTER 4, BUT HERE WE'VE REACHED THE STAGE WHERE WE TAKE WHAT WE LEARNED BY OBSERVING THE ZOMBIES AND PUT IT TO USE IN BATTLE.

grabs, and how hard the zombie's nails actually are. This information will help you determine which defensive clothing is most effective in hand-to-hand combat.

Although this is a lower priority, you should also add into your investigations just what caused an outbreak of zombies in the first place. What is allowing the dead to move? Can it be reversed? These are questions that will allow all of human society to prevent the creation of more zombies and eventually eradicate zombies altogether. Whatever answers you do find, though, will not provide aid in the more pressing needs of survival.

After all, since the problem has taken the form of walking, hungry corpses, it's already gone well beyond the realms of science. It's best to think that the basic principles behind zombification can only be found in corners of science that man has

yet to even think of exploring. Also, considering the years of observation and discovery that went into the scientific exploration of a theory like nuclear fusion, as an example, you might reasonably conclude that we still have an extremely long way to go before science can discover how the dead walk again. Expecting science to discover this secret and deliver an answer to the problem within just a few months of siege warfare is setting some unrealistically high expectations.

RECONNAISSANCE AND RESUPPLY

Zombie survival is basically siege warfare. You are defending against a siege of zombies, but you can't win by simply keeping the zombies from ever getting in. Here, winning means staying alive.

In human-versus-human siege warfare, the besieging troops fear for their own safety. The larger the besieging force, the more food they have to consume, which places a burden on the supply corps. If it can't hold out, the attacking force has to withdraw. And in past ages of combat, infectious diseases could also sap one side's military might.

But an army of zombies doesn't need supplies. They can stay on the attack virtually forever, keeping up the siege for as long as it takes. And, of course, dead people don't get sick. It is possible that the zombies will probably do significant damage to their own bodies over the course of time, finally resulting in their inability to move at all. But it won't happen quickly enough to do you any good.

On the other hand, supplies among the besieged will be a fragile commodity.

To continue to defend against enemy forces, the besieged need food, water, emergency stores of fuel, and all of these things will eventually start to run short. The number of weapons will be practically zero, and you won't have enough building materials. The people inside the "fortress" may become a disorderly mob.

RECONNAISSANCE & RESUPPLY (MOVEMENT BEYOND CAMPUS)

IT'S BETTER TO DO MANY SMALL RECONNAISSANCE AND RESUPPLY MISSIONS THAN ONE BIG ONE. AN IRONCLAD RULE IN ZOMBIE MOVIES IS THAT THE PEOPLE WHO OVEREXTEND THEMSELVES OR GET TOO COCKY USUALLY WIND UP DEAD.

When these factors add up, they can result in the loss of the "fortress." Unless these weaknesses are addressed, the longer the siege goes on, the more likely it becomes that this college campus will fall. Even if you are not attacked by zombies, you simply won't be able to function inside the walls anymore. The only option left will be to run away from there.

Those are the weaknesses you must overcome, and to do that, you must be proactive in reconnaissance and re-provisioning your supplies. Do your reconnaissance during the day. Strike out in the morning, and maintain a schedule by which you will be sure to return before evening. Use bicycles or motorcycles to get around. There is no guarantee that the roads will be clear enough for four-wheeled vehicles.

Be sure to check out the surrounding area as much as possible before setting out. Use your observation posts on the

roofs of buildings or from windows. Aside from that, if there is a radio-controlled drone with a camera attachment handy, you can fly it around and check out the vicinity.

With regular observations of the area around the campus, you will be able to tell if there are more zombies than usual, and whether this will present a danger to your recon teams At that point, you may consider luring the zombies to some other location before sending out your reconnaissance missions.

Your reconnaissance missions should be trying to learn how many zombies are in the vicinity. They should also be doing preliminary work to ascertain likely places to resupply.

For fuel, look for gas stations. For food and clothing, watch for supermarkets and shopping malls. For drugs and other medical supplies, keep an eye out for hospitals and pharmacies. For farming tools, check the hardware stores.

Some of these places will have already been looted, while others may have burned down or otherwise destroyed. Others still may have large numbers of zombies wandering around inside them, so it will be hard to determine their suitability with just one reconnaissance check.

When your best resupply spot is a long ways away, you must prepare against meeting zombies on your journey. You will want to confirm several different routes, and you'll determine the success of the reconnaissance mission based on how many hiding spots you can find hide and wait for zombies to pass, along with spots where you can stash your supplies on the way.

Break the reconnaissance mission into a series of shorter missions, and then send out the resupply team that this was all in preparation for. When sending out your resupply team, give them a list of priority items to collect. They should work from the highest priority items down the list, and if zombies start to gather, they should withdraw. They should take the collected supplies to a predetermined storage location, then leave them there and beat a fast retreat. Supply runs should be done in

many steps as well. Even if you can gather all the supplies you need in one or two trips, short, repeated bursts of activity will help your team gain valuable experience. You will also increase the chances of successful supply runs.

With the exception of emergency runs for medical supplies, you should challenge yourself to a number of short, easy runs.

CONTACT AND COOPERATION WITH OUTSIDE GROUPS

In mid-to-long-term siege-warfare survival situations, while the information infrastructure is still up and working with TV and radio broadcasts, you should be able to gather a lot of information on local zombie movements and obtain quite a bit of survival knowhow.

That was true of the early-stage survival in the shopping mall, but it was still early days. We were assuming it was hard to find useful information online from the general public because of the chaos. In a college campus, you may not be able to count on supplies, but you can reasonably expect to count on some expertise in information.

One vital thing you need is advice that those survivors on campus with you cannot give. If there are no doctors on campus at the time, then they can't give advice on diagnosis and treatment. Also, knowledge about weather forecasting will also help.

Needless to say, Japan has experienced earthquakes, typhoons and other disasters. Zombies could be thought of as another disaster of this type. Although zombies are tougher than humans, they aren't able to decide for themselves to evacuate in the event of a natural disaster. When such a disaster hits, it will reduce the zombies' numbers. After a disaster would be the best time to go on reconnaissance and resupply missions.

But be careful, there may be a zombie buried under the rubble who could still try to take a bite of your leg. Whoever goes out will need boots that are able to withstand the pressure of a zombie's bite.

Defense Tactics Against Zombies

Let's assume that you are holed up on a college campus, that zombies have appeared, and that you will need to fight them.

There are two ways of combating zombie forces, depending on the strength of the force that is attacking you. In the first one, you can lure zombies in to reduce their numbers, and in the second one, you can deal with a larger-scale zombie attack.

A SMALL-TO-MID-SIZE GROUP OF ZOMBIES LURED IN AND EXTERMINATED

When a small-to-mid-sized force of zombies starts wandering around the perimeter of your campus, one way of waging defensive warfare is to entice them in and eradicate them.

There are two good reasons why you would lure them onto your base.

The first is that you can attack after all your preparations have been made. We're not simply talking about arranging your security forces to take on the zombies, but also going into battle with the knowledge that all non-combatants are safely away in some sort of evacuation shelter.

The second pattern is to take the battle initiative yourself. If you go out and do battle on a bright, sunny morning, you may be able to finish up the battle before the afternoon's over. You pick your battles on nice, sunny days because if something goes wrong, you have the best sightlines possible.

Before the battle starts, check the location and strength of your barricades. Also, confirm that your communication devices work in the area and that people are on standby in case the communication devices don't work. Call a briefing and go over all the steps in the mission, what kind of trouble you should expect, and what common-sense steps you can take if and when trouble arises. Try to reduce the number of spontaneous decisions you need to make during the operation.

Once all preparations are complete, open a portion of the fence and lure the zombies in. You should only lure in a small

number of zombies, ten at the most. Once they're through, have helpers close off the barricade again to stop the rest of the zombies from entering. If there's some defect in the barricade, don't fight it—let them through. You will have set up movable backup barricades for just such an occasion. Pitfalls will be waiting for the zombies.

You will need bait or some other kind of decoy for the traps. This is where the knowledge gained through your observation and experience of the zombies comes in useful. If they hunt purely by sight, then a mannequin or other human-like form should lure in the zombies. If they react to sounds, use a music player to entice the zombies to your trap.

But, if they sense life forces or have some other sense that is difficult to pinpoint, then you will have to put someone in danger and get them to stand near the pit to lure the zombies in. If that's the case, you will need to set up some sort of plan that will allow the person playing the bait to escape effectively.

You may not even need to hide the trap at all. Review your observations of zombie behavior. If zombies have many individual characteristics, then you may need to set up multiple traps and lure each zombie into the one they would most likely fall into. It may be a lot of extra work, but it's work you must put in. It's better to prepare a trap and not need it than to need a trap and not have it prepared.

We say that the pitfall is the most basic trap, but you might also lead the zombies into a narrow passageway, block them off using movable barricades, and then attack their heads from above via the second floor or the building-to-building overpasses. Use stones you can throw and long poles to attack. Assuming that the college campus is rather large, you may be able to set effective fire traps as well.

Battle tactics are the same as they were in the shopping mall. Use traps to hunt your zombies. Launch one-sided attacks from a place where their nails and jaws can't reach you. If, for any reason, you do find yourself in a place where their nails or jaws can

reach, you need to run. At that point, you should have one combatant held in reserve with a large shield-like item, to assist in your escape. Hopefully the shield is one you can afford to throw away, and if you're the one who's wielding the shield, you can abandon it and run once your comrade has escaped.

No matter what kind of trap you make, there will be a limit to the number of zombies the trap can hold. Someone behind the action should be counting how many zombies enter a trap. Once it's full they should signal the commander, who will then give the order to close off the path and direct the next zombies to the next trap.

This is all quite similar to how defensive battles played out in castles during Japan's history. They used moats, canals, and stone walls to restrict the enemy's movements to certain paths, and they built their gates and other vital areas into areas of overwhelming advantage for themselves.

Because both sides are human in a battle around a castle, the attacking troops can use bows or guns to support their allies or engineers to fill up moats or otherwise render fortifications useless. But here, you're up against an enemy who cannot use tools or intelligence, so you have a distinct advantage. On the other hand, zombies don't retreat after suffering damage. Every single zombie is, quite literally, a soldier who isn't afraid to die since they are already dead. If they have the numbers, they can overcome any moat or other obstacle by filling them in their own bodies.

The entire reason for this bait-and-trap battle strategy is to increase the safety in the vicinity of the campus and to prevent the zombies from building up into a zombie horde.

When you're heading out on reconnaissance or resupply missions, you must never get cocky or let your guard down. If a zombie near the campus gate happens to see you, the sight, sound, or smell of you could stimulate a group of massed zombies to come toward campus, which will bring other zombies to the attack.

CHAPTER 5

BATTLING ZOMBIES (LURE IN AND EXTERMINATE)

 MAKE SURE YOU'VE CALCULATED HOW MANY ZOMBIES YOU LET IN TO MAKE SURE THEY DON'T OVERWHELM YOUR TRAPS. THEN, BEFORE EACH PITFALL GETS TOO FULL, MAKE SURE YOU MOVE THE BARRICADES EARLY AND LEAD THE ZOMBIES TO THE NEXT TRAP. IT'S A PROACTIVE TACTIC, BUT YOU HAVE TO BE PREPARED FOR *EVERY* CONTINGENCY!

That's what these small-to-mid-size battles with the zombies are for. They allow the combat-ready people on campus to reduce the overall threat level by luring in a number they can handle and finishing them off.

ATTACK BY A LARGE-SCALE HORDE OF ZOMBIES

A series of unfortunate coincidences, a mistake on the part of your reconnaissance teams, or some other mishap has brought a horde of hundreds of zombies to surround your campus. At this point, it is impossible for you to send out reconnaissance teams or resupply teams. And something has clued the zombies in to the fact that there are humans on campus, so they are attacking the campus from all sides.

A siege by a large-scale horde of zombies is the most dangerous scenario in all of siege warfare. Depending on how the battle

goes, your campus could be overrun by shambling zombies, causing your "fortress" to fall.

The battle tactics against a large-scale horde of zombies are the same as with a small-to-mid-sized invasion. You lure them into traps. But in this instance, you need to prepare for what to do when the traps can't hold them all anymore.

There are troubles on the battlefield, too. When facing a horde of zombies, the weakest part of your fence will fall, allowing them to pour in. If your guards aren't careful, they may be turned into zombies and attack their former comrades, forcing chaos in the ranks. Then your traps will be overrun, and other systems will fail as well.

This is when you call in a group that you've set aside for just such an occasion—your reserves. What the reserves are ordered to do depends on the commander. If communications break down and you cannot receive orders from the commander, then the reserves' executive officer has to make the decisions. The reserves' executive officer has trained and equipped his people to offer support in the battle against the zombies.

Even if the reserve troops don't use traps, they still try to avoid any close contact with the zombies. Use guns, bows, or any thrown tool to attack the zombies from a distance. For that reason, the reserves should be made up of people who are skilled with weapons or people who possess other skills that go beyond the average Japanese person.

In an attack by a large-scale horde of zombies, the zombies will probably take complete control of the grounds while invading the ground floors of buildings, so that's what we'll assume has happened now. You need to prepare your living quarters for this eventuality. You will need to move at least the most vital living sections on campus at a moment's notice from the first floor to the second floor and quickly install barricades at any access points to that floor. Access from the second floor of your main building to a second floor of a neighboring building should be accessed only by ladder-bridges that can be

WHAT DO YOU DO IF A ZOMBIE HORDE INVADES?!

I DON'T LIKE THINKING ABOUT IT, BUT WE HAVE TO. WE HAVE TO DECIDE WHAT KIND OF MOVES WE'LL NEED TO MAKE IF THE UNTHINKABLE HAPPENS.

WHETHER YOU FIGHT OR RUN, YOU'RE NOT GOING TO BE ABLE TO USE COORDINATED MOVEMENTS WITH YOUR GROUP LIKE YOU USED TO! THIS COULD BE TROUBLE...!

retracted after use, so that zombies cannot follow. You will, of course, have to block the elevators.

Even if the ground floors have been occupied by zombies, you should be able to continue the siege for at least a little longer if you can escape to the second floor.

This is where the commander must make the decision. Do you continue the fight for the campus, planning to destroy all the zombies who have gotten onto the grounds? Or do you give up on the base and make your escape?

If your commander decides to continue the siege, you will have to start disposing of all the zombies. You'll need to launch attacks from the second floors in the ways previously described, where the zombies cannot reach you. However, you will only be left with the stores of food and water placed on the second floor or above. This means that you'll be fighting

under a time limit.

But if you see that there will be no way to clear all the zombies from the first-floor area and the grounds, then you will have to open your escape routes and flee the campus.

In a best-case scenario, all of you would be able to escape. But the battle with the zombies may have used up all your fuel or you may also have been cut off from your gassed-and-ready escape vehicles. Any number of things could have gone wrong.

Who should you save? Who gets left behind? These are the bitter decisions that haunt every commander of a lost siege.

The End of the Siege

This simulation presupposes a siege that lasts about six months to a year. And as indicated in the simulation, a fully-equipped university with inhabitants on the order of several hundred people will not be able to live independently for a period of years without significant time for preparation. And this is done on the assumption that it will have to be abandoned eventually.

There are two ways a siege can end. The first is that humanity begins an organized resistance, and the resistance makes it as far as the area of your campus.

Perhaps the Self-Defense Force or some other ally figures out effective ways to fight the zombies, and using urban warfare techniques, they have taken the land back section by section. They wipe each section clean of zombies until they get to your area, finally liberating the campus. If this were a movie, this would be a happy ending.

You bid a fond farewell to the campus that has protected you for so long. Now you must devote yourselves to destroying the remaining zombies and to the recreation of human civilization.

But it might also go the other way.

A SURVIVAL SUCCESS?

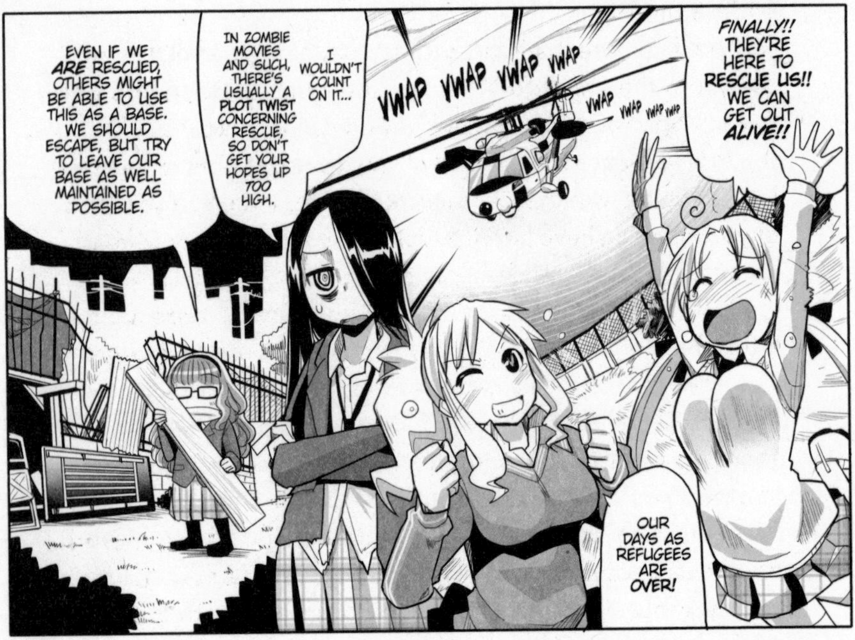
FINALLY!! THEY'RE HERE TO RESCUE US!! WE CAN GET OUT ALIVE!!
VWAP VWAP VWAP VWAP VWAP VWAP VWAP VWAP
I WOULDN'T COUNT ON IT...
IN ZOMBIE MOVIES AND SUCH, THERE'S USUALLY A PLOT TWIST CONCERNING RESCUE, SO DON'T GET YOUR HOPES UP TOO HIGH.
EVEN IF WE ARE RESCUED, OTHERS MIGHT BE ABLE TO USE THIS AS A BASE. WE SHOULD ESCAPE, BUT TRY TO LEAVE OUR BASE AS WELL MAINTAINED AS POSSIBLE.
OUR DAYS AS REFUGEES ARE OVER!

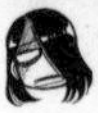
YOU KNOW, HELICOPTERS DON'T DO VERY WELL IN ZOMBIE ENTERTAINMENT. IT DOESN'T SAY CAPCOM ON THE SIDE, DOES IT?

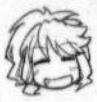
THE ODDS WERE AGAINST US, BUT IT LOOKS LIKE WE MANAGED TO SURVIVE!

TACTICS OF EVACUATION

You are now located deep inside zombie-controlled areas, and you don't have the personnel or capabilities to hold out. So you abandon the campus and try to retreat to human-held areas. In Japan, mountains run straight down to the beach, and fast-running rivers cut through farmland.

Since the landscape is so mixed, it will probably be very difficult to take back even a limited area of mainland Japan from the zombies. However, humans may be able to use some of these distinct terrain features to segregate themselves from the zombie-infested areas, maintaining a humans-only location. It'd be nice if your university was in that very location, but just in case it isn't, you should prepare to find a way of evacuating to the human areas.

The first thing to arrive would probably be helicopters. Perhaps the Japanese government (assuming it still exists) has someone in charge of the human retreat to secured areas. The helicopters would probably take your sick, your pregnant women, and your children back with them to the human area. And it would be nice if the helicopters could make the round trip to take you all to freedom. But it's unlikely that they would have the fuel for that.

Or maybe they have the fuel, but since the campus is such a well-maintained fortress, they may want to keep it—and you—as a forward base. They may also want to just use the campus to retrieve items that will be difficult for them to manufacture. Then they would take the items and the surviving humans back to the human area.

In this case, you would close up the campus to try to keep zombies from coming in and make your retreat. This would be the zombie equivalent of the "scorched earth" policy that is sometimes used in human-on-human combat, when one side retreats and leaves the land unusable by the opposition. You could set fire to the place, but your enemies here are zombies. Even if you were leaving vital resources behind, there is no way zombies could use them. And as long as there are no humans inside, there is no reason for zombies to even come in.

Before you head back to the human area, we suggest you leave behind a memento of yourself. Someday, you may want to come back and reclaim it.

THE FINAL VICTOR

No matter which way the siege warfare goes, in the end the ones who will finally achieve victory in the battle between humans and Explosive Pandemic-type zombies will be, without a doubt, humans.

Nations may fall. It's doubtful that all that much of human civilization and culture will remain. But the fact is, in the battle between humans and Explosive Pandemic-type zombies, the

humans had an unbeatable advantage right from the start.

Zombies have no intelligence. Zombies don't learn. Zombies have no imagination. Zombies are dead, and as such, they have no possible way to change or adapt to new circumstances and environments. All they can do is repeat a behavior programmed into them to try and attack humans and turn them into zombies.

But humans are very different. Humans have intelligence and can learn from experience. In fact, they can even use their imaginations to figure out what to do if zombies invaded their town, just as we've done here.

Certainly intelligence, the ability to learn, and the ability to imagine can work against humans, too. During the resulting confusion when an unknown, fearful element like zombies causes chaos, humans can take the wrong action and make the problem worse. Intelligence, the ability to learn, and an active imagination can all lead humans into failures.

But humans can learn from both success and failure. Eventually, humans will learn that zombies are ultimately an easy enemy to handle. Zombies always show the same reaction to the same stimulus. Their programming is simple and easy to predict. They can be easily outsmarted.

Early man, with no skills or culture to speak of, used to hunt down mighty mammoths. Zombies are presumably even easier to manipulate than that.

Any battle between zombies and humans will lead to a human victory. Of that, there is little doubt. Still, no one knows how long that will take. And no one knows how many lives will be sacrificed before it happens.

How short a time it takes, and how few sacrifices have to be made, depends on each of you, individual humans, your intelligence, and your ability to learn. And it depends on your imagination.

 WE'VE DONE TWO SIMULATIONS, SO LET'S RECAP HOW EVERYTHING PLAYS OUT IN EACH OF THEM.

to SUM up...

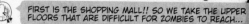 FIRST IS THE SHOPPING MALL!! SO WE TAKE THE UPPER FLOORS THAT ARE DIFFICULT FOR ZOMBIES TO REACH...

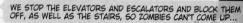 WE STOP THE ELEVATORS AND ESCALATORS AND BLOCK THEM OFF, AS WELL AS THE STAIRS, SO ZOMBIES CAN'T COME UP...

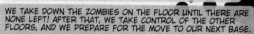 WE TAKE DOWN THE ZOMBIES ON THE FLOOR UNTIL THERE ARE NONE LEFT! AFTER THAT, WE TAKE CONTROL OF THE OTHER FLOORS, AND WE PREPARE FOR THE MOVE TO OUR NEXT BASE.

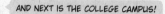 AND NEXT IS THE COLLEGE CAMPUS!

 WE EXTERMINATE ALL ZOMBIES FROM THE CAMPUS GROUNDS AND SET UP FENCES TO ISOLATE OURSELVES FROM ANY WAY THEY MIGHT SENSE US.

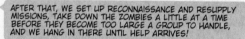 NEXT, THE PEOPLE INSIDE FORM AN ORGANIZATION, DECIDE WHO DOES WHAT, AND START PREPARING DEFENSES.

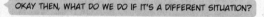 AFTER THAT, WE SET UP RECONNAISSANCE AND RESUPPLY MISSIONS, TAKE DOWN THE ZOMBIES A LITTLE AT A TIME BEFORE THEY BECOME TOO LARGE A GROUP TO HANDLE, AND WE HANG IN THERE UNTIL HELP ARRIVES!

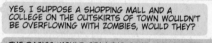 I THINK YOU'VE ALL GOT THE GIST OF IT. BUT SINCE THIS IS AN INTRODUCTION, THE DEGREE OF DIFFICULTY WAS SET TO BE PRETTY LIGHT.

OKAY THEN, WHAT DO WE DO IF IT'S A DIFFERENT SITUATION?

YES, I SUPPOSE A SHOPPING MALL AND A COLLEGE ON THE OUTSKIRTS OF TOWN WOULDN'T BE OVERFLOWING WITH ZOMBIES, WOULD THEY?

THE BASICS WOULD STAY THE SAME. THE SHOPPING MALL WAS ABOUT SECURING A BASE IN A SINGLE BUILDING AND WHAT TO DO FOR A SHORT-TERM STAY...

THE COLLEGE CAMPUS EXPANDED THE RANGE AND LIVING SPACE TO A WIDER AREA. IF THE MALL WERE A SINGLE BUILDING, THEN THE COLLEGE MIGHT WORK FOR THE SIZE OF A SMALL TOWN AND FOR A LONG-TERM SIEGE.

I GUESS THAT'S TRUE. INSTEAD OF A MALL, YOU COULD SUBSTITUTE A LARGE DEPARTMENT STORE OR AN OFFICE COMPLEX, AND THINGS WOULDN'T CHANGE THAT MUCH.

SO INSTEAD OF A COLLEGE CAMPUS, YOU COULD DO THIS WITH A GRADE SCHOOL OR HIGH SCHOOL?

ESSENTIALLY. OF COURSE, THERE WOULDN'T BE AS MUCH IN THE WAY OF FACILITIES IN EITHER OF THOSE.

BUT ONE PROBLEM IS THAT, IN REAL-LIFE SURVIVAL, NOBODY KNOWS WHAT IS GOING TO HAPPEN. ALL YOU CAN REALLY DO IN PRE-CRISIS DAYS IS TRY TO THINK UP AS MANY PROBLEMS AS YOU CAN AND HOW THEY COULD BE SOLVED, SO YOU CAN BE MENTALLY PREPARED.

WAIT! AREN'T YOU, LIKE, ENDING YOUR STORY WAY TOO SOON HERE?

WHAT DO YOU EXPECT? WE'RE ABOUT TO GO BACK TO THE MANGA WORLD, SO MY JOB HERE IS DONE.

OH MY GOSH, I FORGOT ABOUT WHAT HAPPENED TO YOU IN THE MANGA!

BUT YOU ALL SURVIVED, SO HAVE FUN IN THE LAND OF THE LIVING, FOLKS!

HUH? YOU'RE *REALLY* NOT COMING BACK?!

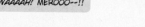 WAAAAH! MEROOO--!!

THE BRAVEST ONE OF THE BUNCH USUALLY HAS A REALLY HIGH CHANCE OF DYING.

MUNCHA MUNCHA

OR WHEN GUYS SAY, "LET'S STAY HERE AND KEEP WATCH."

"WE'RE SAFE NOW," MEANS THAT ZOMBIES ARE ABOUT TO BREAK IN.

THE GUY WHO GOES OUT ON HIS OWN...

ALWAYS DIES!

PLANNING OUR NEXT MOVE

OKAY, JUST SO WE DON'T DO SOMETHING STUPID, WHAT ALWAYS HAPPENS IN ZOMBIE SHOWS AND GAMES?

WELL, THAT DOESN'T APPLY TO ANY OF YOU!

NOT A BOYFRIEND IN THE BUNCH!

WE GO TO AN ALL GIRLS' SCHOOL TOO.

WE'LL HAVE TO BE EXTRA CAREFUL ABOUT THAT!

THAT ISN'T JUST ZOMBIE MOVIES. THAT'S ANY HORROR MOVIE.

OR ONE OF THEM WILL TURN OUT TO BE A ZOMBIE.

THE COUPLE THAT HAS THE HOTS FOR EACH OTHER IS GOING TO DIE.

MNCH MNCH

LOOK. MY BAD, OKAY?

GUESS I TOUCHED A NERVE.

GUESS...

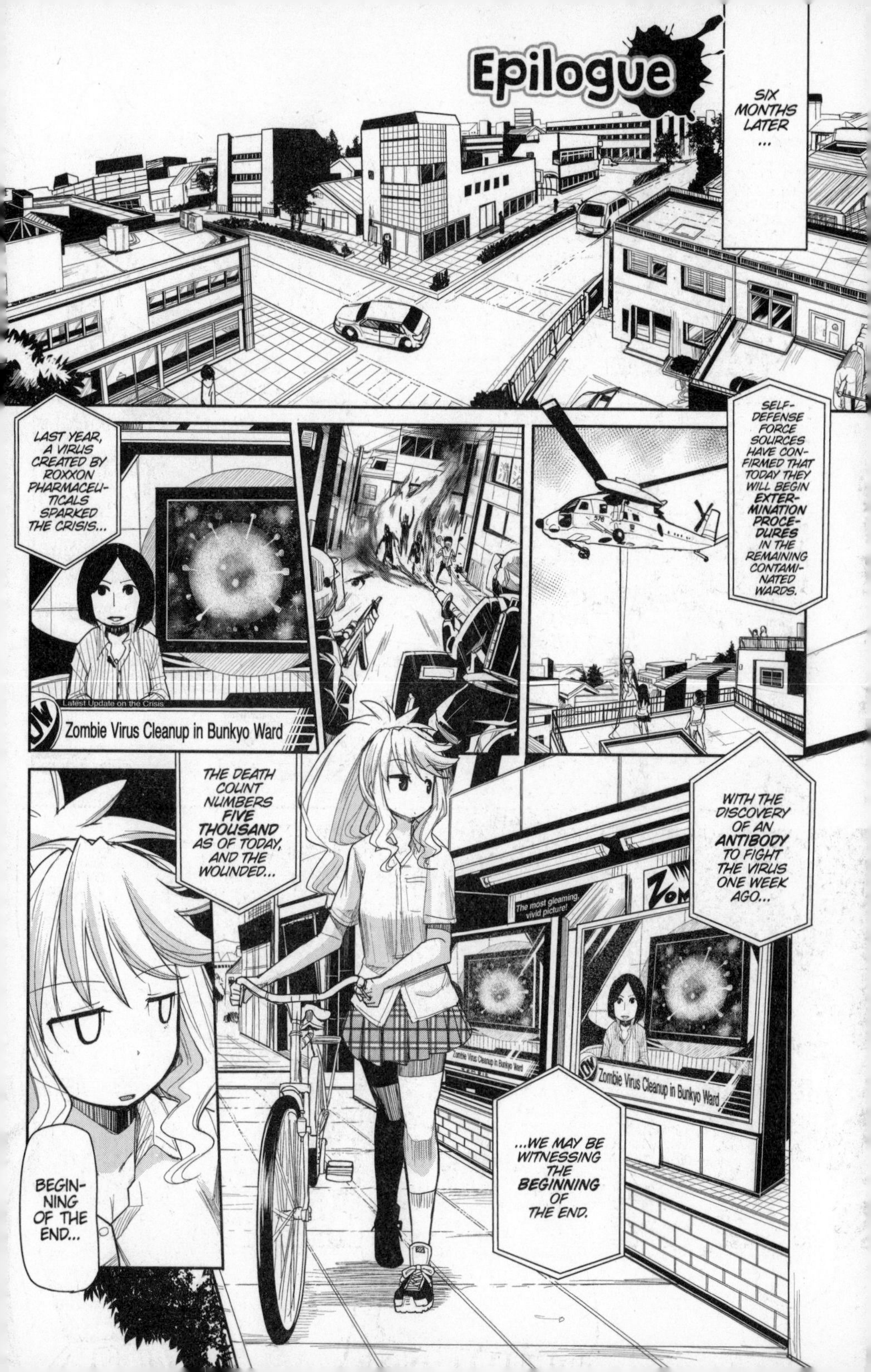
Epilogue
SIX MONTHS LATER ...
LAST YEAR, A VIRUS CREATED BY ROXXON PHARMACEUTICALS SPARKED THE CRISIS...
Latest Update on the Crisis
Zombie Virus Cleanup in Bunkyo Ward
SELF-DEFENSE FORCE SOURCES HAVE CONFIRMED THAT TODAY THEY WILL BEGIN EXTERMINATION PROCEDURES IN THE REMAINING CONTAMINATED WARDS.
THE DEATH COUNT NUMBERS FIVE THOUSAND AS OF TODAY, AND THE WOUNDED...
WITH THE DISCOVERY OF AN ANTIBODY TO FIGHT THE VIRUS ONE WEEK AGO...
The most gleaming, vivid picture!
Zombie Virus Cleanup in Bunkyo Ward
Zombie Virus Cleanup in Bunkyo Ward
...WE MAY BE WITNESSING THE BEGINNING OF THE END.
BEGINNING OF THE END...

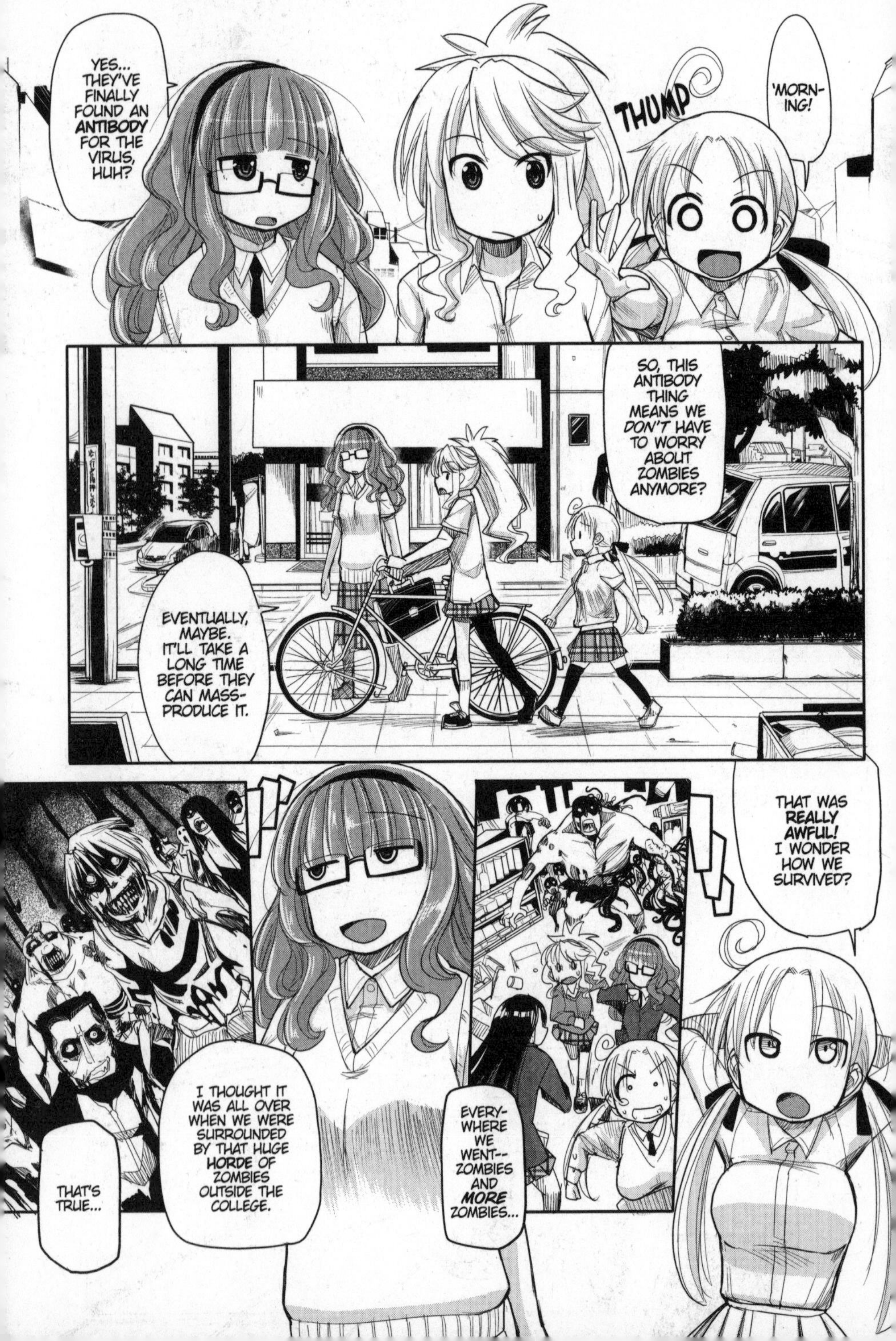
'MORN-ING!
THUMP
YES... THEY'VE FINALLY FOUND AN **ANTIBODY** FOR THE VIRUS, HUH?
SO, THIS ANTIBODY THING MEANS WE *DON'T* HAVE TO WORRY ABOUT ZOMBIES ANYMORE?
EVENTUALLY, MAYBE. IT'LL TAKE A LONG TIME BEFORE THEY CAN MASS-PRODUCE IT.
THAT WAS **REALLY AWFUL!** I WONDER HOW WE SURVIVED?
EVERY-WHERE WE WENT--ZOMBIES AND ***MORE*** ZOMBIES...
I THOUGHT IT WAS ALL OVER WHEN WE WERE SURROUNDED BY THAT HUGE **HORDE** OF ZOMBIES OUTSIDE THE COLLEGE.
THAT'S TRUE...

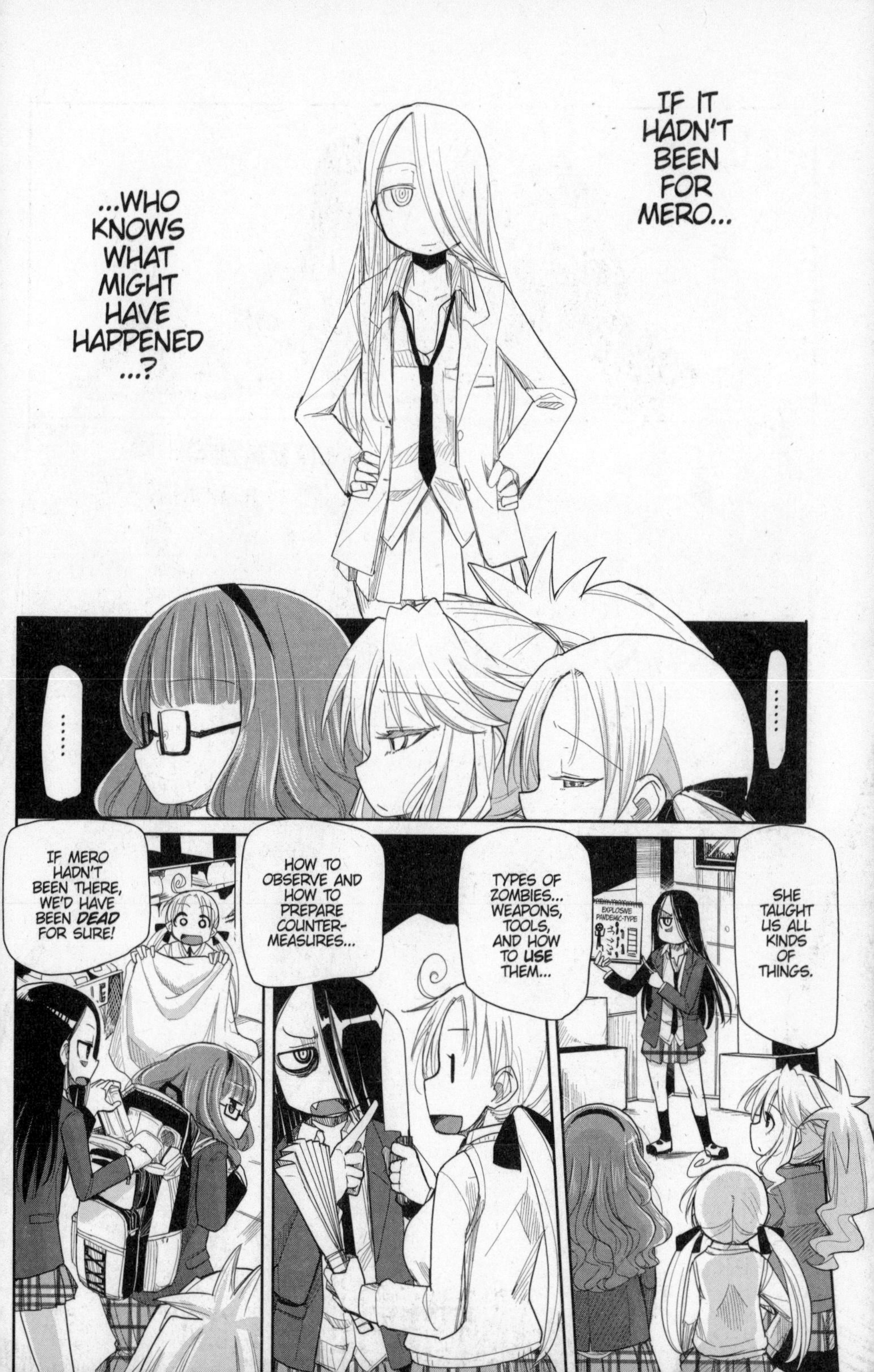
IF IT HADN'T BEEN FOR MERO...
...WHO KNOWS WHAT MIGHT HAVE HAPPENED ...?
......
......
SHE TAUGHT US ALL KINDS OF THINGS.
EXPLOSIVE PANDEMIC-TYPE
TYPES OF ZOMBIES... WEAPONS, TOOLS, AND HOW TO *USE* THEM...
HOW TO OBSERVE AND HOW TO PREPARE COUNTER-MEASURES...
IF MERO HADN'T BEEN THERE, WE'D HAVE BEEN *DEAD* FOR SURE!

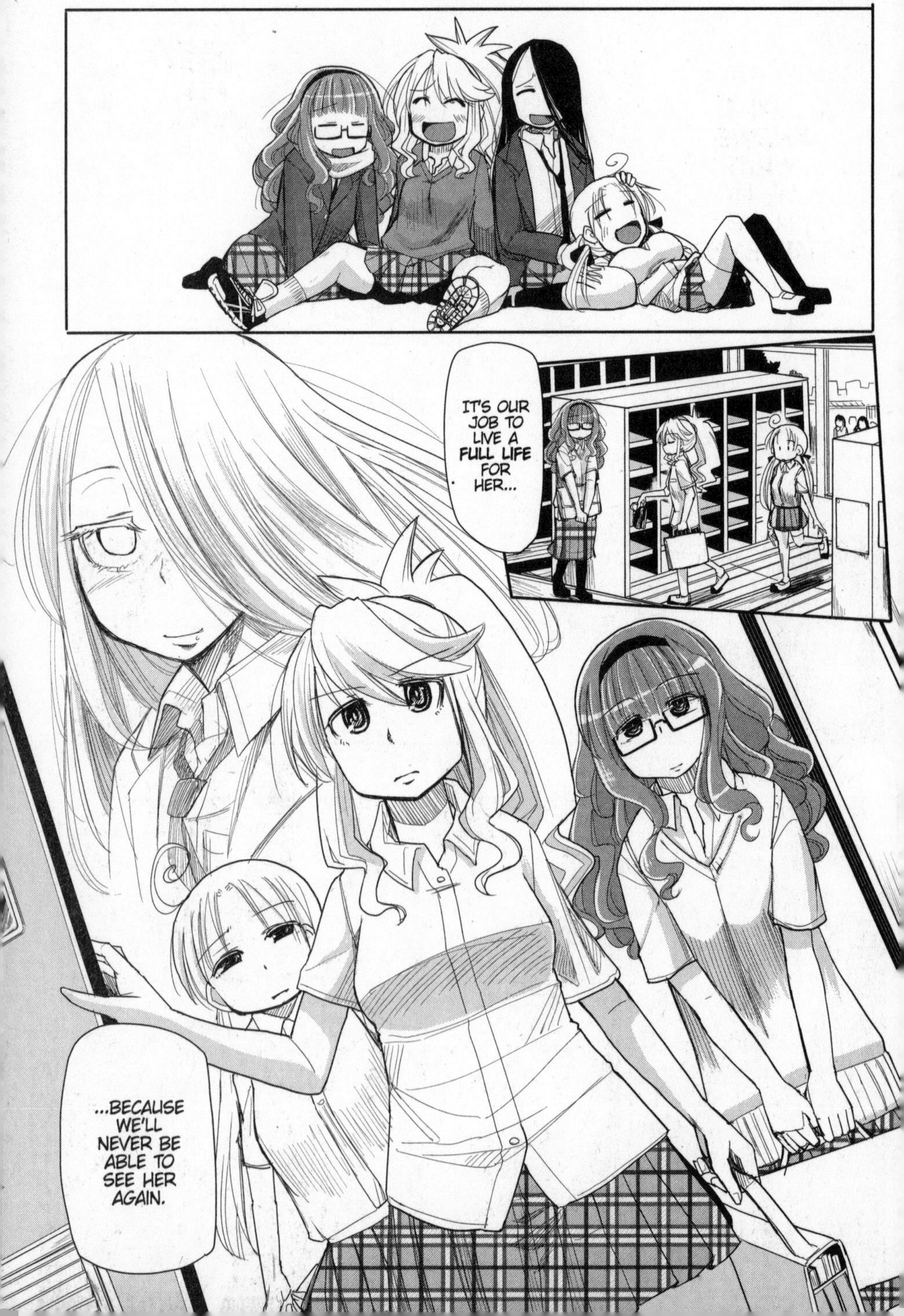
IT'S OUR JOB TO LIVE A FULL LIFE FOR HER...
...BECAUSE WE'LL NEVER BE ABLE TO SEE HER AGAIN.

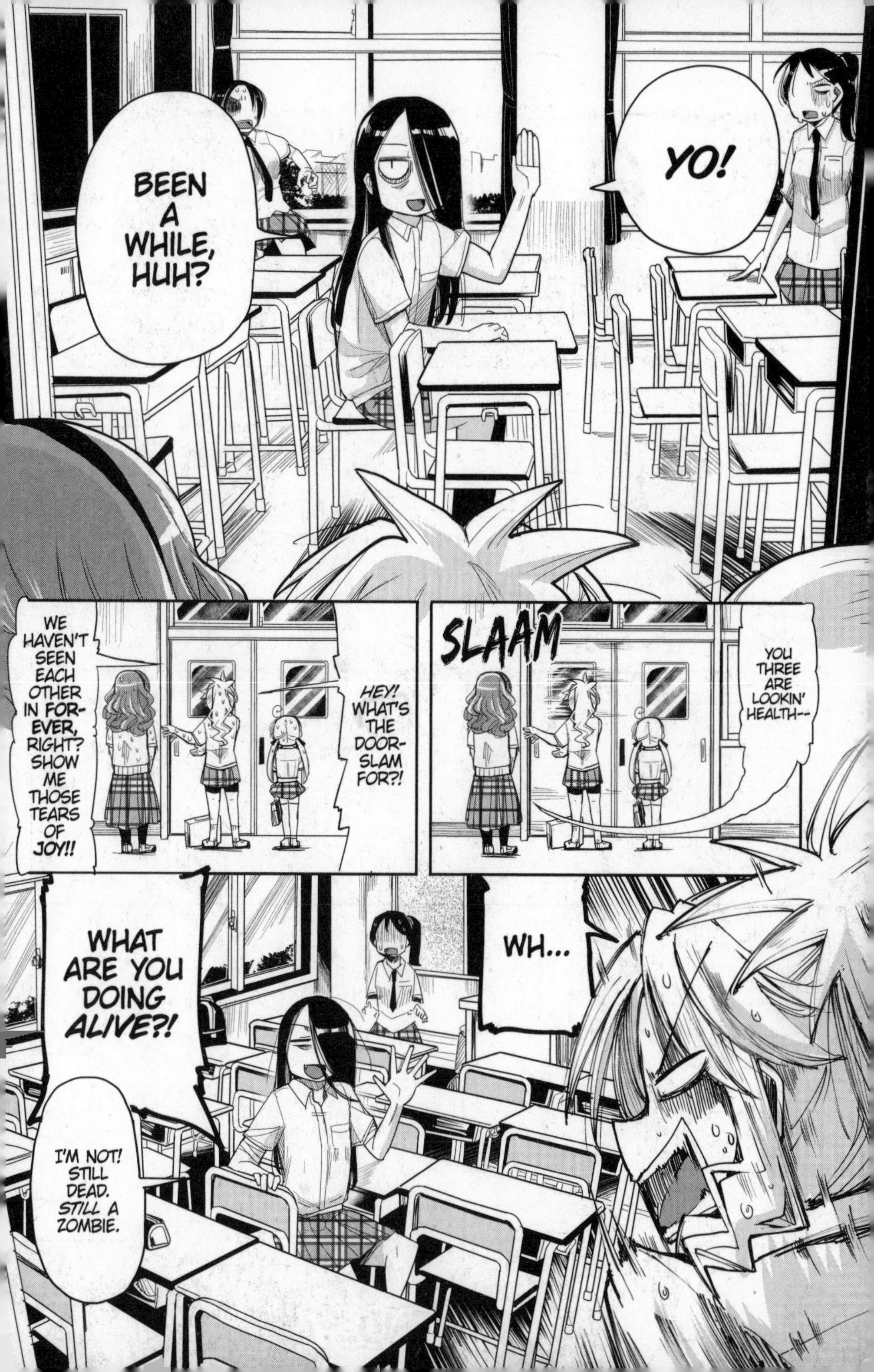
YO!
BEEN A WHILE, HUH?
WE HAVEN'T SEEN EACH OTHER IN FOR-EVER, RIGHT? SHOW ME THOSE TEARS OF JOY!!
HEY! WHAT'S THE DOOR-SLAM FOR?!
SLAAM
YOU THREE ARE LOOKIN' HEALTH--
WH...
WHAT ARE YOU DOING ALIVE?!
I'M NOT! STILL DEAD. STILL A ZOMBIE.

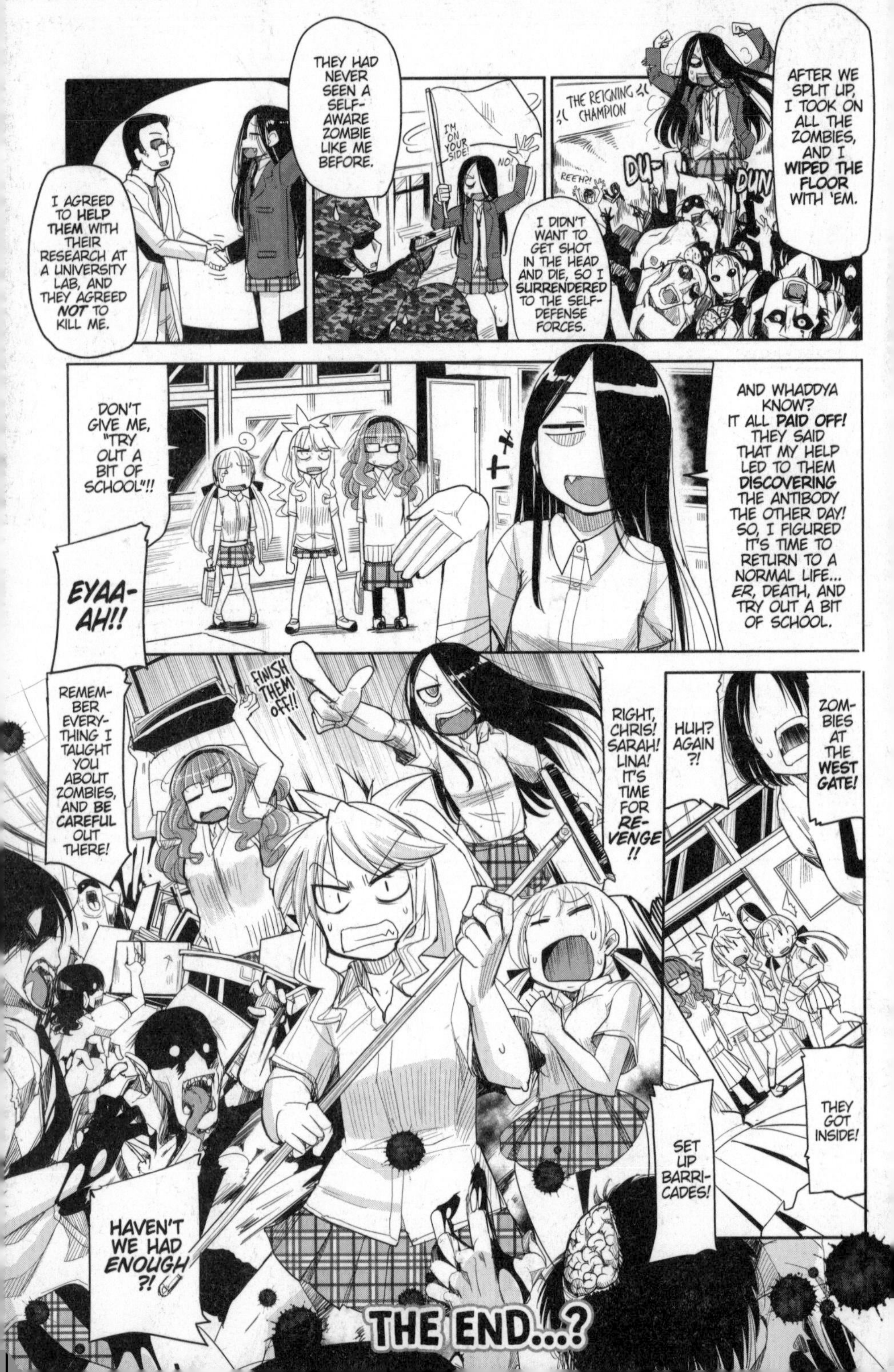
AFTER WE SPLIT UP, I TOOK ON ALL THE ZOMBIES, AND I WIPED THE FLOOR WITH 'EM.
THE REIGNING CHAMPION
DU-DUN
REEH?!
THEY HAD NEVER SEEN A SELF-AWARE ZOMBIE LIKE ME BEFORE.
I'M ON YOUR SIDE!
NO!
I DIDN'T WANT TO GET SHOT IN THE HEAD AND DIE, SO I SURRENDERED TO THE SELF-DEFENSE FORCES.
I AGREED TO HELP THEM WITH THEIR RESEARCH AT A UNIVERSITY LAB, AND THEY AGREED NOT TO KILL ME.
AND WHADDYA KNOW? IT ALL PAID OFF! THEY SAID THAT MY HELP LED TO THEM DISCOVERING THE ANTIBODY THE OTHER DAY! SO, I FIGURED IT'S TIME TO RETURN TO A NORMAL LIFE... ER, DEATH, AND TRY OUT A BIT OF SCHOOL.
DON'T GIVE ME, "TRY OUT A BIT OF SCHOOL"!!
EYAA-AH!!
ZOMBIES AT THE WEST GATE!
HUH? AGAIN?!
THEY GOT INSIDE!
SET UP BARRICADES!
RIGHT, CHRIS! SARAH! LINA! IT'S TIME FOR RE-VENGE!!
FINISH THEM OFF!!
REMEMBER EVERYTHING I TAUGHT YOU ABOUT ZOMBIES, AND BE CAREFUL OUT THERE!
HAVEN'T WE HAD ENOUGH?!
THE END...?

About the Authors

Bakagane (Dai Akagane)

Game designer, author of *The Age of the Galaxy (Game Field)* and *Toaru Chinjufu no Ichinichi* ("A Day on a Certain Military Base," Sneaker Bunko) among others. First encountered zombies as a child while watching western movies on TV (*Dawn of the Dead*). Helped to make it fashionable at his school to thrust out one's arms and say, "Arrrgh!"

Wataru Araizawa

Archaeologist, writer.

Norimitsu Kaihou

Gamer, writer, translator. Heart-felt lover of American comics and tabletop RPGs. Just a few days ago, played a zombie role as a voice actor, putting one more tick on his bucket list. Take a look at the manga and anime, *Gakoukurashi* ("School Living").

Morihiro Matsushiro

Military writer. Chief literary works: *Hontou ha Yatte Ikenai Gomon Manual* ("The Torture Manual You Really Shouldn't Try," Sanwa Publishing), *History of the World Weapons* (Gakken Publishing), *Nyotaika! Sekai no Dokusaisha Retsuden* ("They're Girls Now! Biographies of World Dictators," Ikaros Publications), and *Nyotaika! Sekai no Shougun Retsuden* ("They're Girls Now! Biographies of World Generals"). Sometimes writes articles for the magazine *Rekishi Gunzo* ("History Fans").

Basically *Sharknado*

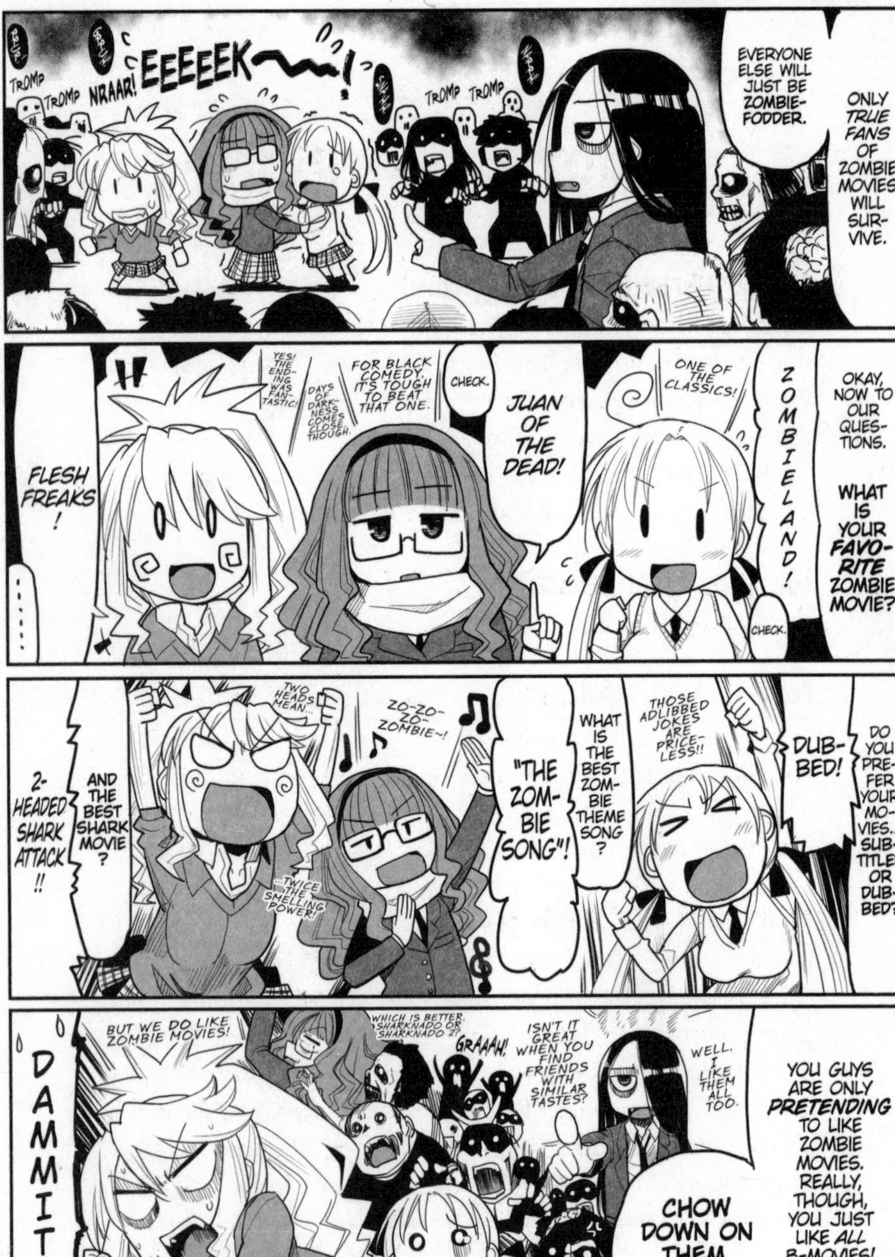
ONLY TRUE FANS OF ZOMBIE MOVIES WILL SURVIVE.
EVERYONE ELSE WILL JUST BE ZOMBIE-FODDER.
EEEEEK~~!
OKAY, NOW TO OUR QUESTIONS. WHAT IS YOUR FAVORITE ZOMBIE MOVIE?
ZOMBIELAND!
CHECK.
ONE OF THE CLASSICS!
JUAN OF THE DEAD!
CHECK.
FOR BLACK COMEDY, IT'S TOUGH TO BEAT THAT ONE.
DAYS OF DARKNESS COMES CLOSE, THOUGH.
YES! THE ENDING WAS FANTASTIC!
FLESH FREAKS!
......
DO YOU PREFER YOUR MOVIES... SUBTITLED OR DUBBED?
DUBBED!
THOSE ADLIBBED JOKES ARE PRICELESS!!
WHAT IS THE BEST ZOMBIE THEME SONG?
"THE ZOMBIE SONG"!
ZO-ZO-ZO-ZOMBIE~!
AND THE BEST SHARK MOVIE?
2-HEADED SHARK ATTACK!!
TWO HEADS MEAN...
...TWICE THE SMELLING POWER!
YOU GUYS ARE ONLY PRETENDING TO LIKE ZOMBIE MOVIES. REALLY, THOUGH, YOU JUST LIKE ALL B-MOVIES!
CHOW DOWN ON THEM, ZOMBIES!!
WELL, I LIKE THEM ALL TOO.
ISN'T IT GREAT WHEN YOU FIND FRIENDS WITH SIMILAR TASTES?
GRAAAH!
WHICH IS BETTER, SHARKNADO OR SHARKNADO 2?
BUT WE DO LIKE ZOMBIE MOVIES!
DAMMIT!!

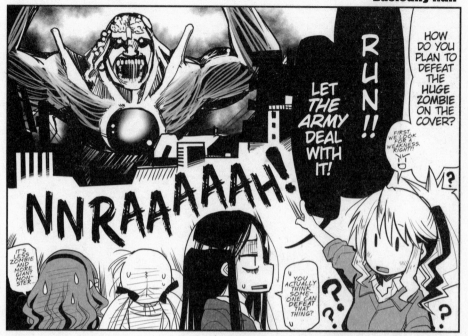

Tough Questions During Break Time

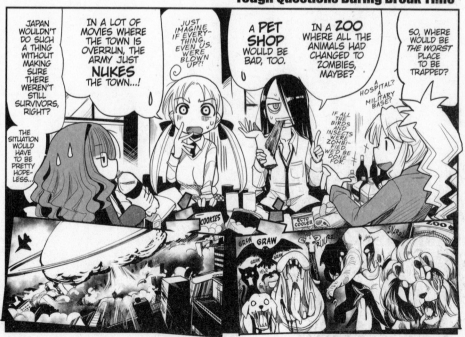

LAND OF THE RISING DEAD

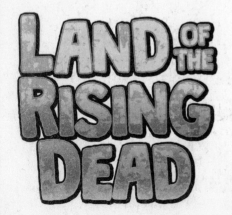

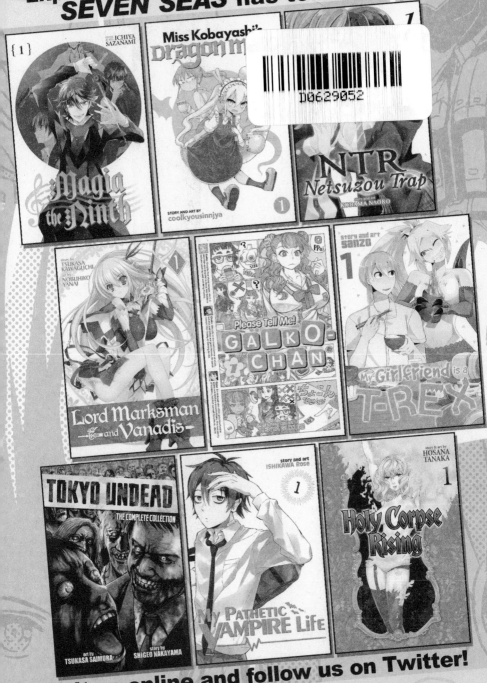